Studies in Emotion and Social Interaction

Paul Ekman
University of California, San Francisco

Klaus R. Scherer
Université de Genève

General Editors

Gestures and Speech

Studies in Emotion and Social Interaction

This series is jointly published by the Cambridge University Press and the Editions de la Maison des Sciences de l'Homme, as part of the joint publishing agreement established in 1977 between the Fondation de la Maison des Sciences de l'Homme and the Syndics of the Cambridge University Press.

Cette collection est publiée en co-édition par Cambridge University Press et les Editions de la Maison des Sciences de l'Homme. Elle s'intègre dans le programme de co-édition établi en 1977 par la Fondation de la Maison des Sciences de l'Homme et les Syndics de Cambridge University Press.

Gestures and speech:
Psychological investigations

Pierre Feyereisen
Faculté de Psychologie, Université Catholique de Louvain

Jacques-Dominique de Lannoy
Faculté de Psychologie, Université de Genève

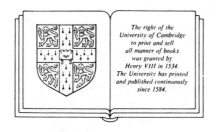

The right of the
University of Cambridge
to print and sell
all manner of books
was granted by
Henry VIII in 1534.
The University has printed
and published continuously
since 1584.

Cambridge University Press

Cambridge
New York   *Port Chester*   *Melbourne*   *Sydney*

Editions de la Maison des Sciences de l'Homme

Paris

Published by the Press Syndicate of the University of Cambridge
The Pitt Building, Trumpington Street, Cambridge CB2 1RP
40 West 20th Street, New York, NY 10011, USA
10 Stamford Road, Oakleigh, Melbourne 3166, Australia
and
Editions de la Maison des Sciences de l'Homme
54 Boulevard Raspail, 75270 Paris Cedex 06, France

First published 1991

Printed in the United States of America

Library of Congress Cataloging-in-Publication Data
Feyereisen, Pierre.
Gestures and speech / Pierre Feyereisen, Jacques-Dominique de
Lannoy.
p.   cm. – (Studies in emotion and social interaction)
Includes bibliographical references and index.
ISBN 0-521-37762-5 (hardback)
1. Gesture. 2. Speech. I. Lannoy, Jacques-Dominique de.
II. Title. III. Series.
BF637.N66F47   1991
153.6'9 – dc20   90-28283
                                                          CIP

British Library Cataloguing in Publication Data
Feyereisen, Pierre
Gestures and speech. – (Studies in emotion and social
interaction).
1. Humans. Communication
I Title. II. Lannoy, Jacques-Dominique de
302.2

ISBN 0-521-37762-5 hardback
ISBN 2-7351-0404-4 hardback (France only)

Contents

Acknowledgments

This book was written while Pierre Feyereisen was Research Associate of the National Fund for Scientific Research (Belgium) at the University of Louvain and Jacques-Dominique de Lannoy was Professor at the University of Geneva. These institutions provided the facilities for the realization of the project. Gratitude is expressed for the editorial services of Edward Haasl, who improved the English translation of the manuscript.

Introduction

I.1 Historical background

The relationships between gestures and speech have been discussed throughout the history of thought. The first writings in the field concerned the gestures of professional speakers: orators and actors. Ancient treatises of rhetoric, such as Cicero's *De Oratore* and Quintilian's *Institutio Oratoria* in the first century A.D., gave advice that is still used in the training of public speakers. Besides practical aspects, these texts presented theoretical perspectives and raised questions from which the discussion in contemporary psychology derives. For Quintilian and others after him, the language of the hands seemed to be universal, an idea that was very popular in the 17th and 18th centuries (for reviews, see Hewes, 1976; Kendon, 1982b; Knowlson, 1965).

Thus, the use of gestures was thought to represent a former, "natural" state of language. Such a hypothesis stresses the similarities between gestures and speech: "For other portions of the body merely help the speaker, whereas the hands may almost be said to speak. Do we not use them to demand, promise, summon, dismiss, threaten, supplicate, express aversion or fear, question or deny?" (Quintilian 11.3.85–86). Nevertheless, gestures would constitute a primitive way of communication shared by human beings and animals. The power of gestures in the expression of feelings gives them the quality of a language, yet the language of emotions is not that of understanding. Human specificity must be sought elsewhere than in cries and body movements. "Infants mumble the noise of their emotions, as animals do, but is not the language they learn from humans quite another language?" (Herder, 1772, p. 61 – our translation).

This property of gestures – their being a language but a primitive or even an "animal language" – is emphasized in Diderot's "Lettre sur les sourds et muets, à l'usage de ceux qui entendent et qui parlent." Diderot

1

conceived an experiment with a "conventional" mute who, without using speech, would try to make himself understood by means of gestures.
To order a drink, for example, it would first be necessary to draw the
waiter's attention before any other movement. From the succession of
gestures, it would be possible to infer "what the succession of ideas is
that would have seemed to the first men to be the best one to communicate their thoughts" (1751/1821, p.13 – our translation). However, gestures and speech cannot wholly substitute for each other, because each
sense modality has specific characteristics. "There are gestures so sub-
lime that the noblest eloquence could never translate them," Diderot
wrote (1751/1821, p. 19).

Psychology has inherited these issues. In some respects, gestures are
considered to have the property of expressing the content of conscious-
ness as words do (Wundt, 1900/1973). This means, in contemporary
terms, that gestures and words both relate to the mental representations
that constitute thinking (Kendon, 1986; McNeill, 1985). Thus, a language
of gestures exists that exhibits variations from one culture to another,
that follows rules, and that allows, like writing, the substitution of visible signs for symbolic meanings. From this point of view, human communication consists, in equal proportions, of verbal and nonverbal behavior, an idea well illustrated in the "kinesics" of Birdwhistell (1970). But
gestures are also considered specific and mainly devoted to the expression of emotions. This gestural mode of expression in human beings
resembles animal communication, and its study suggests hypotheses
about the phylogeny of human behavior. Darwin wrote: "The habitual
use of articulate language is, however, peculiar to man; but he uses, in
common with lower animals, inarticulate cries to express his meaning,
aided by gestures and the movements of the muscles of the face. This
especially holds good with the more simple and vivid feelings, which are
but little connected with our higher intelligence" (1881, p. 85). Similarly,
Wundt held that "the primary cause of natural gestures does not lie in
the motivation to communicate a concept, but rather in the expression of
an emotion. Gestures are first and foremost affective expressions. . . .
Only secondary, insofar as every affect contains strong emotional concepts, does the gesture become a conceptual expression" (1900/1973, p.
146).

I.2 Overview

The relationships between gestures and speech may be viewed from
different perspectives. First, commonalities may be stressed. To some

extent, gestures identify with speech and can be studied as a "body language" (chap. 1). Other similarities are demonstrated by the analysis of vocal and gestural communication from a comparative and evolutionary point of view. Whether signals are displayed by an animal or by a human being, ethology will raise the same questions: What releases them? What are their functions? What is their ontogeny and their phylogeny (chap. 2)? Second, a system of nonverbal communication may be assumed, distinct from language and specialized in the expression of affective states and interpersonal attitudes (chap. 3). From such a perspective, gestures separate from speech. However, social interactions usually involve a conjunction of verbal and nonverbal aspects. Apart from particular situations like telephone calls, speech does not occur in isolation, and similarly, excepting deaf-mutes, dancers, mimes, and some neuropsychiatric patients, people usually do not gesture without some speech processing. Strangely enough, language has most often been studied independently from its nonverbal context, and gestural behavior has been studied independently from language use (Kendon, 1981).

In the following chapters, we will attempt to specify the nature of the interactions between gestures and speech. Two related perspectives on these interactions are difficult to distinguish on the basis of empirical evidence. One is to assume a central stage shared by gestures and speech and modality-specific stages in input and output processing. The other is to assume multiple connections between a diversity of specialized processing units. With respect to these discussions, three kinds of data will be reviewed: the analysis of the relationships between gestures and speech in cognitive psychology (chap. 4), the study of the development of these associations (chap. 5), and neuropsychological observations bearing on lateral differences in gesture production by normal subjects and on the gestural behavior of different pathological populations, especially aphasics (chap. 6).

I.3 Definition problems

To some extent, any movement or change in position of a body segment may be considered a gesture. Accordingly, the very notion of gesture refers to a great variety of phenomena. In an extended sense, the term encompasses technical gestures that are used in various professions and that often involve tool use. From such a perspective, gestures are mainly actions before becoming means of communication. They are also visually guided to reach a goal in the physical environment (for a motor-control perspective, see, e.g., Keele, 1981; Schmidt, 1988). The attempt here is neither to analyze the diverse relationships between language and action nor to examine the multiplicity of anthropological studies proceeding from Mauss's (1935) suggestion concerning "techniques of the body" (see, e.g., Mathon, 1969; Meyerson, 1986; and the journal *Geste et Image*).

Many disciplines use the notion of *body language* with a wider extension than that given here. For example, social sciences describe bodily expression as an image of the society (e.g., Douglas, 1973). In psychology, correspondences between physical and psychological characteristics are sought, or beliefs that such correspondences exist are described as social stereotypes (see, e.g., Asendorpf & Wallbott, 1982; Chaiken, 1986; Jodelet, 1984; Wallbott, 1982). In a different perspective, bodily techniques aiming at nonverbal expression are proposed (Ancelin-Schützenberger & Geffroy, 1979). These investigations of bodily symbols have valuable objectives, but they shed little light on the relationship between gestures and speech. Indeed, it is significant that these endeavors are more concerned with the body than with the gestures as such. Describing body language in such a way does not explain why a particular movement is produced at a given moment. Moreover, from a methodological point of view, it may be noted that access to the meaning of bodily movements is given by verbal mediations: the inquiries and the reports of informants in social sciences, the patient's free associations and the therapist's interpretation in psychoanalysis, and questionnaires in psychology. In some cases, even the direct observation of movements is dispensed with. One study, for example, examined the meaning of self-touching behavior by correlating the results of several questionnaires, some bearing on diverse aspects of temperament and one on the description by the subject of his or her own fidgeting habits (Mehrabian & Friedman, 1986).

The purpose of the present book is different. Research on actual movements, observed or recorded in situations of verbal intercourse, will be surveyed. What movements will be examined? Gestures may be defined in a narrow sense in which only symbolic hand movements used for communication are considered. This is the case with daily-life gestures produced in order to insult, reprimand, command, etc. Such a restricted definition neglects nonrepresentational movements and unintentional gestures, like those of a speaker on the telephone to which the correspondent has no access. According to a wider definition, gestures are any kind of movement performed during speaking, not only hand movements but also head, eye, and face movements. Indeed, movements of various parts of the body may express skepticism, approval, interest, etc. (They may also be disregarded by the listener.) Moreover, many gestures combine movements of several body parts, like pointing in one direction with the index finger and looking elsewhere or shaking one's fist while frowning.

It seemed useful for the present purpose to find a compromise between a narrow definition of the domain restricted to representational and symbolic gestures and a broad definition encompassing any movement that relates by necessity or contingency to verbal interchanges. Indeed, the literature devoted to the communicative value of bodily movements is now extensive. Furthermore, the study of some problems results in the formation of specialized domains that focus on questions other than the relationship of gestures to speech. This is the case for most of the research on the facial expression of emotion and for a good deal of the studies on the social functions of gaze (see, e.g., Ekman, 1982; Feyereisen & de Lannoy, 1985; Kleinke, 1986; Oster, Daily, & Goldenthal, 1989; Rutter, 1984). An exhaustive review of the literature was not attempted; rather, our concern is centered on specific questions: Why do people move while speaking? What role does this activity play in verbal exchanges? What kind of relationship does it exhibit between the verbal and the nonverbal domains?

1. Body language

For a long time, gestures were studied under the assumption that human beings communicate not only with words but also with body movements. Several observations, indeed, support the hypothesis that the processes underlying verbal and nonverbal behavior may be analogous. First, gestures, like spoken languages, vary according to place, time, and socioeconomic factors. Second, body movements, like speech sounds, convey symbolic meanings, and some conventional gestures belong to a given language as truly as do lexical items. Third, regularities in gestural performances while speaking resemble syntactic rules. Thus, it may be that linguistic methods can be used in the study of gestures.

1.1. The cross-cultural study of gestures

As one learns the language or the dialect of the group one belongs to, one reproduces the gestures, the facial movements, and the bodily expression typical of this group. Mauss (1935) defined the "techniques of the body" as the ways by which people, in their own society, know by tradition how to use their bodies. Resting postures like sitting, lying, crouching, etc., illustrate this notion. Hewes (1957) described the world distribution of more than a hundred variants. These postures also receive different connotations according to the culture: the "open" posture of a woman (elbows far away from the body, legs stretched out, knees apart, etc., versus the "closed" posture: elbows next to the body, arms crossed, knees pressed together, etc.) is judged positively in the United States but considered immoral in Japan. More generally, the connotative meaning of postures and gestures verbally described to subjects and rated on several bipolar scales is influenced by different considerations in different cultures: for example, mainly by status in Japan and by the evaluation as pleasant or unpleasant in the United States (Kudoh &

6

Matsumoto, 1985; Matsumoto & Kudoh, 1987; McGinley, Blau, & Takai, 1984).

The best known example of cultural differences in the use of gestures is the case of head movements expressing affirmation and negation. According to Jakobson (1972), three patterns may be distinguished in Europe: (1) vertical nod for "yes" and horizontal shake for "no," (2) horizontal shake for "yes" and throwing the head back for "no," and (3) forward head bending for "yes" versus backward movement for "no." The hypothesis was proposed that when negativity is expressed by horizontal shaking, the movement begins to the right or to the left according to the ocular dominance of the subject. This hypothesis was not supported, and when requested to answer several yes–no questions, the subjects showed little consistency in the direction of the first move (Collett & Chilton, 1981). There are other examples of similar gestures expressing different meanings. For instance, tongue showing may be used to tease in Europe or to greet in Tibet; forming an O-shape with the thumb and the index finger may signify "OK," money, zero, or an insult; hand raising with fingers making a V is an obscene gesture for the British when the palm faces the performer but means "victory" when the palm faces the audience, whereas for continental Europeans, the two versions of the gesture have the same victory meaning (Calbris, 1981; Kirch, 1987; Kirk & Burton, 1976; Morris, Collett, Marsch, & O'Shaughnessy, 1979; Morsbach, 1973; Scott & Charteris, 1986).

Communication between people from different cultural backgrounds may thus suffer from comprehension problems. By way of illustration, there was a Soviet leader who, after a conference in the United States, expressed the friendship between the two nations by joining his hands over his head, a gesture by which American athletes indicate triumph. The observation of similar misunderstandings has led teachers of foreign languages to propose the inclusion of the study of gestures in the acquisition of a second language. Many emblems, indeed, are equivocal if their meaning has not been learned (Calbris & Montredon, 1986; Erikson, 1979; Safadi & Valentine, 1990; Saitz & Cervenka, 1973).

It is also well known that gestures accompanying speech are more frequent in some cultures than in others and that they may take different forms for different ethnic groups. One of the first and most systematic analyses of cultural differences in gestural behavior was conducted in New York by Efron (1941/1972). Gestures performed while speaking by Jewish immigrants from Eastern Europe were compared with those performed by immigrants from Italy. Some differences appeared in spatial and temporal characteristics, that is, the planes and axes used, the gesture shapes, the tempo, and the body segments involved. The gestures of the Jewish immigrants were narrower and shorter in duration, their rhythm was more irregular, and their shape more complex, with frequent changes of direction, than those of the Italian speakers. The Jews executed the movements in the frontal and vertical planes and used mostly their hands and forearms unilaterally; the broader gestures of the Italians also occupied the lateral plane and involved the use of both arms simultaneously. Other differences concerned the social and ecological aspects of gestures. The Jewish immigrants often spoke close to or while touching their partner whereas the Italians maintained greater interindividual distances. Gestures with held objects or simultaneous gestures by the listener were observed only among the Jewish people. On the semantic level, the gestures performed by the Jews described the thought pathways or showed the different steps of an argument; the Italian gestures conveyed symbolic or illustrative meanings and referred to concrete aspects rather than to abstract processes. After Efron described these differences among the immigrants of the first generation, he observed the second-generation immigrants. These people of Jewish or Italian origins were considered assimilated. The ethnic characteristics of the gestures faded. Furthermore, some "hybridization" had occurred; some typical items of Anglo-Saxon behavior appeared with traditional items, so a genetic interpretation of the original differences was ruled out. A more recent comparison of American Jews and Anglo-Saxon American Protestants, both groups observed while leaving a religious service, confirmed Efron's results. Similar investigations might be conducted to analyze other cultural differences between or within societies (Argentin, 1985; Ricci-Bitti, 1976; Sainsbury & Wood, 1977; Shutter, 1979).

It should be stressed that even when some movements seem to bear a universal meaning, as is the case with some facial expressions and gestures of emotion used in social encounters, culture may exert an influence by prescribing or repressing their public manifestation. Consequently, people from different ethnic backgrounds may vary in their ability to understand nonverbal signals. For instance, the gesture of touching the arm or the shoulder of others to express sympathy or reassurance is not allowed in the same circumstances in all societies. The culture may also confer a particular meaning to a particular movement. For example, a rapid eyebrow raising in a social context, or eye flash, universally indicates a readiness to interact, but depending on the culture, a particular connotation of friendship or hostility is added (Eibl-

Eibesfeldt, 1984; Gallois & Callan, 1986; Giovannini & Ricci-Bitti, 1981; Grammer, Schiefenhövel, Schleidt, Lorenz, & Eibl-Eibesfeldt, 1988; E. T. Hall, 1959; Watson, 1970; Willis & Reeves, 1976; see particularly reviews by Ekman, 1977; Gillespie & Leffler, 1983; LaFrance & Mayo, 1978; Sogon & Masutani, 1989; Vogelaar & Silverman, 1984).

While obvious for the observer, cross-cultural differences in gestural behavior remain difficult to explain. On the one hand, they may be compared with regional accents that simply result from traditional transmission of "habits" and serve no other function than to reveal the social or geographical origins of individuals. On the other hand, it may be that differences in gestures relate more deeply to the systems of symbols and values of the groups being compared and thus to cross-cultural differences in other domains.

1.2. The semiotic meaning of gestures

Movements as symbols

The meaning of some gestures originates in their symbolism, as shown by many insulting gestures or by a gesture like covering the mouth while yawning, now a sign of civility but formerly a protection against malign forces. These gestures derive from beliefs in the evil eye or in demoniac influences within magic practice (Röhrich, 1960). Beyond these vestiges of almost past times, some movements reflect social divisions according to gender, age, status, or kinship and are explained by the members of a society by reference to a symbolic system. For instance, gestures and postures expressing hierarchical relationships may be linked to the proper way of representing the world. In his study of the Tikopia of the Pacific, Firth (1970) was told that the natural orientation of the body divides space into an anterior and a posterior region. The center of interest – the leader or the guest – is faced, and subordinates are shown the back. Proximity implies similarity of status. This structure of attention may be compared to the results of investigations made in a different context in primate ethology (see chap. 2). In human societies, however, bodily signals are explicitly conceived in relation to general views, including the understanding of the natural or built environment within social categories (see Schmitt, 1990, for other examples; see also Hinde, 1976, for further discussions).

This way of conceiving the relationships between body language and symbolic systems has the advantage of showing that terms opposed in often sterile controversies are not true dichotomies: Here, nature is captured in the terms of culture. The critical issue is not to demonstrate the biological foundations of behavior – for instance, to relate gender differences to anatomical and hormonal factors or to relate handedness to cerebral asymmetry. It seems more important to see that social representations invest natural reality and that people behave according to these second-order phenomena. Thus, societies, by formulating sex roles, may modify the influence of biological differences. Similarly, if the use of the right hand is mandatory in judicial or religious rituals, it is more because of its symbolic meaning than because of its motor ability (Hertz, 1909).

In the different examples presented above, a capacity was assumed for members of a society to "explain" or to justify in some way the reason for the symbolic gestures that relate to beliefs and values. However, this is not necessarily the case with the entire set of gestures performed by a group. Most often, the origin of a tradition is lost. It just seems "natural" to express disdain by shrugging or by spitting and to greet by hat tipping or by handshaking. The informant is rarely able to comment on these habits, and their symbolic meaning cannot be discovered.

Sign arbitrariness: conventional and iconic gestures

Some gestures, like words, signify by a convention established within a community. A group of adolescents, for example, may create a secret gestural code meaningful only to themselves. These gestures do not need to be justified by reference to a symbolic system. Linguistic signs are characterized by an arbitrary relationship between the material (visual or auditory) form of the sign and its referent. From this point of view, iconic and deictic gestures that relate to the referent by similarity or spatial contiguity differ from true linguistic signs. Actually, conventional and iconic gestures cannot be distinguished as sharply as it may seem.

Gestures may be shaped to resemble what they refer to, like onomatopoeia, although they are arbitrary to the extent that different cultures choose different ways to establish similitude. For instance, a counting gesture may begin with the thumb or the little finger, drinking may be expressed by pretending to hold a glass or by describing the flow of the liquid with an extended thumb, etc. (Calbris, 1987).

The issue of sign arbitrariness has elicited investigations on the "transparency" of gestures used in sign languages like the American Sign Language (ASL) and the manual communication system of the North American Indians (Amer-Ind). In these languages, many iconic or deictic gestures exhibit relationships of similarity or contiguity between the sign and the referent. Sign languages might thus be considered more restricted in their ability to convey abstract meaning than oral languages built from arbitrary signs. Several studies have demonstrated the fallacy of the argument, however, by showing that hearing subjects do not understand sign language without training. If a manual sign is presented together with its written translation in a language like English, subjects judge it to resemble its referent far more than the word does. But if the gesture is presented alone, hearing people cannot guess the meaning. Only some signs are transparent, that is, understood by all the hearing subjects; some are never understood; and some fall between these extremes. Thus, the extent to which the meaning of gestures of this kind may be accessed varies according to both the signs and the subjects. These observations lead to defining arbitrariness or iconicity in a different way. From such a perspective, three terms have to be considered: not only the material sign and its referent, but also what Peirce (1932/1974) called the ground of the sign, that is, the aspect by which the sign evokes the referent. Iconicity would then not relate to the relationship between the sign and the referent but to the relationship between the sign and its ground, an arbitrarily selected characteristic from which the gesture shape stems (Bellugi & Klima, 1976; Daniloff, Lloyd, & Fristoe, 1983; Mandel, 1977; Page, 1985).

Semiotic classification of gestures

Several semiotic classifications of gestures have been proposed, most derived from the study of Efron (1941/1972), who opposed two kinds of gestures. Some convey a meaning that does not depend on the verbally expressed contents – they may be performed in isolation – whereas others have meaning only in relation to spoken utterances. Among the former, Efron distinguished, following Wundt (1900/1973), deictic, illustrative, and symbolic gestures. Note that this classification corresponds to Peirce's trichotomy of indices, icons, and symbols. A second category of gestures encompassed "batons," which are related to the utterance rhythm, and "ideographs," which describe thought processes. Other authors similarly contrasted "motor primacy" and "speech primacy" movements or distinguished "pantomimes" from "semantic modifying and relational movements." In other versions of the classification, the boundary of the two categories is moved. Only symbols or emblems belong to the category of autonomous gestures. "Illustrators," iconic or metaphoric gestures, are not thought to be able to convey meaning independently from the verbal context (Calbris, 1980; Cosnier, 1982; Dahan & Cosnier, 1977; Ekman & Friesen, 1969, 1972; Freedman, O'Hanlon, Oltman, &

Witkin, 1972; Johnson, Ekman, & Friesen, 1975; Kendon, 1983; McNeill, 1985; Wiener, Devoe, Rubinow & Geller, 1972; for a review, see Rimé & Schiaratura, 1991).

It remains to be established whether the borders of these categories are clear or blurred. Do autonomous gestures form a class that must be sharply distinguished from speech-related gestures or may a continuity be seen between these different kinds of gestures? Emblems are separate from illustrative gestures: They are often performed silently and can be understood without accompanying speech. However, when repertoires of these autonomous gestures are closely examined, one wonders whether a given movement, for example, the gesture for "money," may sometimes be used to convey autonomous meaning and sometimes to illustrate a spoken utterance. Thus, the distinction between semiotic categories relies on conditions of use, the gesture being performed inside or outside a verbal context, rather than on intrinsic qualities. Furthermore, in the history of a gesture, a movement may pass from one category to another without changing its form. Some emblems might derive from illustrative gestures: Originally produced in relation to spoken language they would later be used independently.

Similar questions arise within the category of speech-related gestures about the distinction between iconic and batonic gestures. The performance of iconic gestures may relate to the intonation of the spoken utterance, and some dimensions of batonic gestures may relate to the verbally expressed content. Thus, the two categories of gestures are not exclusive and one might merge them (Bolinger, 1983; Feyereisen, Van de Wiele, & Dubois, 1988).

However, if gesture classification does not reflect ontological differences, some distinctions, considered relative and provisional, remain useful as observational tools. High interobserver agreement can be achieved about the mere occurrence of illustrative gestures that are discriminated from a residual manual activity of lower amplitude. Similarly, speech-related movement may be distinguished from other gestures like body-focused movement, even if in some contexts like a medical examination, self-touching can serve illustrative or deictic functions (Friesen, Ekman, & Wallbott, 1979; see Rosenfeld, 1982, for a review).

1.3. The syntax of gestures

The influence of culture on gestural behavior suggests that a social model shapes individual practices outside awareness. Sapir conceived the existence of a collective "unconscious," that is, a set of rules or a grammar that everyone applies in bodily expression without being able to make the rules explicit. "We respond to gestures with an extreme alertness and, one might almost say, in accordance with an elaborate and secret code that is written nowhere, known by none, and understood by all" (Sapir, 1927/1949, p. 556).

Interaction rituals

A similar perspective was developed by Goffman (1959, 1971) in his analyses of numerous daily-life events in Western societies. A social encounter is conceived as a game in which people behave in order to manage the impressions made on others. The rule is to keep a "normal" appearance, that is, to follow norms; and the goal is to look good or, better, to win prestige. Goffman described two general kinds of interaction: remedial and supportive interchanges. Remedial interchanges attempt to transform the meaning of an act: They make acceptable what might be thought offensive. Several types of behavior may serve that purpose: (i) reoriented or pretended behavior, for instance, someone ill at ease in a public place may look at his watch as though he had an appointment; (ii) circumspect behavior or apology, such as leaving a meeting with a busy appearance only to slow down outside; (iii) excessive behavior, like the exaggerated clumsiness of beginners who try to elicit laughter or pity instead of reproach.

By supportive interchanges, people show respect and consideration toward objects or persons. The greeting and parting rituals described in the next section are of this sort. They may be conceived as programmed sequences of simple and stereotyped transactions. Avoiding collision on a pedestrian crossing results from exquisite collaboration in the nonverbal communication of intended trajectories (Collett & Marsch, 1974). "Togetherness" may be expressed by trunk or head orientation, postural congruence, or touching gestures. In these ways, bodily expression and gaze behavior of interacting individuals display the quality of their ties (Kendon, 1973). Eye contact in encounters on pedestrian crossings or during elevator rides obeys the rule of "civil inattention." It is acceptable to look at someone from a distance but one must avoid a too intimate eye contact in close quarters. Children, handicapped people, and beggars are not considered in this way but, instead, stared at or completely ignored. There are, however, contradictory findings about this behavior, so the proposed rule cannot account for all the observations. It should also be noted that from a different perspective like that of social psychology in equilibrium theory, many studies concern the determinants of gaze direction and bodily orientation, and other interpretations are proposed (e.g., Cary, 1978a, 1979; Edelman, Evans, Pegg, & Tremain, 1983; Edelman et al., 1984; Sigelman, Adams, Meeks, & Purcell, 1986; T. L. Thompson, 1982; Zuckerman, Miserandino, & Bernieri, 1983; for reviews, see Kleinke, 1986; Rutter, 1984; and this volume, chap. 3).

Close to the notion of interaction rituals, the concept of "behavioral program" presented by Scheflen (1968) concerns the execution of coded, standardized, hierarchically integrated acts through successive stages. These structures of invariant behavior are revealed in diverse situations. To illustrate, Scheflen (1965) described a "quasi-courtship" sequence. The program uses some of the actions of sexual courtship: high tonus, face-to-face orientation, eye contact, and, in women, leg crossing, arm folding, wrist stroking, or a hand-to-waist posture. However, these actions are completed only in abridged or modified forms in order to signal that the program is not to be understood as a seduction attempt. From these different examples, it appears that people behave in certain ways to get expected responses from others. In this manner, control is exerted in situations where verbal exchanges occur (Edinger & Patterson, 1983; Scheflen & Scheflen, 1972).

The analysis of conversation

Conversation seems to be the most clearly rule-governed social interaction. In this respect, the study of its organization constitutes a paradigmatic case in sociology and sociolinguistics. Conversational rules concern the framing of the verbal exchanges, turn-taking alternation, and the establishment of coherence between successive utterances. Indeed, dialogue implies not only reversals of speaker and listener roles but also some continuity from one turn to another. It might plausibly be supposed that together with diverse linguistic devices, nonverbal means are used to maintain coherence, for instance, through gestural anaphoras, deixis, or expressions of connection (see, e.g., Hobbs & Evans, 1980). However, these latter functions of gestures have never been systematically investigated, so only the former, regulatory functions will be discussed here.

Opening and closing

Talking to unknown persons requires preambles, and nonverbal behavior may serve this "starting" function. For instance, in a waiting room, two subjects more willingly begin to converse if a mutual gaze occurred when the later arrival entered the place (Cary, 1978b). Kendon and Ferber (1973) have described the behavior of opening conversations during informal meetings. When someone has perceived a possible partner, he or she orients the body in that direction, approaches, announces his or her presence, tries to be introduced or introduces himself or herself, and imitates the posture of the target person. Specific greeting behavior is sometimes observed: waving at a distance or head nodding or raising. During the approach, the gaze is often averted, grooming is displayed, or an arm is crossed over the chest. In the last phase, the head is raised with a smile and ritualized forms of touch may occur: an embrace, kiss, or handshake according to the circumstances or the gender, the familiarity, or the status of the partner (see also Collett, 1983; Greenbaum & Rosenfeld, 1980; Heslin & Boss, 1980; Riggio, Friedman, & DiMatteo, 1981).

In these analyses, attention is drawn not only to the signals that people choose to display but also to the sequence. Kendon (1982a) has studied greeting as one of the clearest cases in which the acts of the interacting parties coordinate. These situations cannot be described by considering the behavior of single individuals or by assuming mechanical and stereotyped exchanges (P. M. Hall & D. A. S. Hall, 1983; Plume, Zelhart, & Markley, 1985; Schiffrin, 1974).

Closing rituals may be analyzed in similar ways. Conversations usually do not end abruptly but a conclusion is prepared by different verbal and nonverbal means. As the time to leave approaches, gestures like self-touching face or chest, smiles, head nodding, leg movements, and gaze avoidance are more frequently performed. Postural changes are also observed: A foot or a leg is oriented outward, the trunk is leaned forward, one's knees or the arms of the chair are touched. This behavior could express inaccessibility and increased interpersonal distance but a simpler alternative is to interpret these gestures and postural changes as movements signifying intention to depart (Gunderson & Lockard, 1980; Heath, 1985; Knapp, Hart, Friedrich, & Shulman, 1973; Lockard, Allen, Schiele, & Wilmer, 1978; O'Leary & Gallois, 1985; Summerfield & Lake, 1977).

The organization of turn taking

The system of rules most exhaustively studied concerns the way smooth transitions between speaker and listener roles are managed. A first attempt was to propose a limited set of rules that would suffice to describe several characteristics shared by any conversation, like the alternation of roles and the variable length of turns. The conversation is then considered to be built from a series of units. Rules generating turn taking are the following: (*i*) At the transition between the first two units, the speaker is allowed but not forced to designate the next speaker, but if someone is designated, turn taking is obligatory; (*ii*) if nobody is designated, the listener is allowed but not obliged to intervene; (*iii*) similarly, the speaker is allowed but not obliged to continue to talk, unless the listener has taken the turn; (*iv*) when this third rule is followed instead of the first two, the three rules again apply at the next transition (Sacks, Schegloff, & Jefferson, 1974).

Such a system may be conceptualized by means of a mathematical Markovian model assuming stationary probabilities of transitions between four states: one person is speaking while the partner is listening; the target person is listening to the speaking partner; both are speaking simultaneously; or both remain silent. However, observations fit the model only poorly, for at least two reasons. The first is that other factors have to be considered to explain rule breaking, particularly the frequency of simultaneous speaking, such as the hierarchical relationship between the two partners. A second reason, which probably relates to the first, is that fragmenting conversations into elementary units raises problems. There is unavoidable subjectivity in setting the criteria of completion in real-time discourse listening. The task of determining the moment when the speaker has reached a transition state that allows turn taking is not easy. In this respect, nonverbal signals and especially gaze direction inferred from head and eye movements could play a crucial role by providing the listener with cues of speech segmentation (Beattie, 1983; Beattie, Cutler, & Pearson, 1982; Feldstein & Welkowitz, 1978; Jaffe & Feldstein, 1970; Rosenfeld, 1978; Taylor & Cameron, 1987).

The role of gaze. Speaker gaze orientation could relate to readiness to hold the floor. Indeed, direction of gaze might signal a disposition to keep or to leave the speaker role. It was observed, first, that a speaker looked at the listener less during the beginning of a speaking turn and, second, that orientation toward the partner was more frequent at the end than at the beginning of a speaking turn. Similarly, gaze avoidance during a hesitation pause could convey the message that a momentary difficulty is encountered that does not allow for turn taking (Kendon, 1967). However, controls elicited by these initial observations yielded contradictory findings. Thus, gaze could serve regulatory functions only in particular conditions: for long but not short turns, between familiar partners but not between strangers, for conversations involving more than two partners, etc. (Craig & Gallagher, 1982; Craig & Washington, 1986; Harrigan & Steffen, 1983; Hedge, Everitt, & Frith, 1978; LaFrance & Mayo, 1976; for reviews, see Beattie, 1980b, 1983; Rutter, 1984).

Another difficulty arises from the diversity of functions involving eye movements. Accordingly, several hypotheses may account for differences between the speaker and the listener as far as visual behavior is concerned. A first interpretation relies on the equilibrium theory proposed in social psychology by Argyle and Dean in 1965 (see chap. 3). Within this framework, it may be suggested that the speaker discloses himself or herself, especially if the subject matter is personal, and that, in order to keep the interaction within the limits of optimum intimacy, eye contact would be avoided.

A second hypothesis is that the speaker avoids eye contact in order to disregard visual information provided by the listener's face that would interfere with discourse planning. Supporting evidence is that gaze avoidance is more frequently observed during nonfluent than during fluent phases of speech production. However, there is little difference in the amount of interference when the speaker is requested to monitor the televised face of the listener and when the speaker is told to interact normally with the televised listener (free viewing conditions), and thus, the mere presence of the partner could play a critical role. Moreover, the speaker, as will be shown in the next section, is influenced by the listener's facial expressions and body movements, and thus, a minimum amount of attention has to be paid to these visual cues (D. E. Allen & Guy, 1977; Beattie, 1980a, 1981a; Beattie & Hughes, 1987; Cook, 1980; Ehrlichman, 1981).

From a third perspective, the problem is less to account for the speaker's gaze avoidance than to explain the listener's fascination. The basic condition would be continuous ocular motility by the speaker, with variations relating to the imagery of speech content. There would be a general tendency to avoid staring at the listener's face. The listener would also exhibit this tendency but to a lesser extent and would inhibit natural eye movements in order to gain information from the speaker's face. Lipreading and perceiving facial signals like frowning may indeed modify the comprehension of utterances (see chap. 4, this volume; and also Bergstrom & Hiscock, 1988; Ehrlichman & Barrett, 1983; Hiscock & Bergstrom, 1981; Weiner & Ehrlichman, 1976).

Patterns of gaze in speakers and listeners are influenced by still other variables: speech content, the relative expertise of the partners in the topics under discussion, information provided by environmental elements such as maps and blackboards, and, in three-part conversations, speaking order. It should be added that elimination of visual cues in conversations by telephone, for example, does not greatly disturb the turn-taking system. To summarize, the relationships between visual and verbal behavior may depend on systems other than the specific device aimed at turn-taking regulation, and this one obviously encompasses other elements than gaze orientation (e.g., Abele, 1986; Argyle & Graham, 1976; Dovidio, Brown, Heltman, Ellyson, & Keating, 1988; Dovidio, Ellyson, Keating, Heltman, & Brown, 1988; Lesko & Schneider, 1978; for reviews, see Rutter, 1984, 1987; and also chap. 3, this volume).

The traffic regulation model. Another turn-taking system was described by Duncan and co-workers (e.g., Duncan, Brunner, & Fiske, 1979). Just as there is a set of rules to avoid collisions at intersections, several cues in conversation could signal the priority of the speaker's role or the possibility of a reversal. The system assumes a distinction between two kinds of utterances: actual turns and "back-channel responses," that is, "uh-uh" interjections or sentence completions and utterances like "I see," by which the listener signals that the communication channel is efficiently functioning. Smooth transitions would be managed by the speaker providing one or more cues to indicate turn completion. Some of these cues are linguistic in nature (sentence well-formedness, expressions like "you know" or "well"), some are paralinguistic (intonation fall, voice lowering, syllable lengthening), and some are nonverbal (gesture ending). The greater the number of cues displayed, the lower the probability of simultaneous speaking attempts. Back-channel responses, on the contrary, do not follow transition cues and are distributed in time according to other patterns. As will be shown in the next section, the listener also signals intentions by giving cues of attention or by claiming the speaker's role by audible inhalations, head turning, or incipient hand movements, other than the ritualized gesture of hand raising to request a speech turn in formal meetings (Duncan, 1972, 1973; Duncan & Niederehe, 1974; Duncan & Fiske, 1977; Duncan et al., 1979; Harrigan, 1985).

Illustrative and batonic gestures have been observed to play a role within this system. The speaker performing a gesture other than self-touching is less often interrupted. If, nevertheless, the listener attempts to take the turn in spite of this cue, simultaneous speech is likely. These kinds of hand movements have thus to be interpreted as floor-holding intention movements. Gestures are performed within a lapse of time between the mental construction of the message meaning and its actual production, which Schegloff (1984) called a "projection space." Because movements often anticipate the parts of speech they relate to, in sentence reformulation or "repairs," for the most obvious example, they show that the turn is not completed. By gesturing while speaking or during hesitation pauses, the speaker indicates to the listener that the time has not come for a role reversal. However, other signals, head orientation toward the listener, for instance, would allow a transition. Looking at the partner is more usual during questions than during statements or answers, for example (Duncan & Fiske, 1977; Duncan et al., 1979; Goodwin & Goodwin, 1986; Thomas & Bull, 1981).

Duncan's system presents two peculiarities. First, signals belonging to it concern elements that are not specifically aimed at turn-taking regulation. Second, several cues may serve similar functions. This redundancy explains why the elimination of visual cues in communicating by telephone does not disturb turn taking (B. Butterworth, Hine, & Brady, 1977; Cook & Lalljee, 1972; Rutter, 1987).

The listener's contribution

An essential feature of conversation is the active participation of both partners. Among other contributions, the listener is responsible for the smooth unfolding of the discourse by displaying attention. To be sure to be understood, the speaker most likely relies on nonverbal and particularly facial signals sent by the listener. Receptivity may be expressed nonverbally by bodily attitudes and gaze orientation. Cues of possible distraction such as gaze avoidance exert a disturbing influence on the speaker, who, by filled pauses or "repairs," summons the distracted listener. Vocal and gestural intention movements in the partner attempting to take the turn may also be interpreted as requests for attention, and illustrative gestures of the speaker may be intended to sustain listener's receptivity (Goodwin, 1981; Heath, 1982, 1984).

The listener is also supplied with other ways to influence the speaker. Receptivity can be expressed in different ways, verbally and nonverbally by back-channel responses like smiling, head nodding, and forward leaning. Facial and bodily signals also can convey skepticism, disapproval, incomprehension, or boredom. To qualify these displays, Cosnier (1988) prefers the term *piloting,* which suggests a closer control of the listener on speaker behavior. There is a long tradition in psychology, within learning paradigms, of studies showing that many aspects of verbal behavior may be influenced by positive or negative reinforcement (for a review, see Rosenfeld, 1978; see also Brunner, 1979; Dittmann & Llewellyn, 1968; Ekman, 1979; Forsyth, Kushner, & Forsyth, 1981; Hadar, Steiner, & Rose, 1985; Machida, 1986; Maynard, 1987; Miller,

Lechner, & Rugs, 1985; Patterson, Cosgrove, & O'Brien, 1980; Rosenfeld & Hancks, 1980; Rosenfeld, Shea, & Greenbaum, 1979).

One wonders about the extent to which all these observations support the sociological model proposed by Goffman and demonstrate obedience of behavior to established "rules." The problem arises from the ambiguity of the notion of a rule that concerns both empirical regularities and social prescriptions (Taylor & Cameron, 1987). Some sociologists do not distinguish these two meanings, so temporal contiguity is interpreted as an indication of social determinism. For instance, sending leave-taking signals may be explained without reference to a concept of rituals but by considering that readiness to depart motivates intention movements like weight shifts and repositioning of the feet (Lockard et al., 1978; Gunderson & Lockard, 1980). Thus, beyond the metaphoric uses of the notion of rules, one should specify how societies modify the behavior of individuals involved in interactive settings.

1.4. Linguistic descriptions of gestural behavior

Until de Saussure, linguistics nurtured the hope of a general science of signs, or semiotics, that would unify the studies of all the systems of meanings, verbal and nonverbal (see discussions in Barthes, 1964; Eco, 1988). A special branch, called zoosemiotics, would even be devoted to the study of animal communication (Sebeok, 1972). Scholars also wondered whether linguistic methods would not apply to the analysis of gestural behavior. From another perspective, however, linguists like Chomsky (1979) stressed the specificity of phonology and syntax and the inadequacy of linguistic methods for the analysis of communication systems other than language.

Kinesics

From the assumption that human communication involves undissociable verbal and nonverbal aspects, "kinesics" attempts to extend linguistic methods to the study of gestures (Birdwhistell, 1970). Units of body movements are considered bound morphemes; that is, they are analogous to parts of speech that cannot be used in isolation, such as verbal inflections marking past time, which cannot appear without being preceded by a verb root. By analogy with the different articulations of linguistic levels, Birdwhistell proposes that several kinesic levels of gesture organization be distinguished.

At the first level, "kinemes" correspond to phonemes. These units do not convey any meaning to themselves, but they create contrasts in one or several relevant dimensions. Moreover, the same unit may be realized in several ways if variations concern irrelevant aspects. Thus, users of the communication system may consider physically different signals to be equivalent. For instance, many forms of head nodding may be understood similarly just as the sound /r/ may be pronounced in several ways, according to the speaker's characteristics and contextual influences. These gestural variants that may be substituted are called allokines. Accordingly, analyzing gestures into kinemes differs from a physical description of bodily movements in the same way that phonology does not reduce to phonetics. The distinction between -emic and -etic perspectives is made in the two modalities, oral and gestural. Birdwhistell identified a limited number of kinemes and proposed a list of written symbols, or kinegraphs, for the transcription of the movements of the head, the face, the shoulders, the hands, etc. This repertoire was not intended to be exhaustive, and scholars were invited to add units discovered in the use of gestures. In principle, however, the number of kinemes should be less than the number of different movements because contrasts in motor execution are not necessarily relevant for communication.

At the second level, the sequential or synchronous association of permutable kinemes results in the building of kinemorphemes, or structures that are analogous to morphemes and that, like them, may have related forms with shared stems, inflections, or affixes. Some units would play a similar role to that of identified parts of speech: Birdwhistell mentioned kinesic pronominal, verbal, manner, pluralization markers, and so on. Other kinemorphemes concern suprasegmental analysis, or "parakinesics." These forms are involved notably in stress assignment. Last, at the third level, complex kinemorphic constructions, similar to words, sentences, and paragraphs, may be identified.

The idea that kinesics might succeed in describing gestural communication with the same precision as that achieved in the study of language by linguistics opened the way for a broad field of investigations. However, Birdwhistell's suggestion resulted only in the study of some exemplary cases. The complexity and tedium of the methods developed in kinesics and difficulties with a continuously evolving terminology do not suffice to explain the disappointment in the enterprise. Kinesics also faced intrinsic theoretical shortcomings (see, e.g., Bouissac, 1973; Kendon, 1972a). To begin with, the very point of view of kinesics, the relevance of a distinction between two structural levels concerning the kinemes and the kinemorphemes, can be questioned. How is one to isolate units analogous to phonemes in the nonverbal realm? A phoneme is known to be meaningless in itself and must combine with other phonemes to form distinctive meaningful patterns. Yet, in contrast to a phoneme like /p/, an isolated kineme like eyebrow raising may convey a meaning apart from any combination with other kinemes, even if, of course, the verbal and gestural context plays a role in reducing the ambiguity of such a signal. A resulting difficulty is how to distinguish a true contrast between two kinemes from allokinetic variations in the realization of a unique kineme. Indeed, only linguistic competence and shared conventions allow one to determine whether two different speech sounds correspond to a single unit or to separate units. As a methodological consequence, the number of kinemes cannot be established without a profound insight into the morphemic contrasts shaping the stream of body motion.

Quite different is the situation with the study of established sign languages, which are structured with a morphophonology and a syntax (Klima & Bellugi, 1979; Stokoe, 1980). Four parameters define the formation of a sign in the ASL (Friedman, 1977): hand configuration (about 30 shapes may be listed), movement (direction, manner, etc.), place of articulation in relation to the signer's body, and hand orientation in the three spatial dimensions. Similar distinctive features may be discovered in the study of other sign languages used by deaf-mute people or in the analysis of repertoires of gestural symbols, like those used in Iran (Kendon, 1980; Sparhawk, 1978). Spontaneous gestures performed while speaking do not seem to obey formative rules of this sort. Some regularities can surely be found, for example, in the correspondence between forms and meanings (Hadar, 1986; McNeill & Levy, 1982). Spontaneous gestures might also be described by using the same morphological dimensions as those underlying ASL. But it remains impossible to devise tasks analogous to the lexical decision or the grammaticality judgment where subjects are required to state whether a context-free movement is a gesture or not or whether or not it is well formed, tasks that can be carried out with spoken or signed utterances. This lack of constraints in gestural behavior hinders the development of kinesics. Furthermore, if gestures are not built from a combination of empty elements, is not the field of possible expressed meanings inescapably limited? Would language thus demonstrate a specificity that prevents any attempt to assimilate spontaneous gestures?

Design features of human language

There are, of course, other communication systems than language and gestural behavior. The issue has been raised as to whether some universal and genuine properties characterize all the natural languages in their diversity without being shared by nonlinguistic systems. Thus, the attempt has been made to define language in contrast to other kinds of communication, particularly, by stressing similarities and differences with animal behavior that might constitute phylogenetic precursors of language. (Actually, it would be preferable to reverse the perspective and to wonder whether among all the defining properties of human language, some correspondences can be found in the animal realm. Human language would then have evolved from a convergence of these antecedent achievements.) This endeavor would allow one to assess the relevance of a linguistic approach to gestural behavior.

One of the most exhaustive formulations was proposed by Hockett and Altmann (1968), who presented a list of 16 "design features" (see also Altmann, 1967). Some of them may, in some respects, be found in nonlinguistic communication systems, but only human language possesses the complete set of characteristics:

1. Channel: usually vocal and acoustical or gestural and visual in written languages or in sign languages (the tactile channel may be substituted in Braille reading but chemical senses [taste and smell] are never used)
2. Broadcast transmission and directional reception: signals are addressed and localized
3. Rapid fading
4. Interchangeability of sender and receiver roles
5. Total self-feedback: the speaker hears the uttered sounds
6. Specialization of signals for communication uses
7. Fixed semantic association between elements of the message and elements of the world
8. Arbitrary denotation (see discussion in previous sections)
9. Digital versus analog communication and use of discrete, rather than graded, signals
10. Displacement: signals do not relate in space and time to what they refer to
11. Productivity: anything may be talked about, and new messages may be formed
12. Duality of patterning: the shortest meaningful unit is compounded of meaningless elements
13. Traditional transmission
14. Prevarication: ability to say things that are not true (fiction, deception, error)
15. Metacommunication or reflexiveness
16. Learnability

Difficulties in accounting for spontaneous gestural behavior in the framework of linguistics might result not only from differences in the nature of the analyzed objects but also from differences in the respective purposes of linguistics and psychology. The object of the latter discipline is the description of structural rules used by an ideally competent speaker, whereas the former tries to explain verbal or nonverbal performances. Such a goal being set, psychologists are more interested in the functional perspectives of language, examining how forms are determined by conditions of use rather than by delicate analyses of the code. Thus, links may be found with pragmatics, the study of language in its social and physical context.

Pragmatic perspectives on gestural behavior

From a functionalist perspective, gestures may serve other functions than conveying precise meaning. Conversation analysis suggests a role in the turn-taking system. Gestures may also contribute to message elaboration rather than to its transmission. For example, Kristeva considered that gestural behavior as "a productivity anterior to the product, and so anterior to representation" fulfills a pure enunciative function without autonomous content (1968/1978, p. 267). The nearest paraphrase would be "I am speaking." Similarly, according to Dray and McNeill (1990), gestures relate to the process of defining contrasts that is essential for speech production: The semantic focus has to be differentiated from the context, related contents have to be distinguished, or similarities have to be underlined. Beat gestures, which can be placed at the end of a continuum of referential to nonreferential gestures, seem to be "metaphors for contrast itself."

Pragmatics also draws attention to the social conditions in which gestures occur. The context of the verbal emission, gestures included, must be taken into account to understand the meaning of an utterance. Like speech forms, gestures are shaped by communication intentions, and the receiver often has to guess the intended purpose to understand elliptic messages (Halliday, 1973; Levinson, 1983). Within this framework, attempts have been made to enumerate all the possible functions of language uses, but unanimity about the repertoire has not been achieved. Some of the functions of speech acts may also be fulfilled by gestural means, whereas others cannot (Cosnier, 1982, 1987). For example, supplication may be conveyed by clasping the hands, but a promise requires verbal engagement. Thus, it remains to be determined whether gestures influence speech comprehension. For instance, the role of nonverbal signals in the comprehension of ambiguous utterances like indirect requests has never been systematically investigated. Other questions also have to be answered: For which functions can gestures substitute for speech? And, more generally, are gestures and speech understood in similar ways?

To show the relevance of a pragmatic approach, these questions are probably best addressed by studying deixis. The analysis of a pointing gesture used by the Cuna Indians in Panama is illustrative in this respect (Sherzer, 1973). The gesture consists of head raising, looking in a specific direction, mouth opening, and lip protrusion. It can be observed in several contexts: (*i*) raising or answering questions about location or direction, (*ii*) commands or declarative statements with a possessive or demonstrative meaning, (*iii*) joking with or teasing the target person, (*iv*) greeting. In each case, the gesture may be performed alone or with a spoken utterance. Thus, it may play diverse roles according to the circumstances, and correct interpretation requires information on context and rather sophisticated inferences. Other analyses of deictic expressions, and more particularly of the cognitive processes underlying their communicative uses and development, will be presented in chapters 4 and 5.

1.5. Concluding remarks

The analogy drawn between gestures and speech by means of the notion of "body language" allowed a wealth of empirical evidence to be gathered. Nevertheless, the increased knowledge raised new questions that probably can be answered only by choosing different perspectives.

First, the heterogeneity of the gestural domain has to be stated. Perhaps it would be preferable to define the field more narrowly and avoid considerations about learned sign languages like ASL or about the symbolic gestures called emblems and focus on gestures accompanying speech. But the interest of comparing different phenomena involving the same manual modality and raising related problems was also demonstrated in some of the discussions of this chapter.

Second, it appears that even a limited category of gestures may be investigated from several perspectives. In some cases, meaning may depend on execution. For example, social groups can be distinguished by the overall stylistic quality of their gestures. Furthermore, among people sharing the same habits, quite different messages may be conveyed by similar gestures that vary only by subtle differences in performance. These qualitative dimensions of gestures justify attempts to use with speech-related movements the descriptive tools conceived for choreography, where details of execution play a critical role. Gestures are analyzed according to physical dimensions or with reference to anatomy. Automatic recording techniques were also proposed to bypass the tedious phase of coding (Frey, Hirsbrunner, Florin, Daw, & Crawford, 1983; Rosenfeld, 1982). In other cases, however, gestures of different forms will be recognized as belonging to the same category. Irrelevant variations in the shape of the pointing gesture, for example, may depend on the position of the speaker relative to the referent, on the initial posture, and on the intention of the message. Similarly with illustrative gestures, discovering a similarity between the form of the hand movement and that of its referent requires extraction of perceptual invariants. Still other aspects of gestural meaning, finally, rely on conditions of use and, more particularly, on the relationship between the communication partners.

Thus, it appears that conceiving a body language gives rise to two related problems, one bearing on descriptive methods, the other on the establishment of signification. Should gestures be listed according to their morphology or according to their function? How does one determine their meaning: by contrasting forms, by analyzing conditions of use, or by relying on a verbal translation (the danger being that one would then study language about gestures instead of gestures themselves)? Human ethology, under quite different assumptions about gestures and speech relations, might offer other ways to answer these questions.

2. Language as gesture: an ethological approach

A tradition stemming from Darwin (1881) invites us to consider the relationship between gestures and speech as having been shaped by the phylogenesis of the human species. The higher mental functions that characterize *Homo sapiens* would have evolved from lower ones, and language and speech-related gestures from primitive, nonverbal behavior. Some candidate precursors of these achievements might involve competences other than those used in communication, such as tool making or tool using (Leroi-Gourhan, 1964). In some respects, gesture and speech would share a common origin, but the two domains could also have progressively differentiated during evolution in relation to functional specializations.

Within a neo-Darwinian perspective, there are two approaches to the investigation of gestures and speech. First, one can focus on factors that, during evolution, may account for the emergence of verbal and nonverbal behavior in human communication. Obviously, clues for reconstructing the phylogeny of gestures and speech are very scarce. Nevertheless, the results of paleontology, comparative anatomy, and comparative psychology may be used to formulate hypotheses on language origins (e.g., Lieberman, 1984). More specifically, one may search for competences shared by human and nonhuman primates as a basis for speculating about the development of species-specific human behavior. In this effort, there are two opposing viewpoints. For some authors, the biological foundations of verbal behavior are quite specific. They see a gap between *Homo sapiens* and the related apes due to the extinction of early hominid species. This hypothesis may be supported by the results of the study of some congenital language disorders and by the discovery of "language areas" in the brain (Lenneberg, 1967). For others, however, linguistic competence rather relates to general motor, social, and cognitive abilities whose roots may be found in proximate species like chimpanzees, gorillas, and orangutans. Language might thus indirectly originate from nonlinguistic factors, such as changes in growth rates of anatomical structures resulting in associated modifications of the brain and the speech apparatus (Bates, 1979). Of course, intermediate solutions may be defended by assuming both general factors in the cognitive and social aspects of communication and specific factors by which speech dissociates from other modalities in information transmission (see, e.g., Dingwall, 1979).

Second, one may simply compare human and animal behavior during social interactions. To begin with, modes of communication (necessarily nonverbal) are described and apparent similarities are found between distant species in the phylogeny. Hypotheses are then proposed assuming commonalities in the mechanisms underlying overt behavior, or abstract models are conceived for the formalization of both human and animal communication. Correlatively, by focusing on these limit conditions where the specificity of verbal behavior is not considered, the role of language in social interactions can better be identified by a "subtractive" method concerned only with the nonverbal aspects of communication.

2.1. The phylogeny of gestures and speech

The gestural hypothesis of language origins

The hypothesis of a gestural origin of language was a subject of lively debate during the 18th and 19th centuries and is still considered today (Hewes, 1973, 1976; Kendon, 1975a). Supporting evidence for this hypothesis and arguments against an alternative proposition that language evolved from vocal communication are found in several fields of inquiry. As far as neuroanatomy is concerned, the areas of the brain involved in language processing differ from those of structures controlling vocal communication in nonhuman primates. Furthermore, gestural performance and speech production rely on shared physiological mechanisms (Kimura, 1976; see discussion in chap. 6, this volume).

Comparative analyses of vocal repertoires in nonhuman species show a limited range of signals; about 20 different calls may be differentiated by human ears (see, e.g., Marler, 1976). Moreover, these vocal signals seem to serve only well-defined social functions, to occur in a limited number of contexts, and to be triggered automatically by the situation. If correspondences with human behavior are sought, they would be found in nonverbal aspects of vocal communication such as emotional expressions like laughing and crying, partially lexicalized interjections, or even speech prosody, rather than in language proper (Scherer, 1985, 1986). By contrast, the manual activity of nonhuman primates would be more diverse and more complex. It would depend less on emotional expression or social interactions, and it would be under "voluntary" control. These aspects are also present in language use.

Finally, comparative anatomy demonstrates characteristics of the vocal apparatus of nonhuman primates that limit the capacity to produce humanlike speech sounds. It has also been suggested from the analysis of fossilized traces that the evolution of the contemporary human vocal tract occurred relatively late. Moreover, it has been stressed that these anatomical changes would only have utility for a species endowed with the cognitive capacity for language. Thus, processes underlying verbal behavior should have developed in another domain, plausibly in manual activity as rule-governed behavior. A stronger version of this hypothesis assumes true sign languages among early hominids, of which our present-day gestures are a vestige. The weaker version only supposes antecedents of serial organization of speech in object manipulation (Allott, 1989; Bradshaw & Nettleton, 1982; Lieberman, 1985; MacNeilage, Studdert-Kennedy, & Lindblom, 1984, 1987; Parker, 1985).

The vocal hypothesis of language origins

The gestural hypothesis, nevertheless, remains disputed, and recent arguments support other views. It is suggested, for instance, that human language evolved from early vocal communication similar to the behavior of contemporary nonhuman primates (Steklis, 1985). First, these animals may display a much larger repertoire of vocal signals than hitherto supposed, for human ears may be unable to capture all the auditory nuances. Human hearing is the most sensitive in the frequency range used in spoken languages. Moreover, as is the case with foreign languages whose phonology differs from one's own, some meaningful contrasts made in animal vocalizations may not be perceived. Second, the affective and referential dimensions of a message are not easily distinguished (Marler, 1984). Alarm calls simultaneously mean fear, presence of danger, and incitement to flee because information may concern the sender, the environment, and the receiver. Accordingly, it has been assumed that vocal behavior manifests semantic properties in nonhuman species (Cheney & Seyfarth, 1982; Gouzoules, Gouzoules, & Marler, 1984; Seyfarth, Cheney, & Marler, 1980). Finally, it has been demonstrated that the vocal response of a macaque monkey may be conditioned (e.g., Sutton, Trachy, & Lindeman, 1981). Thus, vocal utterance is not always an automatic reaction, and some control may be exerted over it. Parallels with human speech processing have also been found on the receptive level, notably as regards lateral differences in the perception of species-specific sounds and coding of auditory signals (Petersen, 1982).

Social origins

The skilled use of verbal and gestural forms in communication implies assumptions by both the sender and the receiver about the state of knowledge and the disposition or intentions of the partner. Premack and Woodruff (1978) proposed calling these mental representations the "theory of mind," in order to stress their inferential and predictive nature. They also considered social cognition to be a prerequisite for language acquisition and devised nonverbal tasks to study it in chimpanzees. Deception, for example, requires the social competence of representing what is known in another mind and of controlling one's own behavior accordingly. Numerous cases of deceptive strategies have been reported in nonhuman primates (Whiten & Byrne, 1988). These observations raise the question of whether they demonstrate assumptions about another "mind" or are simply learned associations between performed action and expected consequences.

The hypothesis that communication develops within the evolution of a social competence has inspired studies on primate gestural behavior. Some of these works explicitly relate to analyses of human mother–infant interactions in a pragmatic perspective (see chap. 5). For instance, Plooij (1978, 1979) described the emergence of "intersubjectivity" in infant chimpanzees during play with their mothers. Some biting movements, first directed toward their own body, reach the body of the mother, who reacts with a "play face" and by tickling the baby. In this way, the contingency between action and reaction is established. The infant chimpanzee also learns to regulate arousal by approach and withdrawal movements. In this stage, infant behavior may be seen as analogous to the "perlocutionary" functions of early human communication, that is, the simple exchange of messages aimed at influencing the partner. The "illocutionary" functions, that is, the intentional attempts to influence another by conventional means, correspond to the display of signals specialized for communication, for example, lying down and exposing the belly to be tickled or presenting the back or another body part to be groomed. Similar observations of gestural communication in later stages of development have been made in young chimpanzees. First, between 14 and 20 months of age, ritualized requests for contact, food, or play appeared. Then, during the third year of age, chimpanzees show response expectation, for instance, by keeping the arm outstretched for a while. The third stage is reached between 40 and 52 months of age and is characterized by alternating eye movements toward the partner and toward the requested object (Tomasello, George, Kruger, Jeffrey, & Evans, 1985; Tomasello, Gust, & Frost, 1989).

Other attempts to describe the gestural behavior of apes with the tools of human pragmatics rely on classifications of messages seen as "speech acts" (commands, requests, apologies, protests, etc.). Several gestures of chimpanzees are interpreted by human observers as "greetings," "sexual invitations," and "demands for food" (de Waal, 1988; Nishida, 1980; Savage-Rumbaugh, Wilkerson, & Bakeman, 1977). Some controversies about sign language in anthropoids bear on the functional status of these learned performances. A reductionist view would interpret all these utterances as "requests" for reinforcement or simple conditioned responses. Against this notion, it is stressed that communicative acts, in anthropoids as in human infants, serve a larger range of functions. Indeed, apes may sign or point as a pure "statement." Note that similar discussions concern the pointing gesture in the human infant, which is seen either as derived from reaching or as a specialized act, a forerunner of naming (see chap. 5). Actually, the two functions might correspond to different forms: pointing with the extended index finger and reaching with the open hand. Anthropoids usually display the latter behavior but not the former (Nelson, 1987, 1988; F. G. Patterson, Tanner, & Mayer, 1988; Savage-Rumbaugh, 1987; Savage-Rumbaugh, McDonald, Sevcik, Hopkins, & Rubert, 1986; Seidenberg & Petitto, 1987)

These studies on gestures in nonspeaking species illustrate a more general conception of communicative behavior as a product of the evolution of social cognition (see reviews by Cheney, Seyfarth, & Smuts, 1986; Steele, 1989). A related suggestion, along the lines of the previously mentioned remark about the necessity of cognitive enhancements before changes in the vocal apparatus can be exploited, focus on another competence that anticipates language – the use of symbols.

Symbol uses in nonhumans

According to the last hypothesis on the phylogeny of communicative functions that will be considered (we limit ourselves here to studies concerning the relationships between gestures and speech), language evolved from a general capacity to form concepts and to use symbols (Premack, 1985). This hypothesis parallels similar suggestions in developmental psychology (see chap. 5), where it is proposed that language is acquired by children on the basis of the latest achievements of sensorimotor intelligence, and in neuropsychology (see chap. 6), where associations of verbal and nonverbal disorders are explained by reference to an impairment of a single central communication system. In this perspective, the cognitive abilities of anthropoids have been examined by studying their ability to learn nonvocal symbolic systems (for a review, see Ristau & Robbins, 1982). Some of these attempts rely on the use of artificial languages devised from lexigrams or colored plastic shapes. These experiments are beyond the scope of this book. Another procedure was to teach apes the American Sign Language (Gardner & Gardner, 1971, 1980; F. G. Patterson, 1978; Seidenberg & Petitto, 1979; Terrace, Petitto, Sanders, & Bever 1979, 1980).

With training over several years, 100 to 200 manual signs can be learned. However, the syntax of these utterances remains underdeveloped in comparison with the achievements of deaf children acquiring sign language. According to Terrace et al. (1979, 1980), most combinations used by the chimpanzee Nim involved only two signs. Three-part or four-part utterances were often redundant (e.g., "play-me-Nim" or "eat-drink-eat-drink"). Nevertheless, in two-part utterances, some orders were preferred to others ("more + X" was recorded eight times more often than "X + more"). Transitive verbs were often signed in the initial position ("tickle me" was more frequent than "me tickle"). Thus, some analogies are seen with syntactic rules followed in protogrammar by young children. However, human and nonhuman utterances differed in three respects: (*i*) the structure of the dialogue (Nim interrupted the signer's turns more often and rarely used signs from the trainer's antecedent utterances); (*ii*) the mode of acquisition (the chimpanzee rarely imitated new signs or pointing gestures and never asked questions about signs for new referents, which human children do; moreover, signs were slowly and systematically learned, whereas human young children rapidly and spontaneously integrate new items into their vocal or gestural repertoires); and (*iii*) relation to context (as discussed in the preceding section, use of symbols by apes may often be interpreted as request because the referents are present in the near environment and because signing provides the subject with immediate or delayed reward; Sanders, 1985; Savage-Rumbaugh, Pate, Lawson, Smith, & Rosenbaum, 1983; Vauclair, 1990; see also Blaschke & Ettlinger, 1987).

The mechanisms of the evolution of human communication

Observation of nonhuman primates has led to different hypotheses on the phylogeny of communicative behavior. These hypotheses are not mutually exclusive but emphasize diverse aspects of communication. Moreover, intermediate solutions may be found by assuming mixed communication systems combining vocal and gestural signals. In any event, it seems reasonable to consider a convergence of several factors in that phylogeny. But how is it possible to account for such an evolution? Is a neo-Darwinian theory relevant to the biology of communication? Two assumptions are central within this classic perspective. The first is gradualism, that is, the progressive accumulation of genetic mutations. The second is adaptation, that is, the notion that gene distribution in a population changes under environmental selective pressure. Verbal and gestural behavior relies on multiple modifications of the genetic material. How could this set of changes be saved before their phenotypic expression in speech? What is the selective advantage they would have provided in early human populations? Should specific genetic foundations of language be supposed, allowing, for instance, for the distinction of parts of speech and contextual rules in syntactic structures? How is the biochemistry of the genes linked to their behavioral expression? From a biological point of view, language origins are very problematic (Premack, 1985). It is largely admitted that human beings have evolved from ancestors shared with other living primates. Disputed issues do not concern the mere fact of evolution but its process, the rhythm and the time of the changes during phylogeny, their continuous or discrete character, and their adaptive value (see, e.g., Gould & Lewontin, 1979; Stebbins & Ayala, 1981). Thus, the framework into which the origins of language and gestures should be placed must be questioned.

Since Darwin (1881, 1872/1955), it has been argued that human expressive movements and their resemblance to animal signals should be interpreted in an evolutionary perspective. Speech and song have been assumed to derive from vocal communication used by some animals during courtship and, thus, to serve sexual selection. Yet, strangely enough, Darwin did not invoke natural selection to explain the evolution of affective gestures but rather three other principles: the association of serviceable habits, the antithesis, and the direct action of the nervous system. Instead of simple similarities in behavior, it would be similar mechanisms underlying communication that would demonstrate phylogenic continuity from animals to humans.

The first principle of serviceable associated habits is now difficult to accept. Some movements that would be useful in a given situation would be performed in a specific mental state. Becoming habitual, they would appear without utility in association with a similar mental state. For example, as Darwin wrote:

> A vulgar man often scratches his head when perplexed in mind;
> and I believe that he acts thus from habit, as if he experienced a
> slightly uncomfortable bodily sensation, namely, the itching of his
> head, to which he is particularly liable, and which he thus relieves.
> Another man rubs his eyes when perplexed, or gives a little cough
> when embarrassed, acting in either case as if he felt a slightly
> uncomfortable sensation in his eyes or windpipe. (*The Expression of
> the Emotions in Man and Animals*, 1872/1955, p. 32)

Thus, it is assumed that different situations trigger similar mental states.
In the cited example, itching, discomfort, and perplexity have been associated, and a single movement, scratching, has become the response to
each of those situations.

The second Darwinian principle is antithesis. When a situation elicits a
mental state that opposes another, like resignation instead of aggression,
movements that oppose those associated with the latter state are also
triggered. For instance, helplessness or apology may be expressed by
shrugging the shoulders, in combination with palm presentation, head
tilting, and eyebrow raising. For Darwin, none of these movements
would be of the "least service." The explanation would lie in the principle of "unconscious antithesis."

> Let it be observed how an indignant man, who resents, and will
> not submit to some injury, holds his head erect, squares his shoul-
> ders, and expands his chest. He often clenches his fists . . . , he
> frowns. . . . The actions and attitudes of a helpless man are, in
> every one of these respects, exactly the reverse. (*The Expression of
> the Emotions in Man and Animals*, 1872/1955, p. 271)

According to the third principle, some movements would simply be
reflex activity resulting from the structure of the nervous system.

With Lorenz (1950) and Tinbergen (1951), "objectivistic" ethology also
tried to account for human behavior by the same mechanisms as those
described in the study of animal behavior. However, no special process
was assumed as far as expressive movements are concerned. Intention
movements, like threatening by fist showing, or "displacement" activities, like hair grooming in puzzling situations, would demonstrate the
existence of so-called innate releasing mechanisms in humans. Furthermore, ethology attempted to show the universal distribution of gestures
performed in social interactions like greeting, courtship, or agonistic encounters (Eibl-Eibesfeldt, 1979, 1984). The assumption underlying such
research is that universality relates to innate, genetically programmed,
probably species-specific "instinctive" structures. This assumption may

be criticized on several grounds. A behavior that is observed in all human beings could simply result from similar constraints in groups living in different environments; it does not prove genetic influence. Reciprocally, genetic determinism of behavior does not imply universality but variability (E. O. Wilson, 1975). Gene distribution differs among human populations. If behavior were genetically determined, as resistance to some diseases may be, interethnic differences would result.

Beyond these issues, the relevance of an evolutionary theory for the analysis of human communication has to be discussed. If it is admitted that evolution concerns exclusively the repartition of genotypes within populations, it follows that only the aspects of behavior influencing that distribution are of interest. Little attention need be paid to gestures that do not offer the same selective advantage as reproductive behavior or environmental resource exploitation. Or, as did Darwin, a different explanation should be provided for communicative behavior like the expression of emotions, probably an indirect consequence of other aspects of behavior. Moreover, even if concern is restricted to the selective advantage of a particular form of behavior in the context of its occurrence (e.g., by considering speech a courtship behavior), it is focused on the genetic programming of this behavior, which is more probably the result of a general disposition belonging to the repertoire of individuals than a specification of the conditions of use. Thus, an evolutionary perspective would limit the analysis to the study of the programmed releasing mechanisms. If similar processes exist in human behavior, there would be only a few, and it would be very difficult to demonstrate them.

Partly for these reasons, ethology moved out of the narrow evolutionary framework to join comparative psychology in the study of proximate causation and ontogeny of behavior (see, e.g., Hinde, 1983). Experience was found critical in shaping many aspects of communication, and analogies or convergences were found in the behavior of loosely related species, for example, between birdsong and human speech. In these two domains, the use of sensory templates and the formation of dialects were discussed (see, e.g., Baker & Cunningham, 1985; Johnston, 1988; Marler & Peters, 1980; Wickler, 1986). Consequently, emphasis was put on processes like social learning and tradition transmission, which constitute modes of evolution in animal behavior not addressed by population genetics. If cultural evolution must be studied in a Darwinian framework, basic units corresponding to genes have to be discovered. Thus, the notion of "memes" was introduced to refer to the nongenetic replication of units that exist in the brain but are phenotypically expressed outside it, like words or gestures. These external events may be recorded by another individual and thus be copied in another brain. Information can thus be transmitted from individual to individual. According to Wickler (1986), a narrow parallelism with genetic transmission is displayed. Instead of cellular mechanisms by which genes, that is, protein chains, are duplicated, memes use communication and imitation processes to reproduce. Just as the phenotypic expression of a gene influences its distribution in the population, so, too, does the influence of a meme on the behavior of the bearer affect its probability of survival. For instance, a meme whose effect is the utterance of pleasant and easily perceived sounds would have a good chance of being copied. Whereas genes group together into genomes, memes combine to form complex sets whose effects do not reduce to the sum of those produced by individual memes. There is nothing to prove, however, that there is more here than simple analogies, and the materiality of units involved in cultural transmission has yet to be demonstrated (see also discussions in Bateman et al., 1990, and Lumsden & Wilson, 1982).

Comparative psychology has attempted in diverse ways to apply animal models to the study of human behavior. These approaches are of methodological and theoretical interest. As a general rule, the use of observational methods and statistical procedures developed for the analysis of animal communication has contributed greatly to the comprehension of human nonverbal behavior, independent of any assumption about the relationships between animal and human behavior. The hypothesis was proposed that human social behavior and particularly the use of nonverbal signals rely on underlying mechanisms that are similar to those discovered in animals, even in distant phyla. Numerous observations were made that enhanced our knowledge of human behavior, whether or not they supported the hypothesis. This point of view will now be discussed.

2.2. Gestures and speech in a comparative perspective

The study of animal communication shows similarities and peculiarities in the social behavior of different species. Some expressive movements like touching a companion or self-scratching are observed in several animals and in human beings, whereas speech and gestures like pointing are specific to our species. Nevertheless, ethology asks the same questions in all these cases. What causes behavior? What functions does it serve? How does it develop in ontogeny and phylogeny? In the search for answers, human ethology shed new light on gestural communication.

Behavioral repertoires

The first objective in ethology is to list the signals used in the observed population in the most reliable way. Accordingly, repertoires of human gestures were published, principally concerning the behavior of pre-school children (see, e.g., Blurton-Jones & Konner, 1973; Brannigan & Humphries, 1972; McGrew, 1972; P. K. Smith & Connolly, 1980). The methodological problems raised by these attempts will not be discussed here. These problems result first from the behavior being describable according to several criteria, referring either to the form of the movement or to its function. Second, the hierarchical organization of behavior implies that an act may be segmented at different levels. Thus, the same gesture may belong to several embedded categories. For example, the unit "beat" may be split into beats with object, open hand, or closed hand, or lumped with other gestures in the class of threat, agonistic, or anger movements (for related discussions, see, e.g., Bekoff, 1979; Dawkins, 1976; Drummond, 1981; Slater, 1978).

A simple comparison of the repertoires of related populations is indicative of the proximity of these populations in the phylogeny: The higher the number of overlapping items, the more likely is a shared history (see de Waal, 1988, for a recent example). Some displays are very frequent in some groups of chimpanzees and absent in others; in which cases, cultural transmission is assumed (McGrew & Tutin, 1978; Nishida, 1980). In this domain, qualitative differences may be of importance. Face touching, for instance, was frequently observed in human and nonhuman primates, which shows phylogenetic continuity. But species specificity was also demonstrated, for example, in the part of the face most often touched, the mouth in apes, the chin in human beings, which probably relates to functional differences (Dimond & Harries, 1984; Suarez & Gallup, 1986).

Functional behavioral categories and motivation analysis

Behavioral repertoires encompass a large number of items, and one may wish to define larger categories grouping several movements into meaningful sets. The notion of motivational system opens the way for classifications based on functional criteria: Belonging to a single category or motivational system are acts that are determined by the same range of factors and followed by similar consequences.

Automatic classification of nonverbal signals

Different methods have been proposed to identify the motivational system to which a gesture belongs from the context of its occurrence. One of these procedures relies on the assumption that movements with the same motivation are temporally associated. The duration of the observation session may be segmented in equal intervals, for instance, 3-min periods, and the frequencies of the different movements during these periods correlated. A shortcoming of such a method is that it yields different results according to the chosen interval. Moreover, it is necessary that the durations of the different signals do not vary too much, as is the case with a pointing gesture that would last less than a second and a forward-leaning posture maintained for some minutes. An alternative method is to consider sequential contingencies and to compute correlations between signals from the frequencies of antecedent or subsequent events (for a review, see Van Hoof, 1982).

Another procedure is based on behavior grouping by differences between individuals. It is assumed that age, gender, and other factors each influence similar movements in similar ways. For example, aggressive children more often frown, hit, and fixate and less often smile, manipulate objects, and talk to adults than inhibited children do.

Correlations derived from the first or the second method may be subjected to multidimensional analysis such as cluster analysis, factor analysis, or a nonparametric alternative. These methods, previously used in the study of animal communication, were later applied to the analysis of human repertoires. The results were similar groupings in the behavior of nonhuman primates and human children, and for instance, sets of rough-and-tumble play, agonistic interactions, and "social participation" (which included items like "talk," "point," and "smile") were identified (for human data, see Appleton, 1980; Blurton-Jones, 1972; Blurton-Jones, Ferreira, Brown, & Moore, 1980; R. Roper & Hinde, 1978; P. K. Smith, 1973; for animal data, see Maurus & Pruscha, 1973; for a presentation of methods, see, e.g., De Ghett, 1978; B. J. T. Morgan, Simpson, Hanby, & Hall-Craggs, 1976).

In some respects, however, these methods only constitute preliminary stages in motivation analysis. As will be discussed later, movements belonging to different categories may still be temporally associated in conflict situations. Furthermore, there is a general distrust in ethology of wide-ranging categories like aggression or attachment behavior that encompass activities whose causation and functional status differ. Thus, motivational analysis cannot bypass the study of the causal factors triggering behavior and of the functional consequences of its occurrence. The interest in automatic classification relies less on the resulting grouping than on the distinctions made. For instance, it appears that a gesture like pushing may, according to the context, belong to different categories, such as play or agonistic encounters.

Some sketched perspectives from control theory

Behavior may be conceived as a set of mutually exclusive activities that depend on motivational states. A state, namely the disposition to engage in a particular activity, may be represented by a point in a multidimensional space. The origin of the axes corresponds to the optimum state of the system. Behavior is considered a movement of the point toward the origin or in another direction. It is controlled by feedback and feedforward loops, that is, by the consequences of the movement. For example, there is an ideal ratio of glucose in the body fluids. Food ingestion increases the ratio; physical effort decreases it. Feeding may reduce a deficit or provide a surplus with a view to the next deficit. This system interacts with the drinking system because food may be dry or wet and because the two activities, which follow a "final common path," are incompatible. Thus, behavior depends on attraction toward the optimum state and on a set of variables of the organism and the environment that influence the actual state (McFarland, 1971; McFarland & Houston, 1981; Toates & Archer, 1978).

An illustration of such a conception in the analysis of human communication is provided by the study of the attachment system. Ethological criteria of attachment are the active search for physical proximity and the preferential orientation of behavior toward the object of attachment (Wickler, 1976). Several signals are involved to ensure physical proximity and to express preferences. For instance, human infants attached to their caregivers may cry when separated from them and smile or vocalize to maintain contact. Moreover, interindividual differences and ontogenetic changes are observed. Following Bowlby (1969), it was suggested that such behavior is controlled by the state of a hypothetical "security" system. Distress would result from too large a difference between the actual and the optimum state. Null difference would allow the occurrence of other activities of lower priority like exploration, which depends on a concurrent system controlling arousal (Bischof, 1975). Use of nonverbal signals relating to various motivational systems may be analyzed in similar ways. It may also be noted that some functional models developed in social psychology resemble the conception presented here (see, e.g., Cappella & Street, 1983; Patterson, 1982).

Self-touching gestures and displacement activities

The analysis of motivational systems is of particular interest for the study of movements occurring in conflict situations. Meeting an unfamiliar person, for example, may elicit both wariness and curiosity in young children and sometimes in adults. Self-touching movements are often observed in that context. However, the only function of scratching, grooming, nose touching, and hand fumbling seems to be body care, so their higher frequency in this kind of situation is not easily explained (Daly, Hogg, Sacks, Smith, & Zimring, 1983; Givens, 1978; Greenberg & Marvin, 1982; Jormakka, 1976; Kendon & Ferber, 1973; Stern & Bender, 1974; see also chap. 1, this volume, about greeting rituals).

Such reactions have been called, following Tinbergen (1951), displacement activities. This notion refers to behavior of animals that is irrelevant to the context in which it occurs, such as grooming or preening during courtship or agonistic encounters. Different interpretations have been proposed. The origin of the term is to be found in the conception of accumulated energy that "sparks over" or displaces when the normal activity is thwarted. Another activity, belonging to a different system, would then occur. This model was abandoned because the notion of energy could not be precisely defined and because it was observed that causal factors involved in the usual release of an activity also played an important role in triggering displacement activities. For example, displacement grooming in a conflict situation, like grooming after a rest period, would be a response to stimuli eliciting body care. Accordingly, another explanation was proposed. It was assumed that in conflict situations, among others, the inhibition of an activity by another – for instance, inhibition of grooming by locomotion – may cease, and thus the releasing mechanisms become effective. A more elaborate formulation of this hypothesis was proposed by McFarland (1974). Two modes of alternation between incompatible activities were distinguished. In cases of "competition," the causal factors that relate to ongoing activity remain in a steady state but the level of activation of a concurrent activity increases. When the latter level is higher than the former, concurrent activity is performed. In cases of "disinhibition," the activation level of ongoing activity decreases while the causal factors related to the concurrent activity remain stable. When the former level falls below the latter, ongoing activity is replaced by concurrent activity. When both sets of causal factors fluctuate, a combination of competition and disinhibition would allow "time-sharing." Thus, the release of self-touching gestures would depend on the presence of specific factors like dust, moisture, or parasites on the skin and on the activation level of concurrent activity like illustrative speech-related gestures. Alternative interpretations rely on the observation that disinhibition of displacement activities by thwarting ongoing behavior often results in higher levels of arousal than usual. Less complete or more rapid drinking or grooming movements are performed, which cannot be explained by the mere influence of the relevant causal factors. It is suggested that disinhibition implies a sort of "rebound" in activation level (for human and nonhuman examples of displacement activities, see Barash, 1974; Diezinger & Anderson, 1986; Easley, Coelho, & Taylor, 1987; Feyereisen & Blondiau, 1978; Kehrer & Tente, 1969; Seiss, 1965; for reviews of the theoretical models, see Hinde, 1970; McCleery, 1983; Roper, 1980; see also discussions by Houston, 1982; McFarland, 1983; Roper, 1984).

Interpreting self-touching movements as displacement activities has advantages over other explanations proposed in psychology. Together with fidgeting and nail-biting, they were traditionally considered signs of "nervousness" (M. R. Jones, 1943; Krout, 1935a, 1935b; D. G. Williams, 1973). They are now often seen as indications of anxiety (see chap. 3). Ekman and Friesen (1969, 1972) called them "adaptors" to suggest that they allow the emotional experience to be managed. However, there is no experimental evidence for such a hypothesis but only unprovoked observations – for instance, high incidence of self-touching in cases of depression (e.g., Ekman & Friesen, 1974b; I. H. Jones & Pansa, 1979; Polsky & McGuire, 1979; Ulrich & Harms, 1979; but see the discussions by Bouhuys, Beersma, & Van den Hoofdakker, 1988; and Ellgring, 1989). Neither is this explanation very useful in contexts like free play, narrations, or problem-solving tasks. Actually, self-touching is observed in a greater variety of situations, and it could also relate to resting periods or to transitions between activities (D'Alessio & Zazzetta, 1986; Feyereisen, 1977; Grant, 1969; Hatta & Dimond, 1984; Miller & Bart, 1986; Rögels, Roelen, & Van Meel, 1990).

Thus ethological models invite one to be cautious in proposing functional explanations and to begin by considering two sets of causal factors in the occurrence of self-touching gestures. First, the presence of specific factors has to be controlled. Temperature and ambient humidity as well as anxiety may cause perspiration or itching and, indirectly, body care (see, e.g., Jurich & Jurich, 1974). In this respect, a curious phenomenon has been reported: Subjects engaged more often in body touching while watching a film documentary on insects than while watching another scientific film (Wild, Johnson, & McBrayer, 1983). Visual representations of potential stimuli for body care might suffice to elicit the movements, but other interpretations of this observation are also possible. Second, controls also have to be imposed on the activation level of concurrent activities. Competition between self-touching and illustrative speech-related activity for the "final common path" is suggested by the negative correlations observed between the frequencies of these movements (e.g., A. Campbell & Rushton, 1978; Duncan & Fiske, 1977).

Movements other than self-touching gestures may be explained in similar ways. Solitary speech and vocal activities might be released in the absence of stimulation for other instrumental or social behavior (this hypothesis, however, has never been investigated). Competition between conflicting tendencies results in diverse behavioral manifestations like intention movements, redirected activities, and alternation of these activities (Hinde, 1970, chap. 17). Such a conception fits the observations of closing rituals in conversations (see chap. 1, this volume). The occurrence of illustrative speech-related gestures themselves depends on the activation level of concurrent activities like adopting a folded-arm posture (Feyereisen, 1982). The causation of rhythmical behavior (rocking, kicking, waving, etc.) diplayed by normal human infants resembles that of self-touching in later life. These stereotypies are influenced by context: A lower incidence was observed when the infant was cradled or carried than when placed on the floor and, then, a lower incidence when an adult was near than otherwise. It has been supposed that stereotyped behavior is triggerred by diverse stimuli to which the organism responds in a nonadaptive way. Rhythmic movements occur instead of specific responses because the infants are developmentally unable to respond to the stimuli with appropriate behavior. This inchoate activity would be the support for later motor acquisitions (Thelen, 1979, 1980, 1981a, 1981b). In other contexts, self-touching and rhythmical movements might play a role in filtering external stimulation. Delius (1970) assumed a specific role of grooming behavior in arousal homeostasis. Similarly, with the hypothesis of "cut-off" postures, Chance (1962) suggested a capacity of the organism to direct attention away from harmful stimulations and toward predictable ones. Supporting evidence may be found in the behavior of autistic children, whose rate of motor activity increases in unfamiliar and social environments. The stereotyped behavior could serve to prevent social contact and the receipt of excessive information (Hutt & Hutt, 1965, 1968; Richer, 1976; Van Engeland, Bodnar, & Bolhuis, 1985; Volkmar, Hoder, & Cohen, 1985).

Discovering the functional meaning of gestures

Since its beginnings, ethology has set out to discover the functional meaning of species-specific behavior. This approach may apply to the study of many human gestures, such as head movements. A general rule is to consider that the meaning of a movement is defined by the context in which it is performed and/or by the response of another individual perceiving the movement.

Noirot (1989) emphasized that the true message conveyed by a gesture, its proper meaning, and the whole context are not directly observable. She proposed the combination meaning = movement + form + context. In this formula, only movement and form may be described empirically. As far as context is concerned, it encompasses an indeterminate number of variables, but the observer may still focus on the contingent movements of the sender and the receiver. Indeed, to be effective, communication depends on physical events and, thus, on observable behavior. This statement seems trivial, but as Noirot stressed, it implies that the meaning of a signal cannot be established in some cases. For example, in an art gallery, a person may be observed nodding twice in the same way. The movement would relate once to silent thoughts about a picture and once to focusing visual attention on a detail. If no more information is available, the observer is forced to attribute the same meaning to the two head nods, whereas the true meaning of them both may be different. Thus, communication relies on the interpretation of the signal by a receiver, and the resulting meaning may not correspond to the meaning of the signal for the sender (who is influenced by other contextual variables).

In the next step of the analysis, Noirot proposed defining a complementary equation context = consequences + other variables, where consequences refer to the observable results of the movement. The observer's interpretation of the signal will be influenced by the perceived consequences of the movement, for example, a change in the spatial relationship between the head-nodding person and the picture. Among several possible consequences, some are more frequent and may even be considered constant. Head tilt, for instance, would involve eye movements in all cases where the same object remains under visual fixation. The meaning "interest" or "visual attention" can be inferred. From such a perspective, it may be understood that some movements express a universal meaning in relation to the constant part of conveyed information. At the same time, the variable part of information would explain transmission of different specific messages. For example, the brief "eye flash" signal resulting from eyebrow raising is displayed in a great variety of social interactions and may be interpreted in different ways, such as sexual interest, curiosity, or anger. Morever, this movement may indicate affirmation (in Polynesia) or negation (in Greece). All these particular meanings share a common term: social contact is accepted, either friendly or hostile. On the contrary, contact avoidance would be expressed by signs of neglect or indifference (Eibl-Eibesfeldt, 1972; Grammer et al., 1988).

Ethological study of gestures in social interactions

The motivational analysis of expressive movements studies them as reactions to external stimuli in relation to the internal state of the organism. The signals released in this way may influence another organism or may occur in response to another organism's behavior. Thus, we turn now to the communicative value of expressive movements, which will be examined regarding their role in social interactions.

Functional analysis of behavioral sequences

If the functional meaning of a signal partially depends on its consequences in social as well as in nonsocial contexts, its role in communication may be demonstrated by sequential dependencies in the behavior of interacting individuals. It has been shown in numerous situations that the probability of occurrence of a movement is influenced by nonverbal cues of another individual. Some brief illustrations may be given.

- Attempts to speak to an experimenter were inhibited when the experimenter displayed a tongue-showing signal while reading, compared with a control condition in which only a concentrated expression was shown. This signal may be observed in various circumstances involving physical effort, teasing, embarrassment, etc., all probably involving unwillingness to engage in social interactions (Dolgin & Sabini, 1982; N. Jones, Kearins, & Watson, 1987; W. J. Smith, Chase, & Lieblich, 1974).
- Imitating the behavior of a partner is more often followed by affiliative responses like speaking, smiling, or playing together than by negative reactions or indifference (Grusec & Abramovitch, 1982).
- A great number of observations are of agonistic interactions. It was observed that the probabilities of being attacked or not, of winning or losing, and of staying together or apart after the conflict were influenced by ex-

changes of signals during the interaction (see, e.g., Brownell & Bakeman, 1981; Camras, 1977; H. J. Ginsburg, Pollman, & Wanson, 1977; Montagner et al., 1978; Sackin & Thelen, 1984).

• Courtship is probably the most obvious situation where approach and avoidance movements depend on exchanged nonverbal signals (see, e.g., Kendon, 1975b; Lockard & Adams, 1980; Moore, 1985; Moore & Butler, 1989; Walsh & Hewitt, 1985).

Social interactions that can be analyzed from such a point of view are extremely diverse, and accordingly, the potential information available from nonverbal messages is considerable (W. J. Smith, 1977). Several statistical methods have been devised in ethology to deal with the problem of demonstrating sequential contingencies (see, e.g., Sackett, 1987; Van Hoof, 1982; see also Wampold, 1984).

Asymmetric influences, relationships, and social structures

Sequential analyses often demonstrate that an individual may exert a greater influence on his or her partner than reciprocally. This can be the case with adult–infant and with male–female interactions. Two individuals with a common past experience may also develop a hierarchical relationship, one being dominant over the other. Much effort has been devoted in human ethology to demonstrate the existence of such a social organization and the role of nonverbal signals in its functioning (see, e.g., Keating, 1985; Savin-Williams, Small, & Zeldin, 1981; Sluckin & Smith, 1977; Strayer, 1980; Strayer & Strayer, 1976; Zivin, 1977).

Chance's (1967) hypothesis, according to which hierarchical relationships are found in the structure of visual attention in different primate groups, led to several studies of human behavior. Low-status animals spend more time gazing at high-status animals and are more influenced by them than the inverse. The same results were obtained with human children. It was observed that the children who received the most attention intervened most to propose activities, were most imitated, or were most prone to support other children in conflicts. Similarly, in human adults, the speaker receives more visual attention than the listener, the superior more than the subordinate, the expert more than the non-expert, and these effects combine in a nonadditive way, as shown in several experiments by Dovidio and co-workers (Abramovitch & Grusec, 1978; Anderson & Willis, 1976; Dovidio, Brown, et al., 1988; Dovidio & Ellyson, 1985; Dovidio, Ellyson, et al., 1988; H. J. Ginsburg & Miller, 1981; Hold, 1977; LaFreniere & Charlesworth, 1983; Vaughn & Waters, 1981).

The discussions about the utility of the notion of dominance to describe social structures and its relevance in the study of human groups will not be entered into here (see, e.g., Bernstein, 1981). We intend only to illustrate a general rule followed in ethology to assess the functional value of a signal. The principle is to ask the question, Who does what to whom, and how often? The same act, such as hindquarter presentation in baboons, may convey different meanings according to whether the receiver is male or female, juvenile or adult, of higher or lower status, familiar or unfamiliar (Hausfater & Takacs, 1987; see also Wickler, 1967). This consideration has given rise to studies inspired by human sociometrics where the frequency of a given act, say grooming, is computed in matrices whose rows and columns correspond to the individuals of the group. In this way, studies of animal communication have shown that societies are organized along dimensions like sex, age class, familiarity, as well as status. Other phenomena like the formation of cliques or of asymmetrical relationships were also demonstrated (e.g., Sade, 1972; see also B. J. T. Morgan et al., 1976; Pearl & Schulman, 1983).

Similar observations can be made about human gestural behavior like touching. If it occurs in greetings, different modes of touch are displayed, kissing, handshaking, or embracing, according to the social category of the partner. Similarly, in public places, occurrences of touching and body parts touched vary according to the gender of the partners. In our societies, same-sex touching seems to be inhibited, especially in men. The issue of asymmetry in the use of gesture has also been raised. As a "possessive" attitude, touching would relate to high status and would be more frequently addressed by men to women than the reverse. This interpretation is disputed, however. Contradictory findings have been reported, and alternative explanations may be proposed (gender differences might relate to subjective reactions to being touched, emotional expression, etc.). Again, the methodological problems involving the qualitative aspects of touching have to be taken into account in the assessment of such apparently simple behavior (Heslin & Alper, 1983; Major, Schmidlin, & Williams, 1990; Stier & Hall, 1984; Storrs & Kleinke, 1990; Thayer, 1986).

Comparison of animal and human communication is worthwhile because it leads to the development of new methodologies allowing the study of gestures without verbal mediation. It is also suggested that the same mechanisms may be involved in social interactions and that the same dimensions may organize human and nonhuman groups. These aspects of communication do not depend on processing of meanings coded by cultures or on true linguistic competence. Nevertheless, language could have evolved from such a background involving some social competence.

2.3. Concluding remarks: what is communication?

Human communication relies on processes that also exist in other species. Consequently, ethology may propose formal models of communication that fit both human and animal communication. Let us first consider the nature of the signals exchanged during communication. During evolution, some aspects of behavior, like displacement activities, intention movements, or redirected activities, would become specialized for communicative functions. However, besides these ritualized "social displays," other nonspecific activities, like sitting together or scanning the environment, may also acquire communicative value. The notion of "message" has a wider extension than that of "signal" and may account for such a range of phenomena.

The processes underlying emission and reception of messages have to be specified. Ethological models of communication assuming automatic responses to "key signals" have been supported by some analyses of behavioral sequences in birds and fishes but were found inadequate in the study of primate communication. Behavior like grooming cannot easily be considered a sequence of stereotyped acts. Moreover, responses to signals like genito-anal swelling that resemble social releasers vary too much according to context to be considered wholly automatic. These forms of communication may depend on some kind of learning or even on more complex mechanisms involving mental representations and inferential processes (Andrew, 1972; Rowell & Olson, 1983). It is easy to see that increased understanding of human nonverbal communication can be gained from these discussions (for reviews, see S. Green & Marler, 1979; Slater, 1983; W. J. Smith, 1977).

Communication may also be considered from the point of view of the costs and the benefits it implies for the sender and the receiver. Another kind of discussion concerns the adaptive value of communicating. In some circumstances, hiding intentions may be useful. Why would some signals have evolved to serve communicative functions? One suggestion is to see social interactions as "negotiations" in which any decision about the emission of a signal takes into account the behavior of the partner (Hinde, 1985; Wiley, 1983).

Finally, in a third group of studies, the attempt is made to describe communication by means of simple mathematical tools, like Markov chains or as a reduction of uncertainty as quantified by information theory. Some inadequacies of these models have resulted in alternative proposals of a "grammar of actions" according to which behavioral sequences are derived from generative rules (see, e.g., Fentress & Stilwell, 1973; Losey, 1978; Rodger & Rosenbrugh, 1979; Westman, 1977). In this approach, the relationships found between language and nonverbal means of communication are, obviously, purely metaphorical. The meaningfulness of the analogy can be questioned, however, with reference either to the "design features" of language or to semiotic classification distinguishing symbols from other signs (see chap. 1). In short, it appears that until now, human ethology has offered little insight on the use of language and on speech-related behavior, even if it does demonstrate the diversity and wealth of other modes of communication.

3. Autonomy of gestures and speech: the notion of nonverbal communication

Gestures may substitute for words, as demonstrated by the creation of sign languages, and words may express anything, even subtle feelings or social relationships. Nevertheless, it is difficult to account for these uses of language and gestures in a single framework, which implies that two independent systems, controlled by specific rules and aimed at their own objectives, should be considered. The notion of nonverbal communication reflects such a conception. Over the last thirty years, an increasing number of studies, mainly in social psychology, have been published in this field, and several surveys have attempted to synthesize the present state of knowledge. Actually, *nonverbal communication* refers to a great variety of activities that, for the sake of clarity, may be grouped in several ways. One approach focuses on the "channel" used: face, gaze, voice, bodily expression, use of space, etc. Another way, closer to attempts in pragmatics and ethology, emphasizes the functions fulfilled by nonverbal means: emotional expression, intimacy regulation, leadership, persuasion, etc. Yet another kind of review is organized along traditional dimensions in psychology: psychometric assessment, development, individual differences, psychopathology, etc. (Argyle, 1988; Bull, 1983; Druckman, Rozelle, & Baxter, 1982; Harper, Wiens, & Matarazzo, 1978; Heslin & Patterson, 1982; M. L. Patterson, 1983; Wolfgang & Bhardwaj, 1984).

It is not the intent of this chapter to cover this literature exhaustively but rather to examine studies that deal with the relationships of verbal and nonverbal communication and that assume that they depend on autonomous systems. These studies share common features. First, three underlying assumptions are generally acknowledged: (*i*) language and nonverbal communication serve different functions; (*ii*) emotions and interpersonal attitudes are mainly expressed by nonverbal means; and (*iii*) nonverbal communication allows one to establish, develop, and maintain social relationships (Beattie, 1981b; see also Burgoon, 1985).

The work of Mehrabian (1972), for example, is representative and stems from clinical preoccupations. In this context, Freud's claim is often quoted: "He that has eyes to see and ears to hear may convince himself that no mortal can keep a secret. If his lips are silent, he chatters with his fingertips" (1905/1953, pp. 77–78). This suggestion of a separation between two modes of expression inspired the first systematic studies on nonverbal communication (e.g., Deutsch, 1949; Mahl, 1967).

Furthermore, as noted by Scherer (1984), inquiries into the nonverbal realm most often follow the functionalist program defined by Brunswik in 1952: to demonstrate probabilistic relationships, first, between initial variables and an intermediate nonverbal behavior and, second, between this behavior and terminal variables that depend on it. Nonverbal signals may be compared to a lens through which some conditions triggering overt behavior are perceived. Thus, nonverbal communication involves two processes: encoding, by which signals are sent from an initial state, and decoding, by which the signals are received and interpreted. To the extent the receiver understands the signal as a consequence of an inferred covert initial state, the two processes are linked. For instance, an experimental subject is shown emotion-loaded slides like a tender picture of a woman with her baby or repulsive close-ups of surgical procedures, and the nonverbal reactions are filmed. This film is then shown to another subject who is ignorant of the eliciting conditions and is asked to guess the emotional valence of the slide. Nonverbal signals are interpreted with more or less accuracy depending on the emotional expressivity of the sender and the decoding skills of the receiver (Buck, 1984). Similarly, a meta-analytic survey of the relevant literature demonstrates that the experimenter's expectancy has a significant effect on several nonverbal behavioral variables and that these variables have a significant effect on the experimental outcome. It can thus be concluded that some experimenter bias may depend on nonverbal communication of expectancy (Harris & Rosenthal, 1985; see also Rosenthal, 1982). In some situations, however, the signal reception is distorted by false beliefs, and the interpretation does not really relate to the eliciting conditions. For example, an applicant who displays a high rate of gestures during a job interview may be judged more motivated than another who speaks without gesturing, but motivation as independently assessed by questionnaire has little influence on gestural behavior (Gifford, Ng, & Wilkinson, 1985).

Selected studies will now be examined from two perspectives. First, we will attempt to briefly identify the information potentially available from nonverbal behavior, especially from gestures and postures. Second, it is necessary to ask whether the movements that are usually performed while speaking can also convey meaning without speech and how specific information provided in this way is.

3.1. The role of gestures and postures in nonverbal communication

In summary, current approaches to nonverbal communication try to assess the extent to which bodily signals can translate in visible form unobservable mental states like subjective emotion, interpersonal attitudes, or personality traits, and the extent to which people can, from the perceived bodily signals, infer psychological states that may or may not correspond to the true conditions of elicitation. Thus, studies may be distinguished, first, according to the nature of the conveyed information (i.e., emotions, attitudes, etc.) and, second, in each of these cases, according to the perspective chosen in describing communication (i.e., the emission or the reception of bodily signals).

The communication of emotion by gestures and postures

In emotional expression, the quality and intensity of the affect can be distinguished (Ekman & Friesen, 1967). The hypothesis has been proposed that the quality of emotions is mainly expressed by facial movements whereas bodily cues relate to the intensity of the emotion. Thus, gestures and postures could be interpreted as signs of emotional arousal, but little information about the nature of the emotion would be conveyed through this channel. Such a hypothesis seems counterintuitive when one considers gestures that express states like happiness, anger, or fear (e.g., manifestations of triumph in athletes after a goal, blows or kicks as signs of rage, or face covering in cases of fright). These movements have been described as emblematic expressions of emotion (chap. 1, see, e.g., Sogon & Masutani, 1989) but have rarely been studied as actual emotional expressions, probably because they are not easily elicited in laboratory conditions.

Sending gestural cues of emotion

The frequency and duration of gestures may be influenced by experimental conditions in which emotional arousal is increased or lowered. In some procedures, the subject is requested to read funny, interesting, sad, or boring texts, to answer embarrassing or neutral questions, to discuss intimate or impersonal topics, or to face an experimenter who behaves warmly or coldly. All these different manipulations yielded the expected result of affecting gestural performance. In another kind of procedure, actors were explicitly instructed to express emotions by non-verbal signals (e.g., Bull, 1978; Edelman & Hampson, 1979; Freedman et al., 1972; Natale & Bolan, 1980; Sousa-Poza & Rohrberg, 1977; Wallbott & Scherer, 1986).

There is little doubt that emotional arousal may influence gestural activity, but several questions still remain open. First, different movements – like illustrative, as opposed to self-touching, gestures – might relate to qualitatively distinct states. According to Ekman and Friesen (1969, 1972), automanipulative gestures called "adaptors" allow one to cope with such emotional states as depression and embarrassment (see discussion in chap. 2). Nevertheless, it can be hypothesized that other emotional experiences, such as anger or disgust, might not be managed in similar ways. Similarly, within a single category of gestures, the relationship between arousal and motor activity might vary according to the nature of the emotion. Finally, gestural behavior does not relate to emotional arousal linearly. In role-playing subjects who pretended to react to five suggested journeys, some rated as more pleasant than others, the total duration, amplitude, and speed of illustrative gestures varied according to the journeys suggested, but a maximum was reached for the mildly attractive one (Ricci-Bitti, Argyle, & Giovannini, 1979).

Perceiving gestural cues of emotion

Few attempts have been made to investigate whether facial and bodily indications play separate roles in conveying information about emotional state. Little information is available on the attribution of emotional states like joy, sadness, fear, or anger from body movements isolated from facial expression. Nevertheless, de Meijer (1989) has identified 20 movements that elicit unambiguous attributions of emotional meaning and 21 movements that may be understood in several ways. Furthermore, above-chance-level judgments of emotion may be elicited from spotlights information about gait movements, that is, on the sole basis of the dynamic characteristics of the movements. It has also been stated that gestural cues are used in rating the target person on dimensions like calm–agitated, relaxed–tense, or unexpressive–expressive. Embarrassment may be recognized from body movements, whereas amusement is not. Judges reported looking at the feet and the hands as well as at the face to rate embarrassment, whereas amusement was mainly inferred from facial cues (Edelman & Hampson, 1981; Ekman, Friesen, O'Sullivan, & Scherer, 1980; McClenney & Neiss, 1989; Montepare, Goldstein, & Clausen, 1987; O'Sullivan, Ekman, Friesen, & Scherer, 1985; Walters & Walk, 1988).

Behavioral attitudes

In interpersonal relationships, body movements may reveal whether interaction is desired and may influence the reactions of the partner who perceives them. Together with smiling and eye contact, orienting the torso toward the partner, leaning forward, nodding the head, and gesturing have been studied as expressions of involvement or affiliation; self-touching, leaning backward, and moving the legs are signals of more negative feelings.

Expressing interpersonal attitudes by gestures and postures

To assess the influence of felt attitudes on body movements, one procedure attempts to manipulate the expectations or the disposition of the subject toward the partner or the situation. For instance, subjects were requested during role-playing to either obtain approval or elicit disapproval. Illustrative gestures were performed at a higher frequency in the former condition and self-touching in the latter. It was also observed that posture was influenced by whether the conversation topic was interesting or boring and whether it elicited agreement or disagreement. In other studies, subjects were presented preliminary questionnaires bearing on anxiety or "willingness to communicate," and correlations were computed between verbal answers and measures of nonverbal behavior during conversations. As expected, "reticent" subjects nodded less often and leaned backward or touched the face more often (Bull, 1987; Coker & Burgoon, 1987; Burgoon & Koper, 1984; Maxwell, Cook, & Burr, 1985; Rosenfeld, 1966a, 1966b, 1967).

A more specific hypothesis concerns the display of a posture that, intentionally or not, imitates the partner's. According to Scheflen (1964), postural congruence expresses a privileged relationship between the interacting persons. Several observations support such a hypothesis. For instance, arm and torso positions of students and their teachers were recorded every 5 minutes. The students' ratings of their rapport with the teacher were positively correlated with a measure of the similarity of postures between students and teachers. Likewise, on a beach, bodily attitudes were more similar in man–woman couples than in man–m⁓

dyads. However, contradictory findings were reported by McDowall (1978b), who, by studying synchronization of postures with a finer grained temporal scale, did not observe any difference between pairs of friends and pairs of strangers regarding postural congruence. Nor was there a significant correlation between the extent of posture mirroring and the later rating of the relationships in two persons unaware of being filmed in a waiting room. Furthermore, verification of Scheflen's hypothesis requires a control of the extent of synchrony that simply results from chance (Bavelas, Black, Lemery, & Mullett, 1986; Beattie & Beattie, 1981; Bernieri, 1988; Gatewood & Rosenwein, 1981; Kendon, 1970; LaFrance, 1979, 1985; LaFrance & Ickes, 1981).

Gestures and postures may also be influenced by other variables and thus transmit other information relative to status, competence, assertiveness, or sincerity. For instance, self-confidence or dominance may be expressed by gesturing, touching the partner, or being relaxed. Inversely, shyness, anxiety, low self-esteem, or submissiveness may be manifested by head lowering or increased rates of automanipulations or postural changes. Thus, the stressed appearance may resemble the expression of low status or lack of expertise or the leakage of deception. These alternative accounts of the same bodily signal are not easily disentangled (Ellyson & Dovidio, 1985; Lecompte, 1981; Leffler, Gillespie, & Conaty, 1982; Poling, 1978; Mehrabian, 1972; Waxer, 1977).

Perceiving attitudes from gestures and postures

Judgments of the attitudes of others are influenced by perceived gestural and postural behavior, even if these cues are sometimes of minor importance in comparison with vocal and facial ones. For instance, bodily signals become more decisive in friendliness ratings when a neutral face is kept. With tachistoscopic presentation, judgments of positive–negative or dominant–submissive attitudes are more accurate for moving than for static stimuli, and for bodily cues than for facial ones (Dittmann, Parloff & Boomer, 1965; McLeod & Rosenthal, 1983; Waldron, 1975).

In Western societies, "closed" postures, that is, folded arms and tight knees, give an impression of passivity and coldness. Posture mirroring elicits higher ratings of attentiveness than true postural congruence with respect to the right–left dimension. A listener may be judged more or less involved in a conversation or to agree or disagree by means of head orientation and trunk, arm, and leg positions. Posture may also modify the impression formed from other nonverbal cues like gaze or interpersonal distance (Bavelas, Black, Chovil, Lemery, & Mullett, 1988; Bull, 1987; Harrigan, Oxman & Rosenthal, 1985; Maxwell et al., 1985; Mc-Ginley, McGinley, & Nicholas, 1978; McGinley, Nicholas, & McGinley, 1978; L. M. Schwartz, Foa, & Foa, 1983; Trout & Rosenfeld, 1980).

Appreciation of status is also influenced by nonverbal signals: standing up or sitting down, erectness of posture, gaze orientation, and facial expression (Dovidio & Ellyson, 1985; Halberstadt & Saitta, 1987; Keating, 1985; Schwartz, Tesser, & Powell, 1982; Weisfeld & Beresford, 1982).

As far as gestures are concerned, brief self-touching of the face and palm presentation movements give higher impressions of warmth and naturalness than does immobility (Harrigan, Kues, & Weber, 1986; Harrigan, Kues, Steffen, & Rosenthal, 1987). On bipolar semantic differential scales assessing connotative meanings, hand configurations elicit the same range of ratings as faces, voices, words, and drawings. Multidimensional analysis of these judgments reveals similar structures with three general factors: evaluation on the dimensions of pleasant–unpleasant, power (dominant–submissive), and activation or control (active–passive). Ratings of verbal descriptions of gestures and postures like fist showing or backward leaning yielded comparable results (Gitin, 1970; Kudoh & Matsumoto, 1985).

Person-related attributions

Individual differences in bodily expression: the influence of sex roles and personality traits

It is well known that men and women differ in their nonverbal behavior in many respects. Gender-related differences have been described in sitting postures (men more often lean backward or keep the knees apart), in walking, in greeting (see chap. 1), and in displaying embarrassment (nose touching is more frequent in men, cheek or upper chest touching more frequent in women). However, the factors that determine these differences remain unknown: Effective influence of biological variables is unlikely, but a strong demonstration of imitation learning has yet to be made (see, e.g., Aries, 1982; Klein, 1984; Rekers, Sanders, & Strauss, 1981; and, for reviews, Davis & Weitz, 1981; Vrugt & Kerkstra, 1984).

Moreover, the personal character of gaits, gestural styles, and postural habits has long been acknowledged. Recurrently, the attempt is made to reduce these individual differences to personality types or variables like extraversion, self-esteem, and Machiavellianism. How-

ever, correlations between results obtained from personality questionnaires and measures of nonverbal behavior have rarely reached significance, so there is little support for the ancient "physiognomic"
hypotheses, which assume transparency of inner qualities in bodily
expression. For example, gestural rate was not found to be related to
personality measures derived from the Gough Adjective Check List.
Inconsistencies have also been observed. For example, ability to express emotion by gestural means was related to extraversion as assessed by the Eyzenck Personality Inventory, but frequency of illustrative gestures during interviews was not (A. Campbell & Rushton, 1978;
Cunningham, 1977; Duncan & Fiske, 1977; Kenner, 1989; Riggio &
Friedman, 1986; Wiens, Harper, & Matarazzo, 1980).

*Inferences about gender, age, and personality from gestures and
postures*

Sexual differences in nonverbal behavior lead to some gestures or
postures being judged more masculine or feminine irrespective of the
actual sex of the person acting in this way. Several behavioral checklists
of "sexual differentiation" have been proposed on this basis (Barlow et
al., 1979; Perkins, 1986; see also Frable, 1987; Garcia & Derfel, 1983;
Green, Neuberg, & Finck, 1983).

Likewise, age estimates may be elicited from gait information, and
persons of the same age-group score differently in relation to a rated
"dynamism" (Montepare & Zebrowitz-McArthur, 1988).

Finally, even if correlations between personality assessment by questionnaires and nonverbal behavior generally yield low coefficients, perception of various nonverbal signals by the nonprofessional entails distinct and consistent attributions about the personality of the sender
(Riggio & Friedman, 1986; Scherer, Scherer, Hall, & Rosenthal, 1977;
Wallbott, 1985).

*Comments: implications and limits of studies on nonverbal
communication*

With this mass of studies, the communicative value of gestures and
postures can hardly be questioned. Of course, the inquiry has mainly
addressed only some of the many meanings of bodily signals, and more
particularly those of a socioemotional nature. But even with this bias, the
multiple implications of the analysis of nonverbal communication have
been demonstrated for both theoretical and applied investigations.

From a methodological point of view, the relationships between nonverbal expression and implicit dispositions allow the use of nonverbal measures in the assessment of attitudes and preferences. These measures are less intrusive than questionnaires and, perhaps, also less controlled by the subjects (see, e.g., the cases of racial or ethnic discrimination: Crosby, Promley, & Saxe, 1980). In this way, nonverbal communication may concern almost all the fields of social psychology covered in the chapters of classic handbooks: person perception, attraction, opinion changes, intergroup relations, etc. Moreover, impressions given by nonverbal signals influence social interactions outside laboratory conditions, as in schools, courts, business situations, and medical and counseling practices. From an applied-psychology perspective, the domain for research on nonverbal communication is unlimited. These directions, however, are beyond the scope of this chapter.

Nevertheless, some of the limitations of studies on nonverbal communication and of the framework chosen to present them here have to be discussed. These issues relate, first, to the importance of context in the interpretation of body movements and, second, to the nature of the processes underlying communication.

Contextual influences

The meaning of a nonverbal signal may vary according to the other verbal and nonverbal signals that are simultaneously present or according to the context of occurrence. This proposition may first be illustrated by an analysis of the social functions of gaze during conversations (see chap. 1). Looking at the face of the partner cannot be interpreted in the same way for both the speaker and the listener. Subjects who look at the partner while speaking and who avoid gaze contact while listening are judged of higher status than those who behave inversely, which is the more usual way (Dovidio & Ellyson, 1985). Thus, visual attention cannot be considered univocally as a cue for dominance or submissiveness. Other examples may be drawn from studies on nonverbal communication in psychotherapeutic relations. Impressions formed about the counselor depend on interactions between several variables and on a sort of "halo" effect rather than on a simple additive combination of indices (Tepper & Haase, 1978; Young, 1980). More generally, interactions of bodily or facial cues with speech content or paralinguistic parameters call into question the notion of a nonverbal code distinct from verbal behavior.

Still other contextual influences have been evidenced in studies bearing on intimacy management. According to the hypothesis originally proposed by Argyle and Dean (1965), an "equilibrium" must be found between the diverse variables that relate to intimacy: interpersonal distance, gaze, speech content, postural orientation, and facial and gestural expression. To achieve an optimum degree of intimacy, which varies according to the partners and the situation, any change in one dimension that modifies the global assessment of the relationship must be compensated for by an inverse change in another dimension. Thus, too close a proximity between unfamiliar persons, in crowds or in elevators, for example, would be compensated for by signs of distancing like gaze avoidance or self-touching. This theory has been challenged as far as the underlying mechanisms are concerned, and many contradictory findings have been reported. Predicted changes have not been elicited, or reciprocity instead of compensation has been observed. Mediation of complex cognitive states like expectations with regard to the situation and covert labeling of arousal was assumed. Nevertheless, it seems clear from these discussions that displaying a nonverbal signal depends on several aspects of the situation and that interpreting such a signal must relate to its context of occurrence (e.g., Cappella & Green, 1984; O'Connor & Gifford, 1988; for reviews, see Cappella, 1981; M. L. Patterson, 1982, 1983).

During social interactions, the context in which nonverbal signals have to be understood is mainly constituted, of course, by the behavior of the partner. From such a perspective, the fallacy of the rationale underlying the search for correlations between nonverbal behavior measures and individual characteristics was emphasized. A variable such as the number of gestures performed during speaking time in conversations does not depend on the behavior of one of the observed subjects alone: Both terms of the ratio relate to both the interacting partners. This is one reason why correlations between measures of nonverbal behavior and personality variables usually do not reach significant levels (Duncan, Kanki, Mokros, & Fiske, 1984; Kenny & Malloy, 1988).

Processes underlying nonverbal communication

The notions of "encoding" and "decoding" used in the study of nonverbal communication do not make explicit the processes underlying the performance of body movements and the way they are perceived. There are simply "black boxes" to avoid complex discussions about poorly understood mechanisms.

Let us first consider the proposition that body signals relate to emotional states, namely, patterns of automatic reactions and subjective experiences together with muscular activity. How do these three aspects of emotion relate to others? Is the gestural or the postural behavior shaped by more or less automatic responses to eliciting conditions or, as assumed in the cognitive theories of emotion, by appraisals and expectations of the situation? Does the triggering of the movement follow, precede, or parallel subjective feeling? Controversies resulting from the James–Lange proposition at the end of the 19th century still dominate the study of emotion. In this context, the hypothesis was formulated that posture, like facial expression, had effects on the emotional state of the subject displaying it. A better adaptation to failure situations is, for still unknown reasons, to choose a congruent posture such as head lowering and forward bending instead of "facing adversity" as recommended by traditional pedagogy. Thus, subjects who were presented problems that were actually impossible to solve and who were then invited to stoop in a pretended biofeedback experiment reported self-attribution of a higher chance of success in the future than subjects invited to hold a more erect posture (Riskind & Gotay, 1982; Riskind, 1984). Moreover, the posture of the listener influences receptivity to spoken messages. In experimental situations, student subjects told they were testing headphones were presented messages that expressed counterattitudinal opinions (for instance, on the necessity to increase university fees). Those who were lying comfortably were less opposed to the proposal than those who were standing while listening. Similarly, subjects asked to nod in the vertical plane were more ready to agree than those assigned the horizontal movement condition (Petty & Cacioppo, 1983; Petty, Wells, Heesacker, Brock, & Cacioppo, 1983). These observations raise more general questions about the processes by which mental states like emotions, attitudes, and action readiness are "translated" into nonverbal signals.

The issue of the comprehension of bodily cues is not simpler. Does the perception of gestures and postures rely on a structured body of knowledge, on inferential processes, or on integration with information from different sources, or does it proceed by direct access to the relevant meaning, as assumed in the "ecological theory" of social perception (McArthur & Baron, 1983)? Can modality-specific devices for the recognition of facial, vocal, and gestural units be identified, or should a more general and unitary process for affective judgment be assumed?

Some discussions about the proper definition of "nonverbal communication" have arisen from the diversity of the processes underlying the interpretation of gestural behavior. Ekman and Friesen (1969) distinguished three kinds of signals from conditions of use: informative, communicative, and interactive acts. Informative acts like "emblems" would be decoded in the same way by all the members of a community (meaning depends on conventions). Communicative acts like pointing gestures were performed intentionally (comprehension implies access to the intent of communication). To the category of interactive acts belong all the signals that influence the behavior of the receiver, like those studied in ethology (functional significance is assessed on the basis of sequential contingencies). Of course, categories are not mutually exclusive, and the same gesture may be simultaneously informative, communicative, and interactive.

A similar but more radical position in the definition of nonverbal communication was put forth by Wiener et al. (1972), who tried to impose a distinction between signs and communication. Signs were conceived as nonverbal acts whose meaning was inferred by an observer. Communication would rely on a code. Strictly speaking, nonverbal communication should be limited to coded behavior whose meaning stems from conventions that do not depend on context but often relate to speech contents. Thus, it should be focused on speech-related gestures instead of signs like emotional expression, scratching movements, or eating manners, which elicit attributions but do not convey meaning in the same way verbal behavior does.

Observation of interindividual differences in the ability to express or to understand nonverbal signals also relates to the issue of the processes underlying communication. Several tools for the assessment of these skills have been devised from the assumption that there is an accurate way to encode or to decode emotional information. For example, the Profile of Nonverbal Sensitivity (PONS) was proposed to assess receptive skills (Hall, Rosenthal, Archer, DiMatteo, & Rogers, 1978). This test consists of 220 recorded segments of 2 sec each, presenting 20 scenarios in 11 modalities. The scenarios belong to one of four categories built from the crossing of two dimensions, positive–negative and dominant–submissive. For instance, expressing motherly love relates to positive dominance and asking forgiveness to negative submissiveness. This material is presented under parallel conditions: filtered voice only, face only, body only, and diverse combinations of these modalities. In each case and for each of the two dimensions, subjects are required to select out of two the word that more accurately qualifies the scene. In adult subjects, with the standard version of the PONS, performances in processing bodily and facial cues positively correlate, which suggests a common underlying factor, probably relating to "social competence." Other studies, however, showed the complexity of the assumed "decoding skill." First, developmental analyses evidenced a dissociation between the capacity to understand isolated cues and the capacity to integrate them. Some specificity of the two modalities was also found from age and gender differences. Bodily signals seem to be more "indiscreet," being subject to less control by the sender, than facial ones. During socialization, one learns to disregard them in spite of their informativeness. Age changes and female superiority in decoding skills seem to mainly concern the processing of facial but not bodily cues (Blanck, Rosenthal, Snodgrass, DePaulo, & Zuckerman, 1981; DePaulo & Rosenthal, 1978, 1979; McLeod & Rosenthal, 1983; Rosenthal & DePaulo, 1979; Zuckerman, Blanck, DePaulo, & Rosenthal, 1980).

Furthermore, the validity of the PONS may be challenged on the basis of possible contextual influences in the decoding of nonverbal signals. It is known that gestures or postures may convey different meanings according to the situation. Accordingly, is it relevant to assess communication skills from the processing of isolated signals that relate to only two dimensions, that is, positive–negative and dominant–submissive evaluations? The accuracy in decoding these signals might differ from the true ability to interpret subtle nonverbal cues in social situations. Other criticisms bear on the notion of a general decoding skill. For instance, it was found that capacity to judge a photograph of two persons as showing a casual encounter or a formed couple did not correlate with judgments of dominance–submission from the same photograph. The two performances actually depend on processing different dimensions of the stimulus, such as assessing postural congruence and naturalness in one case and age and dress in the other. Neither of the two responses correlated with the results of the PONS or of an assessment of social competence. These observations open the way to the analysis of the multiple competences involved by the interpretation of bodily cues (Feldman & Thayer, 1980; Sternberg & Smith, 1985).

The present state of knowledge may best be expressed in the interrogative mode. Can a separation be assumed between language and a nonverbal communication system that would specifically concern implicit socioaffective information? What is the extent of the interactions between these two modalities in natural settings? Is it possible for gestures that usually accompany speech to exert an influence that does not depend on language processing?

3.2. The relationships between verbal and nonverbal communication

The demonstration that nonverbal expression may influence social perception does not imply that these signals serve unique functions not fulfilled by verbal means or that they belong to a separate system of communication. Nevertheless, it has been assumed by nonprofessional observers as well as by psychologists studying emotional expression that bodily signals are more effective than language in the communication of affects and interpersonal attitudes. Is the proposition supported by experimental results? Many contradictory findings have been reported, and an explanation must be found for the discrepancies.

Different procedures have been used to assess the respective weights of verbal and nonverbal information in communication. One type of method compares performances in experimental conditions in which some signals are made unavailable. In one procedure, an audiovisual recording of spoken utterances is contrasted to the sound-only recording, the silent videotape, or a written transcription of the verbal content. In some studies, random spliced or filtered speech is also presented; that is, a signal is made unintelligible but retains some of the vocal characteristics of the original utterance. It has also been attempted to isolate different cues in the visual modality: face, body, and background information. Another procedure is to compare actual interactions either in face-to-face conditions or without visual access, back-to-back, from behind a screen, or by telephone. These situations differ as far as the presence of the partner is concerned, which is signaled by subtle auditory cues like sounds of breathing or postural changes. In another kind of method, messages are constructed in such a way that some signals may contradict or supplement others. A special case is lie detection from verbal and nonverbal cues. Some examples of these works will now be examined.

Verbal and nonverbal modalities of presentation

A first set of investigations compares evaluations of material that conveys so-called affective meanings in visual and auditory modalities. From the initial results, the conclusion was drawn that visual information dominates in emotion recognition and in social evaluation. Later research questioned this "video-primacy" effect on the basis of contradictory findings and methodological concerns (for a review, see Noller, 1985).

Several variables were found to be critical in determining experimental issues. Subjects may differ in their reliance on one or another source of information (see, e.g., studies using the PONS). Other variables relate to the types of stimuli, the requested responses, and the statistical methods. One of the stimulus characteristics concerns the behavior of the sender. Some persons display preference for one or another modality to express emotion. Consequently, the evaluation of some messages may be more accurate when based on voice quality and that of other messages when one relies on bodily or facial signals. This was shown, for instance, by the study of Berman, Shulman, and Marvitt (1976), who had actors express warmth or coldness in relationships. Similarly, the capacity to recognize pretended emotions in different modalities varies in relation to the quality of the actor's performance. Strangely enough, judgments were less accurate when the expression was exaggerated (Wallbott & Scherer, 1986). These observations might account for some of the discrepancies in the literature about such things as the respective roles of vocal and visual behavioral cues in the perception of anxiety (Waxer, 1981, 1983).

In many studies, the differences in results were due to qualifications of tasks or rating scales. For instance, subjects were requested to rate on several dimensions excerpts of a televised debate between two candidates for the vice-presidency of the United States. Messages were presented under different modalities, and correlations were computed between responses to these stimuli. The ratings elicited on several bipolar scales differed according to the dimensions. More particularly, for ratings on the positive–negative dimension, responses to the written transcript correlated significantly with those made in the audiovisual condition, whereas responses to the video-only presentation did not. Ratings on the activity dimension yielded the inverse result. Another experiment also demonstrated the importance of semantic information for evaluative judgments. Subjects were unable to rate interviews accurately on the positive–negative scale when content was filtered or when the videotape was presented without sound (Krauss, Apple, Morency, Wenzel, & Winton, 1981). Other examples show that the relative importance of vocal and visual nonverbal information varies according to the requested judgments. In the experiment of Burns and Beier (1973), an actor expressed different emotions, like joy, anger, and anxiety, by bodily and vocal means. Subjects were asked to identify the enacted emotion from filtered or normal audiotape, videotape with or without sound, or the written transcript. The effect of mode of presentation interacted with an emotion effect: The results were generally better when visual nonverbal information was available, but anxiety was better identified from filtered speech. Similarly, in person perception, ratings of "conscientiousness" or "emotional stability" mainly relied on the processing of visible behavior, whereas no modality effect was observed in the ratings of "extraversion," "agreeableness," or "assertiveness." Thus, when several scales are used, correlations between judgments from full and from partial information do not consistently favor one of the isolated sources, that is, isolated bodily, facial, or speech cues. Moreover, many significant positive correlations are observed, which suggests redundancy of the different communication channels (Ekman et al., 1980; Furnham, Trevethan, & Gaskell, 1981; O'Sullivan et al., 1985; Scherer et al., 1977).

It may be noted that most of the studies on modality effects in person perception are concerned with the processing of affective meaning. Nonverbal signals, however, may be used for more diverse attributions. This was the case in a study by Archer and Akert (1977), who showed either filmed sequences of interactions between two or three persons – two women and a child for instance – or a written transcript of the verbal exchanges (see also Costanzo & Archer, 1989). The subjects answered questions about the characters, for example, identifying the mother of the child. As expected, a higher number of correct responses was given in the audiovisual condition than in the transcript condition. Thus, the question of the influence of modalities of presentation may be raised in all the domains where bodily signals were found effective in conveying information and where it was assumed that "actions speak louder than words" (Reeder & Fulks, 1980).

Modality effects in information processing might also be studied from a cognitive perspective in order to identify factors favoring one kind of presentation or another (see chap. 4). Audiovisual messages are generally no better understood or recalled than the written transcription of the verbal content. Nevertheless, an important qualification was made by Chaiken and Eagly (1976). Although a written text of a difficult argument is better understood, is rated more pleasant, and elicits more opinion change than a videotape presentation of the same argument, inverse results were noted for an easy version of the material. Politicians using television or public discourse have certainly grasped the implications of such findings. Further studies are needed to identify the source of these modality effects in text comprehension and memory with closer control of attentional load and cue availability (see, e.g., Furham, Proctor, & Gunter, 1988; Stine, Wingfield, & Myers, 1990).

Communicating without visual cues

The importance of visual signals in communication was examined in several experiments controlling modalities of access to the partner. These studies have implications for the assessment of different telecommunication systems and for improving the social adaptation of blind people (for reviews, see Rutter, 1984, 1987; Short, Williams, & Christie, 1976; Taylor & Thompson, 1982; Williams, 1977).

Four hypotheses are discussed in relation to the effects arrived at by an elimination of visual cues: reduced intimacy, depersonalized exchanges, a disturbed turn-taking system, and changes in content and style of verbalizations. An experiment by Argyle, Lalljee, and Cook (1968) illustrates the first type of study. Subjects were interviewed in one of several conditions: with normal vision, vision impaired by a screen, or reduced vision when either the subject or the experimenter wore dark glasses or a mask. Just after the interaction, the subjects rated the comfort and the ease of the conversation. Asymmetry of access was found more important than simple availability of visual cues. The situations judged most uncomfortable involved the feeling of being seen without seeing the partner. Mutual invisibility had little impact on impression formation (Kemp, Rutter, Dewey, Harding, & Stephenson, 1984; Rimé, 1982; Siegman & Reynolds, 1983a, 1983b; Tartter, 1983).

Little support was found for the depersonalization hypothesis. For instance, no differences were observed between experimental conditions when the use of first-person pronouns or self-references was analyzed. Contrary to the predictions, blind people more often referred verbally to their own personal characteristics, whereas sighted subjects did not mention what may be inferred from visual cues (Kemp & Rutter, 1982, 1986; Rimé, 1982; Rutter, Stephenson, & Dewey, 1981).

The role of visual signals in the regulation of turn taking has also been examined by comparing verbal behavior under conditions of normal or restricted visual access (see chap. 1). Elimination of visible cues does not increase the number of interruptions or the number of words in conversations, but it does affect the temporal structure of the exchanges. In the experiments, lack of visual information may be compensated for by linguistic and paralinguistic means, such as longer transition pauses and the use of shorter sentences and interrogations. However, different results are given by different methods of restricting visual access (use of a telephone, interposition of a screen, or observation of blind subjects). Accordingly, the mere presence of the partner was assumed to be the most critical variable (B. Butterworth et al., 1977; Cook & Lalljee, 1972; Krauss, Garlock, Bricker, & McMahon, 1977; Kemp & Rutter, 1982; Rimé, 1982; Rutter & Stephenson, 1977).

Rutter (1984, 1987) suggested that the lack of visual cues in telephone communication affected the content and style of conversations. The absence of the partner decreases the spontaneity of the exchanges, as shown by the number of filled pauses and the refraining from interruptions. In such a condition, the speakers experience a feeling of "psychological distance" paralleling the physical distance. "Psychological distance . . . is something which is set from the very beginning of the encounter. Subjects make use of whatever social cues are available and form an impression of psychological closeness or psychological distance – the feeling that the other person is 'there' or 'not there' – and the effects upon content, style, and outcome begin immediately" (Rutter, 1987, pp. 74–75). To some extent, this hypothesis refines the earlier depersonalization concept. Increased distance would orient the discourse to the task and exclude irrelevant references to other characteristics of the partners or the surroundings. Supporting evidence was found in the content analysis of genuine conversations between President Nixon and his co-workers published by the *New York Times* in 1974 during the Watergate affair (Wilson & Williams, 1977). Compared with face-to-face conversations, the telephone calls were shorter, used fewer polite formulas, and displayed less intimacy. According to Wilson and Williams, the relative brevity of the telephone exchanges was due to the lack of positive reinforcements by President Nixon. The absence of feedback would disturb the partner, who did not know whether and how he was being understood. Results of the experiments by Rutter and co-workers also demonstrate that cues of social presence, in either the visual or the auditory modality, influence speech content.

Interpreting discrepant messages

The video-primacy hypothesis was also examined in the decoding of incongruent messages constructed for experimental purposes by combining in the auditory and visual modalities cues whose meanings were different or opposite. For example, an actor was requested to utter a sentence expressing superiority with an anxious tone of voice, a nervous, deferential smile, and lowered head. In the control conditions, the cues were congruent (for a review, see Noller, 1985).

How are these messages understood? The receiver may follow three different strategies. (*i*) One would be to combine additively the information from different sources, as was the case with congruent messages in an audiovisual presentation (see earlier discussion and, e.g., Archer & Akert, 1977). (*ii*) An alternative would be to give priority to one of the sources, if, for instance, nonverbal cues were believed to be more important than verbal content in detecting irony or sarcasm. (*iii*) The third possibility is to weight the cues in a nonadditive way, for example, by combining congruent cues but disregarding inconsistent messages as "incoherent."

To examine these issues and, especially, the responses to messages where bodily or facial cues contradict vocal information, DePaulo and Rosenthal (1982) transformed the PONS into the Nonverbal Discrepancy Test. An actor was posed to express dominance or submission in a positive or a negative way. Speech was filtered to prevent access to verbal content. In half of the segments, only the face was shown; in the other half, only the body. As all the combinations of auditory and visual signals were presented, some messages were congruent and others incongruent on one dimension (status or evaluation), and others were incongruent on both. Children and adults were asked to rate the stimuli on three scales: positive–negative, dominant–submissive, and congruent–discrepant. Complex developmental trends were observed. The video-primacy effect interacted with age, rated dimension, and degree of discrepancy. Young children gave priority to vocal cues (or to verbal content in other studies). Older children and adults criticized large discrepancies. The late acquisition of the ability to process ambiguity likely relates to other achievements in the development of social cognition. An important qualification concerning the video-primacy effect was recently introduced by Trimboli and Walker (1987). They showed that experimental results depended on the proportion of inconsistent messages in the presented material and, accordingly, on the strategies elicited by the artificial conditions devised. When discrepant cues are frequent, subjects give priority to nonverbal signals; otherwise, they give priority to verbal information (Argyle, Alkema, & Gilmour, 1972; Argyle, Salter, Nicholson, Williams, & Burgess, 1970; Blanck, Rosenthal, Snodgrass, DePaulo, & Zuckerman, 1982; Bugenthal, Kaswan, Love, & Fox, 1970; Demorest, Meyer, Phelps, Gardner, & Winner, 1984; DePaulo, Rosenthal, Eisenstat, Rogers, & Finkelstein, 1978; Volkmar, Hoder, & Siegel, 1980; Volkmar & Siegel, 1979; Zuckerman et al., 1980).

Detecting deception

Discrepancies between verbal and nonverbal parts of a message may occur during deception if bodily cues contradict speech content. A number of experimental studies have been aimed at the verification of the commonsense hypothesis that gestural signals can reveal a hidden truth. Subjects were requested to speak in pleasant terms about disliked persons, to defend counterattitudinal opinions, to describe as a previous job a never-occupied position, etc. These studies may be reviewed from the deceiver's perspective or from that of the "lie detector" (DePaulo, Stone, & Lassiter, 1985a; Kraut, 1980; Zuckerman, DePaulo, & Rosenthal, 1981;

Zuckerman & Driver, 1985; see also the special issue of *Journal of Nonverbal Behavior*, *12*, 3–4, 1988).

Nonverbal behavior is influenced by instructions to be deceitful or honest. Some effects of the experimental conditions result from the strategies used by the subject and the control exerted on his or her appearance. According to a first hypothesis, the deceiver, in order to be believed to be telling the truth, refrains from releasing behavioral cues that are commonly considered to be signs of lying: self-touching, gaze avoidance, smiling, etc. The hypothesis was not supported in a study in which candidate police officers were instructed to answer some questions honestly and others deceptively. Few differences occurred between the two conditions (Hocking & Leathers, 1980). Nonetheless, other experiments demonstrated that subjects looked more often toward a listener who was presented as an expert in lie detection, both when lying and when telling the truth, than in a control condition. Deception was less often detected from video recordings when the subjects knew they were being observed than when they were unaware of being recorded. Different strategies were also used toward intimates and strangers. Skillful liars are thus able to monitor their nonverbal behavior, which young children sometimes cannot do (Buller & Aune, 1987; DePaulo & Jordan, 1982; Fugita, Hogrebe, & Wexley, 1980; Krauss, 1981; Lewis, Stanger, & Sullivan, 1989).

According to a second hypothesis, proposed by Ekman (1981, 1985), the liars control the signals judged more informative and for which speakers are judged more responsible, mostly speech content and facial expression, but they pay little attention to tone of voice and body movement. Two kinds of cues allow lie detection: (*i*) cues of deception, like nervous movements, and (*ii*) emotional leakage, signals expressing true feelings. As predicted, deception was detected more often from bodily than from facial cues in subjects having to recommend a film that was actually pleasant (truth condition) or unpleasant (deception). Subjects displayed more self-touching gestures and postural shifts while lying than while telling the truth. They also performed fewer illustrative gestures and gave subtle facial signs of not sincerely liking the film. Nonspecific arousal by hearing white noise in nondeceptive conditions did not result in the same behavioral changes as lying. Strangely enough, higher motivation for success in deceit by subjects instructed to feign agreement with the opinion of an attractive person of the opposite sex increased detectability from gestural and vocal cues, probably because increased control over speech content entailed leakage on uncontrolled dimensions, such as eye movements and pause duration (DePaulo,

Stone, & Lassiter, 1985b; deTurck & Miller, 1985; Ekman & Friesen, 1974a; Ekman, Friesen, & O'Sullivan, 1988).

Judges rating the honesty of a message rely most often on nonverbal behavior. Accuracy in the detection of deception was generally low but was better from vocal and bodily signals than from facial expression and speech transcripts (e.g., Ekman & Friesen, 1974b; Littlepage & Pineault, 1979; Manstead, Wagner, & MacDonald, 1984, 1986; Stiff et al., 1989).

However, these modality effects must be qualified in several ways. First, the credibility of a target subject depends mostly on vocal and gestural parameters, but cues used for the attribution of deception do not correspond to the real cues of deception. For instance, in a study where fraud of airport customs was simulated for experimental purposes, a great number of subjects remained unsuspected by professional officers and by novices, but these inspectors agreed on signs of deception actually shared by guilty and innocent subjects: gaze avoidance, postural shifts, slow response latency. Thus, liars able to control these aspects of behavior were not detected (Kraut & Poe, 1980; see also Bond, Kahler, & Paolicelli, 1985; Riggio, Tucker, & Widaman, 1987).

It is also stated that body movements convey ambiguous information. Signs of deception are not specific but resemble manifestations of anxiety or ambivalence. Thus a judge cannot tell whether a subject is lying or is simply anxious. Moreover, detection of deception may depend on some familiarity with the liar: Judges previously exposed to a sample of sincere behavior of a target subject were more accurate in uncovering subsequent lies than were uninformed judges (see, e.g., Ekman & Friesen, 1974a).

Further studies on such highly strategic situations might benefit from a signal detection approach. Bias in the receiver's decision for excessive trust in others or misinterpretation of ambiguous cues may likely be modified by training and differential reward. Refining perceptions of nonverbal behavior and developing efficient heuristics as well as being able to manage the impressions given by nonverbal behavior should be influenced by the respective cost and benefit of success and failure in deceiving or detecting deception. In any event, the matter does not reduce to a simple weighting of verbal and nonverbal cues.

3.3. Concluding remarks: separation or interaction?

It becomes increasingly clear that gestures and postures may convey diverse information that relates, according to the standard nonverbal communication approach, to emotions and socioaffective attitudes. These terms should be understood in a large sense to include conversational conduct and communication of personal characteristics such as age and cultural background, of the degree of intimacy of the relationship, and of the discourse intentions as studied by pragmatics. However, only a few of these aspects have been experimentally analyzed. A focus on some connotative dimensions is probably inherent to the assumption of a separate nonverbal communication system. Nevertheless, the literature reviewed offers little support for the hypothesis of a functional specificity of gestural signals. The video-primacy effect was qualified by numerous variables, and vocal cues were often shown to be as important as facial or gestural ones in social evaluation. Interactions between gestures and speech have been found at the expressive level: Visual access influences speech content, and speech qualities affect gestural performances. Similarly, at the receptive level, the interpretation of bodily signals depends on concurrent speech, and comprehension of a spoken utterance may vary with the nonverbal context. Thus, the present state of knowledge demonstrates a greater gap between the people studying nonverbal communication and those concerned with the psychology of language than the actual separation between the two modes of communication (see also Scherer & Wallbott, 1985).

Investigating the processes underlying encoding and decoding also suggests that gestures and speech may interact in complex ways. Progress in cognitive and developmental psychology or in neurosciences shows that simple behavior, such as confrontation naming, word and picture remembering, and visually guided reaching, depends on multiple operations of input–output transfers. Describing nonverbal behavior does not reduce to discovering stimulus–response regularities but requires sketching a "cognitive architecture" of the multiple components involved in information processing. The study of the interaction between gestures and speech is necessary not only because verbal and nonverbal behavior associate in motor execution and in perception but also because these two systems may relate in several ways that experimental analysis has to distinguish.

4. Cognitive approaches

To determine whether gestural behavior and vocal behavior depend on separate or integrated systems, three kinds of data may be considered: data derived from the experimental analysis of the relationships between gestures and speech within cognitive psychology, developmental data, and pathological data. The research we now propose to examine differs from the work on nonverbal communication in two ways. First, it is focused on the processes underlying the production and the perception of gestures and spoken language. Second, it is assumed that some of these processes are shared by gestural and verbal behavior and others are modality specific. We will first present studies bearing on the production of gestures while speaking and then the mechanisms involved in the comprehension of gestures and discourse.

4.1. Gesture production while speaking

Theoretical considerations

Current perspectives

As Wundt (1900/1973) pointed out, gestures and speech may constitute two ways of expressing the same idea. Their origins are to be found in the thinking process that underlies both manual and oral activity. Accordingly, the study of gesture production can shed light on the mental functioning that also produces speech. More recently, authors like Freedman, Rimé, McNeill, and Kendon put forward a similar position, which will be discussed in what follows. Most of them explicitly refer to the conceptions of Werner and Kaplan (1963), according to whom symbolic representations develop from early "affective–sensory–motor patterns" in infancy. In this perspective, knowing first results from apprehending the world as "things-of-action" and only thereafter from building "objects of contemplation." Persistence of manual activity during speech production in adulthood could be explained by the difficulty the speaker encounters in encoding global-synthetic representations into linearly ordered parts of speech.

Expressing thought by words obviously involves several operations. Freedman (1977) distinguished two main processes. One he called filtering: the focus of discourse has to be determined either by a selection of one content out of several possible ones or by an exclusion of irrelevant associations. The other process is referential linking, by which mental experience is connected to symbolic forms. One particular kind of gesture would correspond to each of these processes: The "body-focused" movements (i.e., self-touching gestures) would relate to filtering, and the "object-focused" movements (i.e., illustrative gestures) to referential activity. Within the latter category, "speech-primacy" movements would depend on prosodic features of the utterance such as rhythm and stress, and "motor-primacy" movements on the intended meaning (see also Freedman & Bucci, 1981).

The hypothesis that different motor manifestations relate to specific cognitive processes and, more particularly, that self-touching gestures are intended to focus attention gave rise to several experiments. In one study, the Stroop interference task was proposed. Subjects named the color of the ink in which words were printed, regardless of their meaning. In interference conditions, the words referred to colors other than that of the ink (e.g., the answer "black" had to be given for the word *red* written in black), and thus the semantic processing of the word had to be inhibited. The frequency of bilateral self-touching, mainly hand-to-hand movements, was found to increase in the interference condition compared with the baseline in a color-naming task. Similarly, in a memory task, bilateral finger-to-hand movements were positively correlated to the number of items recovered. It was suggested that self-touching during recall prevented interference by external stimulation. However, with a dual-task paradigm of probe-reaction time during monologues or during arithmetic problem solving, the reaction time was not shorter during phases of self-touching than outside these phases. Moreover, self-touching differences between experimental conditions during a speech-shadowing task (repetition with minimal delay) did not relate to the relative complexity of the conditions as assessed by number of errors in repetition. Subjects receiving binaurally two texts read by two different speakers and having to report on one of the texts (easy condition) performed better than when requested to attend to one content in a single-speaker, difficult condition. However, similar amounts of self-touching were observed in the two tasks. Thus, empirical support for Freedman's hypothesis is lacking, and its theoretical foundations remain unclear (Barroso & Feld, 1986; Barroso, Freedman, & Grand, 1980; Barroso, Freedman, Grand, & Van Meel, 1978; Kenner, 1984).

Most studies of the Freedman group on illustrative gestures concern individual differences in normal or pathological populations. Following Werner and Kaplan, the symbolizing process consists of a differentiation between the self and the external world. In this context, it is assumed, first, that people differ along this "differentiation" dimension and, second, that "object-focused" movements, mostly "motor-primacy" ones, relate to a primitive mode of symbolization that characterizes poorly differentiated subjects. However, experimental results did not support the hypothesis of an influence of a cognitive style, such as field dependence, on gestural behavior. Observations of illustrative gestures of schizophrenic subjects did not demonstrate peculiar performances in relation to verbal behavior. Subgroups of subjects were more clearly defined from self-touching behavior. Thus, Freedman's hypothesis should be rejected, or the underlying assumptions revised (Bucci & Freedman, 1978; Freedman et al., 1972; Grand, Marcos, Freedman, & Barroso, 1977; Marcos, 1979a; see also Baxter, Winters, & Hammer 1968; Sousa-Poza & Rohrberg, 1977; chap. 6, this volume).

From a similar perspective, Rimé described the relationships between gestures and speech by emphasizing two aspects of motor activity. First, nonverbal behavior, mainly illustrative gestures, may express meaning by analogy, either in shapes and movements referring to objects and actions or in more rudimentary motor activity. It is assumed that "the symbolizing activity of someone verbalizing his experience is never independent of some degree of analogical motor activity, whether in the form of outbursts of highly representational gestures, or of nearly latent or incipient motoric manifestations" (1983, p. 103). Thus, gestures would be triggered during speech production because meaning embodied in motor schemata would be activated. Second, gestural and vocal performances display rhythmic properties. The mechanical conditions of speech production would relate to another kind of gestural activity that may be called batonic. In return, these movements would exert a structuring influence in the control of discourse production. The primary function of nonverbal behavior would not be to communicate information but to support the speaker's encoding activity. For example, gesture frequency was not seriously reduced when the mutual visibility of partners in conversation was experimentally suppressed or while speaking by telephone (Rimé, 1982). Furthermore, restriction of hand movements during interviews induced compensatory motor activity of eyebrows and fingers, as though movements were a necessary component of the speech production process (Rimé, Schiaratura, Hupet, & Ghysselinckx, 1984; Rimé & Schiaratura, 1991; see also Lickiss & Wellens, 1978).

In a comparable way, McNeill challenged the traditional view that considered body movements and language as constituting parallel, separate systems specialized in the expression of connotative and denotative meanings, respectively (see chap. 3). He argued for a close association of the systems controlling verbal and gestural outputs: "Gestures share with speech a computational stage; they are, accordingly, parts of the same psychological structure" (1985, p. 350). In support of this claim, McNeill noted that (*i*) gestures occur only during speech in synchronization with linguistic units, (*ii*) they serve similar pragmatic and semantic functions, (*iii*) there is simultaneous dissolution of linguistic and gestural abilities in aphasics, and (*iv*) gestures develop together with speech in children. Unlike the proposition of Rimé (1983), the distinction between iconic gestures and beats would parallel differences in discourse functions, that is, in narrations and extranarrative comments, respectively (McNeill & Levy, 1982). In subjects telling the story of a cartoon, iconic gestures presented features relating to verb meanings, such as a downward component when a fall was verbally described. This was not the case for beat movements, which were found to relate to discourse functions like emphasis rather than to referential activity. The reason for such a strong connection between gestures and speech might be situated in the nature of the thinking process and its origin in the sensorimotor stage of intelligence ontogenesis. "The basis for synchronization is not that gesture and sentence are translations of one another, but that they arise from a common cognitive representation" (McNeill, 1985, p. 353). In reference to Piaget, the development of the conceptual structure in early childhood is seen as resulting from "semiotic extension" of sensorimotor schemata. Knowledge is constructed on the basis of manipulatory activity, and metaphoric uses of language, which represent nonimageable entities as imageable ones, constitute vestiges of this stage in adulthood (see also McNeill, 1979, 1987a, 1987b, 1989; McNeill, Levy, & Pedelty, 1990; and chap. 5, this volume).

For Kendon (1980, 1983, 1985), too, gestures and speech stem from a single conceptual structure, because both gestural and vocal outputs are suited to express meaning. The structuring of discourse in paragraphs, sentences, and "prosodic phrases" (i.e. "groups of syllables over which a completed intonation tune occurs") is paralleled by the organization of bodily expression: the larger the size of speech units, the greater the number of limb segments involved in movement when a transition between units occurs (Kendon, 1972b). Moreover, a single gesture is sometimes associated with several speech units, but then it appears that these different units express a single idea (Kendon, 1975a). Thus, the nonverbal behavior accompanying speech seems to be intended to make visible the organization of the discourse. Nevertheless, the two modes of expression, verbal and gestural, are not equivalent. First, they are used in different contexts. For example, gestures might be produced more often when the conditions of speech reception are impaired by a noisy environment, by a glass partition, or by limited knowledge of a foreign language. Second, gestures and speech do not obey similar constraints in the turn-taking system. Finally, gestures are particularly adapted to convey information about spatial relations, for example, by describing shapes or directions that are not easily coded verbally. Thus, some kind of monitoring process is assumed by which the speaker chooses the vehicle most appropriate for facilitating understanding.

In summary, there is considerable agreement on the existence of close links between gestures and speech production, but the explanations proposed by the different authors vary. According to Kendon, the communicative value of gestures is a critical factor, whereas other authors assume that the primary function of hand movements, which often cannot be interpreted in the absence of speech, is not to transmit information. Conceptions also diverge with regard to the nature of the distinction between batonic and iconic gestures as modes of symbolizing (motor-primacy versus speech-primacy), levels of processing (semantic mapping versus realization of the utterance), or discourse functions (propositional versus off-propositional). We may conclude that gestures and speech interact in several ways but that the imprecision of the assumed processes hampers experimental analysis. The task of a psychological investigation is to confront alternative propositions in order to identify the mechanisms underlying the production of gestures and speech.

Working hypotheses

Under the assumption of multiple interactions between the gestural and the verbal systems, different hypotheses may be devised according to two schematic distinctions. The first one bears on the excitatory versus the inhibitory nature of the interactions. A coactivation hypothesis would have vocal and manual movements triggered simultaneously from the computational level shared by the two systems. Alternatively, gestures and speech can be conceived as similar but rival activities, so competition would occur in the display of substitutable forms. A second distinction relies on the fact that both gestures and speech express meanings through motor realizations. Thus, the two systems may be connected on a deep, conceptual level where the propositional structure of the message is formed or on a surface, subpropositional level where characteristics of the gestural and vocal outputs are determined. We will discuss these concepts in somewhat more detail before examining the supporting evidence.

Coactivation hypotheses. Some authors have assumed inevitable activation of the gestural system during speech production. This hypothesis is probably anchored in Birdwhistell's (1970) idea that human communication intrinsically combines linguistic and kinesic behavior.

As noted earlier, gestures accompanying speech have been considered visible "manifestations of the speaker's ongoing thinking process" and related to the "initial phase of sentence generation" (McNeill, 1985, pp. 367, 370). In this conception, gestures and speech share origins and then separate into two different output channels. The model has problems, however. One is to identify the processes belonging to the common stage, where interactions occur, and those belonging to the later, output stage, where dissociations may be observed. Either the output processes refer only to the control mechanisms of specific effectors (hands and articulatory systems), or the output processes encompass all the modality-specific operations, for example, in the verbal channel, that of giving prosodic contour and phonological interpretation to the syntacticolexical representation. Whatever the solution may be, gestures are assumed to relate to speech only in the early stages of sentence formulation (see discussions in Feyereisen, 1987; Butterworth & Hadar, 1989).

From another point of view, interactions are assumed on several levels of the speech production process, including the motor realization of the utterance. For example, Birdwhistell suggested that some gestures (especially beats) relate to the prosodic features (stress, melodic contour) or to the syllabic structure of the verbal utterances. Hand movements would depend not only on the expressed content but also on the surface characteristics of the sentences and, thus, on the requirements of motor planning of the utterance. The notion of "coordinative structures" presented by Kelso, Tuller, and Harris (1983) can be applied to this kind of interaction on the level of motor control of gestures and speech.

Thus, facilitative interactions between gestural and verbal systems could occur at different levels of processing: in the elaboration of the message at the conceptual level or in the motor planning, when parameters of vocal and manual movements are determined. Another issue is whether similar connections between the gestural and verbal systems have to be identified for all kinds of movements or whether the distinction between iconic and batonic gestures relates to interactions at different levels of the production process.

Competition hypotheses. Gesture production during speech presents obvious discontinuities: Movement phases alternate with rest phases, just as speaking combines sounds and silences. Speaking people do not gesture all the time they talk, and differences in gestural behavior among speakers are also observed. Thus, it has been suggested that gesture production is sometimes prevented or delayed instead of being simultaneously activated during the process of expression of thought. Gestures and speech might compete and inhibit each other through their connections. Again, different versions of this hypothesis may be formulated, according to the component considered.

One kind of competition could occur during the initial stages of sentence formulation, for example, when the meaning of the selected forms is matched to the intended meaning for control. A momentary inability to retrieve appropriate words or a felt inadequacy of expression in the speech situation would activate gesture production. Pathologies that would block speech production, then, would also release manual activity. Many movements do not express an identifiable meaning, however, and competition in control mechanisms for gesture and speech may occur in another way than in the activation of concurrent message components.

Indeed, competition can also be assumed from studies on attention using the economic metaphor of "processing resources" to account for variations of performance in demanding conditions. Resources are assumed to be limited and, thus, the attention load required for one task reduces the amount that can be allotted to a concurrent task. Resources are assumed to be mobile, and some degree of freedom is assumed to exist in the allocation of attention to parallel processes. From such a perspective, gestural activity while speaking constitutes a particular instantiation of the dual-task paradigm in which subjects are requested to divide their attention between concurrent processes. Thus, a sharing of resources might be assumed at the level of motor planning because gestures and speech both require attention in selecting the response and programming characteristics of execution. Nevertheless, two important qualifications have emerged from research on attentional mechanisms.

First, fully automated tasks no longer require attention, which might be the case with some of the gestures performed while speaking. Similarly, processing load is reduced when parallel activities are coordinated. Two-handed movements might not be more difficult to execute than one-handed ones if they are synchronized for a single purpose such as catching a large object (Jeannerod, 1984, 1988). Second, independent pools of resources have been assumed for tasks that do not share components. No concurrence between gestures and speech would occur if both rely on separate mechanisms. This hypothesis may be examined from a neuropsychological perspective predicting greater interference of verbal behavior in right-hand activities, which both depend on the left cerebral hemisphere, than in left-hand activities (Kinsbourne & Hiscock, 1983; see also chap. 6, this volume).

The experimental literature may be reviewed in relation to these different hypotheses, even though very few studies have explicitly intended to contrast coactivation and competition models or to determine the level at which gesture and speech interact.

Empirical evidence

Temporal relationships between gestures and speech

Coactivation models assume close temporal associations in the production of speech and gestures, whereas competition models suggest a relation between gestures and hesitation pauses, but no precise prediction can be formulated from such perspectives. Indeed, gestures would not interfere with sentence production when made without attentional control or in coordination with speech movements. Moreover, during silence, gesture production could be inhibited by the processing load required by speech planning.

Relationships between speech and body movements may be analyzed on different time scales by identifying large units, like turns in conversation or "paragraphs" in discourse that may be fluent or nonfluent, or by studying smaller segments, like sentences and "prosodic phrases," with microanalytic methods.

Gesture production and speech fluency. If verbal activity is considered over relatively long periods, speech rate may be computed by counting the number of words produced per time unit. A similar measure can be proposed to define "gesture fluency." Speech tempo varies as a function of the time taken to access lexical items and is reduced by hesitation pauses. Because several variables affect this access time, such as word frequency or semantic and syntactic priming, speech tempo may be affected in very diverse ways.

Coactivation models predict a direct relationship between speech fluency and gesture production: The more one speaks, the more hand movements are performed. In some circumstances, the rate of gesture production seems to depend directly on the number of spoken words. For example, when compared with the interview situation, fewer hand movements occurred during a recall memory task like digit-span testing (Rimé & Gaussin, 1982). Ten-year-old children performed more illustrative gestures while explaining solutions found to arithmetic problems than during a color-naming task (Barroso et al., 1978). Nevertheless, in these studies, speech connectivity may be a more critical variable than only the number of emitted words. In other conditions, indeed, gestural rate and speech fluency were inversely related. For example, bilingual subjects gestured more while speaking the nondominant language than the native language, in which they were more fluent. (The frequency of movements other than illustrative gestures, like self-touching, increased similarly during interviews in a nondominant language.) In these cases, familiarity with the spoken language was found more important than speech tempo (Elzinga's unpublished dissertation, 1978, cited by Kendon, 1985; Marcos, 1979a, 1979b; Sainsbury & Wood, 1977).

Temporal associations between gestures and speech may also be analyzed according to individual differences. Do people who speak more or with higher fluency produce more gestures? Does a pathology like depression, which lowers speech rate and vocal intensity, also influence gestural behavior? The numerous studies that relate to these issues have yielded contradictory findings. In some cases, production of illustrative gestures by normal subjects correlated positively to duration of speech. People considered dominant, assertive, extrovert, psychopathic, and the like might speak a lot and use many gestures. However, in other cases, shorter speaking time was not associated with a significant decrease in gesture production (see, e.g., Campbell & Rushton, 1978; Duncan & Fiske, 1977; Rimé, Bouvy, Leborgne, & Rouillon, 1978; but see also chap. 6, this volume).

One way to resolve these contradictions would be to devise experimental situations in which the speech rate is controlled. The first studies relevant to this issue were conducted under the assumption that gestures and verbal dysfluencies might be associated because they would all depend on the speaker's level of anxiety (Boomer, 1963). However, with an experimental manipulation of speech tempo, Boomer and Dittmann

(1964) failed to confirm an association between pauses and gestures: Speeding up or slowing down the verbal rate by specific instructions did not influence the number of movements per minute. Nevertheless, a movement-per-word computation seemed to show a relative increase of gesticulation in the nonfluent condition.

There are certainly other procedures for influencing speech tempo, such as proposing conversation topics in which speakers show different levels of expertise. Unfortunately, studies examining the influence of independent variables on both speech and gesture production are not numerous, and the reports of those that have been done often lack details on the methods used and the relevant resulting data. For instance, subjects are proposed difficult and easy tasks but no measures of verbal behavior are reported to assess the effectiveness of the procedure. Nonetheless, manipulations intended to influence speech output seem to have little impact on manual activity. Discussions on familiar and unfamiliar themes exerted different influences on gestural behavior according to subject characteristics, and giving directions to proximate and distant places did not change the use of illustrative gestures (Baxter et al., 1968; Cohen and Harrison, 1973).

The effect of other variables on speech content and speech tempo complicates the interpretation of these observations. It has been suggested that illustrative gestures are produced when sizes, shapes, and spatial arrangements are described. The same number of gestures was performed while defining concrete and abstract words, but the proportion of gestures called representational differed in the two tasks (Barroso et al., 1978, exp. 2). However, interviews on topics differing in intimacy or in imagery did not elicit different numbers of gestures and did not change the proportion of iconic gestures (Sousa-Poza & Rohrberg, 1977; Marcos, 1979b). Children have also been observed to produce much fewer iconic gestures while telling stories than while describing their own drawings or their daily activities (Riseborough, 1982). This contrast might be due to differences between the situations either in requirements for speech production or in the way the information was encoded, either from narrations or from self-initiated performances. Finally, differences have been noted in the rate of postural change in various speech situations: Trunk, leg, and foot movements were produced more often during new statements than during answers to questions (Bull & Brown, 1977). Thus, it is suggested that body movements are not automatically triggered by the activation of verbal production and that in some conditions, they are inhibited by still unknown factors.

Microanalytic studies. Some pilot studies have analyzed the relationships between speech and gesture production at a finer level. The pioneering observations of Birdwhistell suggested a close association between phonetic and kinesic realizations. This hypothesis was examined in frame-by-frame analysis of short segments of sound films (Condon & Ogston, 1966; Condon, 1970). From such studies, the organization of body motion seemed to be synchronized with the articulated organization of speech. For example, just when a mouth movement related to the utterance of the word *I* began, changes in head, trunk, and hand position occurred. These observations have elicited two main criticisms. First, it is very difficult to achieve high accuracy in detecting the beginning of a movement (McDowall, 1978a, 1978c). Only changes across units of 3 to 6 frames in a 24-frame-per-second film could be noticed, and thus, synchronization could be assessed only within about 125 msec. This discussion concerns both autosynchrony, which is considered here, and interactive synchrony, or mirroring, which was discussed in chapter 3. The second problem arises from the difficulty of defining how much synchronization is actually random. When several limb segments are involved in a movement, it could happen by chance that the movement of one of them will coincide with one of the observed speech movements (Cappella, 1981).

To some extent, automatic recording of different kinds of movements allows these difficulties to be bypassed. For example, Hadar and coworkers recorded head movements with a polarized-light goniometer. During conversation, such movements were almost continuous while speaking, but many fewer movements were detected during pauses or listening. Different movements were distinguished on the basis of amplitude and velocity. These types of movements differed in association with prosodic contours. Small and rapid movements, as well as large and rapid postural shifts, tended to occur in initial phases of utterances, and slower, large movements at the end. The rapid movements and not the slower were associated with loudness peaks. Rapid movements also tended to occur following dysfluencies like hesitation pauses or repetitions, whereas "grammatical" pauses between clauses or sentences were accompanied by larger postural shifts. Related observations have been made of face and head movements in stuttering, which suggest that difficulties in speech production arouse motor activity. Only moderate support for the coactivation hypothesis was provided, because head movement frequency is increased during speech, but across the sample, the amplitude of these movements did not relate to loudness peaks

(Hadar, 1989; Hadar, Steiner, Grant, & Rose, 1983a, 1983b, 1984; Hadar, Steiner, & Rose, 1984; Janssen & Kraaimaat, 1980; Kraaimaat & Janssen, 1985).

In another example, when the temporal association between automatic recordings of head, hand, and foot movements and verbal utterances was analyzed, the movements were found to be related to the rhythmic characteristics of the utterance (Dittmann and Llewellyn, 1969; Dittmann, 1972). More movements were observed than expected in the beginning of the phonemic clauses, that is, during the first word of a verbal unit whose end is marked by a juncture (final syllable stretching and pause) and to which only one stressed word belongs. When dysfluent clauses were considered, movements also frequently occurred after a hesitation pause. The combined effects of starting position, hesitation, and lengthened speaking time led to an increased gestural rate in nonfluent clauses. These results, however, were contradicted by observations using a different procedure.

Other studies used another method, the analysis of video recordings. In 4- and 5-year-old children, movements occurred more often at the end than at the beginning of utterances, and after a pause, movement frequency decreased to rise again at the end of the utterances (DeLong, 1974). Gestures have also been reported to anticipate or accompany, rather than follow, other kinds of dysfluencies, like sentence change, repetition, and stuttering (Ragsdale and Silvia, 1982). During hesitation pauses foot movements and discrete body-touching movements occurred; continuous hand-to-hand contact did not occur during hesitation pauses (Freedman & Bucci, 1981). To summarize, methodological differences in recording nonverbal behavior, in defining dysfluencies, and in statistical analysis make comparison between the studies difficult. Replication of these preliminary observations would be welcome.

Butterworth and Beattie (1978) proposed a more complex answer to the question of the relationships between hesitations and gestures. Utterances were segmented into alternating planning and execution phases, which differed in the number of pauses. Gestures more often accompanied verbalizations during the hesitant, planning phase, but during the execution phase, a greater gesture-per-second ratio was observed during hesitations. In total, more gestures occurred during execution phases, whereas Dittmann and Llewellyn (1969) observed increased gestural rates during nonfluent utterances. Moreover, the morphology of the gestures differed according to time of occurrence: Representational gestures were more often observed during hesitations, especially in the execution phase, but nonrepresentational movements were more frequent during vocalizations, especially in the planning phase. Thus, Butterworth and Beattie showed that the coactivation and the competition models are not really incompatible. Because more gestures were observed during execution phases and more nonrepresentational movements during vocalizations, there is evidence for the arousing properties of speech. The more complex gestural representations during hesitations and reduced movement rate during planning phases could reflect resource allocation between gestures and speech (see also Butterworth & Hadar, 1989).

Experimental approaches

Motor preparation. Studies on the temporal association between gestures and speech demonstrate the limitations of observations in daily-life situations. Indeed, recorded events in these settings do not correspond closely to the mental processes from which gestural and oral productions are assumed to result. By analyzing end products only, it cannot be determined whether previous operations involve activation or inhibition. When words or gestures occur, the largest part of the mental work has already been accomplished.

A laboratory setting allows a closer control of events triggering overt behavior and more precise measurement of temporal relationships between input and output variables. From such a perspective, the synchronization of manual and oral movements has been experimentally analyzed by Levelt, Richardson, and La Heij (1985). Two hypotheses on the coordination of pointing with deictic utterances were contrasted: full autonomy (relation during the planning phase only but no feedback from one system to the other during the execution of the motor programs) and interdependence on the lowest level. The subjects were requested to point to lights turned on near or far from a centerline by saying "this lamp" or "that lamp" as soon as the light came on. As expected, the initiation time of the gesture, the apex time (time to reach the maximum extent), and the execution time (difference between apex and initiation times) were influenced by the distance between the lamp and the subject, the longer movements taking more time to be planned and executed. Moreover, the voice onset time was also influenced by this distance factor, thus evidencing interaction between the two systems. Similarly, the voice onset time was influenced by the relative location of the light and of the responding hand. It was faster in the ipsilateral than in the contralateral condition. These variables had no effect on voice onset time in another task, when the subject responded only verbally. In comparison with the condition where subjects responded only verbally or only manually, initiation time and voice onset time were delayed in the dual-task condition, and the delay was much longer for the vocal than for the manual response. Competition for common resources is thus suggested. However, an unexpected application of a load on the arm after the initiation of the pointing movement delayed the apex time, as one might expect, but did not influence the voice onset time. Thus, as predicted by the hypothesis of autonomy, interaction between the gesture system and the speech system was absent during the execution phase and restricted to the phase just prior to beginning the movement. Gestures and speech may be characterized as "ballistic movements" rather than being subject to continuous control by feedback.

The results of this experiment have to be interpreted within a larger perspective on reaction time. In experimental situations where subjects are requested to process information that is provided, the response time depends on the duration of the different operations involved in the task. These operations may follow each other, occur fully in parallel, or interact, and thus predictions about the total duration of the process depend on specific assumptions. In a procedure like that devised by Levelt et al. (1985), subjects have to detect the onset of the lamp and code its location, select a response and program it (for instance, in a deictic gesture by assigning values "left" or "right," "near" or "distant," to an unspecified "pointing" movement), and finally, execute it. The response time is a function of variables that may relate to one or another of these operations. It is unlikely that the interference between vocal and manual response relates to input processing. Rather, it may result from increased load in response selection or from greater difficulty in movement programming.

Coordinative structures. Interference between gestural and vocal performances may diminish or disappear with automation of one of the movements. With the notion of "coordinative structure," Kelso et al. (1983) proposed another explanation for the efficient execution of complex activities, namely, movements involving numerous parameters. Control requirements for the speech apparatus, for two-handed activity, or for concurrent oral and manual movements may be lightened if different components of a system are coordinated in such a way as to depend on a single parameter. Evidence for this was found in an experimental situation in which the subjects were simply asked to alternatively lift and lower the index finger while repeating the word *stack*. There were a free condition (no instruction about the oral and manual performance), a condition where successive words were uttered with alternately high and low intensity, and a reciprocal condition where amplitude of successive movements alternated during list production. Stress in the utterance of lists of words and movement amplitude were related, as though the motor programs controlling the manual and the vocal movements were exchanging information about the values of the parameters specifying details of execution. Furthermore, some subjects synchronized the repetitions of gestures and words without having been instructed to organize performance in this way (Chang & Hammond, 1987; A. Smith, McFarland, & Weber, 1986).

It could also be the case that in more natural conditions, gesture characteristics are coordinated with speech parameters. From video recordings of public speeches by politicians, it was noted that most loudness peaks were accompanied by a hand gesture. Similarly, in a sample of conversations, 90% of the time a movement of a body part accompanied the utterance of a stressed syllable. One may suppose that body movement would occur less often when unstressed syllables were uttered (Bull, 1987; Bull & Connelly, 1985). From these relationships between vocal stress and gestures, the hypothesis may be proposed that manual activity facilitates control over paralinguistic parameters of utterances.

Motor and verbal memory in recall. Interactions between gestures and speech may be studied in memory tasks requiring subjects to reproduce movements or words that were previously presented. Delayed responses depend on input encoding, trace storage, and information retrieval, and thus, gestures and speech may relate in different ways according to the considered process. Memory performances are influenced by conditions resulting from contexts, presented materials, and instructions given to the subject. Some procedures may be facilitative with regard to a control condition while others may yield disturbances that demonstrate memory limitations.

In some circumstances, motor performance during the presentation of verbal material may enhance recall performance. For instance, 3- and 4-year-old children recalled the names of letters better when tracing the letter contour during learning than when letters were only visually presented (Hulme, Monk, & Ives, 1987). Similarly, enacting a sentence like "The workman was digging a hole in the ground" or single words like *bird* or *flying* resulted in a greater number of recalled items than control conditions in children as well as in adult subjects (Salz & Dixon, 1982). These results were interpreted by assuming that activation "motor images" facilitate the recall of associated material. Further experiments should identify the processes by which the effects are elicited.

Studies on "working memory" more particularly concern limited processing capacities. Under this label, a set of interrelated components is considered, including, among others, a "central executive" for attentional control, an "articulatory loop" used in remembering words, and a "visuo-spatial sketch pad" used in remembering locations. It is assumed that interference between concurrent tasks results when the same component must be used, whereas parallel processing is possible if different components are involved. Thus, empirical results allow one to determine if two performances depend on a single or on separate components. In this kind of experiment, subjects are asked to recall a series of 10 movements (such as raising the left arm or bending the head forward), a list of words, or spatial locations. During the presentation of the stimuli, the subjects have to perform either a repetitive manual task or a vocal task: tapping or counting aloud from 1 to 5. In comparison with the recall performances displayed in control conditions, the recall of movements is impaired by tapping and the recall of words or locations is not. Thus, a modality-specific component seems to mediate memory for bodily movements. Furthermore, vocal activity interfered with movement recall but less when the subjects were previously familiarized with the material than when the movements were new. Thus, the task also involves a verbal coding or a nonspecific attentional component (Smyth, Pearson, & Pendleton, 1988; see also Smyth & Pendleton, 1989, 1990). In another experiment, the subjects had to recall digit positions in a matrix, a task involving the visuo-spatial sketch pad. The performance of "incompatible" movements during encoding impaired recall whereas simple tapping did not. Thus, it is suggested that some gestures may involve a spatial component (Quinn & Ralston, 1986). These studies only indirectly relate to gestural activity while speaking. Nevertheless, they draw attention to potentially relevant variables, like spatial coding of, or familiarity with, gestures.

Conclusions

The simplest explanation for manual activity during speaking suggests that human thinking is built upon representations of actions, so gestures are unavoidably triggered by the process of expressing ideas. But is speech accompanied by gestures at all times and under all conditions and for all individuals? Should not the coactivation hypothesis be qualified? The alternative suggestion of competition between gestural and verbal behavior is supported by some observations, but the level at which interactions occur, the selection of lexical and gestural units from message meaning or motor programming, should be specified. Experimental analysis of these issues is still in its early stages. Furthermore, the preliminary attempts reviewed here show some bias in approaching speech-related gestures. The devised conditions most often involved controlled presentation of the information that the subject has to process in order to produce a manual or a verbal response. The situation with spontaneous gestures performed while speaking differs in an important respect. During conversations, speakers themselves determine the content of the message and adapt the formulation to the expected effects on the partner. Motor control is also dependent on goal setting. From such a perspective, it is essential to specify the extent to which a speaker's gestures may influence the comprehension of the message. The results of such an investigation should allow one to determine whether factors relating to listener reactions must be considered in the study of gesture production.

4.2. Gesture and speech comprehension

The theoretical concepts that introduced this chapter and the experimental studies reviewed in the preceding section mainly concern gestures at the expressive level. One may now wonder whether produced gestures fulfill communication functions in discourse processing and, if so, what information is conveyed. Different aspects of these issues have already been examined in the previous chapters. There are gestures that express conventional symbolic meanings within defined communities (chap. 1). Hand movements also serve social functions, because they simply indicate that speech is taking place. In the visual arts, representing gestures is a common means of indicating discourse. For instance, in religious painting or sculpture, preachers and prophets are often shown with the raised hand typical of speaking people. In this way, gestures may play a role in a turn-taking system because the speaker who pauses while searching for a word is able to express nonvocally his or her willingness to continue to hold the floor. Similarly, the listener who remains silent out of respect for rules of civility can manifest the intention to speak by means of a gesture. Finally, gestural behavior gives rise to diverse attributions that relate to emotional states, dispositions, or personal characteristics of the speaker. Thus, enthusiasm, self-confidence, embarrassment, and so on may be expressed nonverbally. Chapter 3 showed that most of the studies on nonverbal communication bear on this kind of influence of bodily signals on social perception.

The analysis of the mechanisms by which gestures are elicited presented in the previous sections of this chapter suggests still other hypotheses about the communication functions of gestures. If, as assumed by Condon and Ogston (1966), verbal and gestural performances are closely synchronized, body movements may give some indications about discourse organization. In this perspective, we may recall the propositions of Kendon (1972b, 1975a), who suggested that the speaker's gestures are analogous to the devices used in written language to distinguish between paragraphs, sentences, and propositions and that gestures allow one to stress links between associated elements across successive clauses or to mark distinctions between different ideas within a single sentence. A description of gestures made during a narrative by a traditional Touareg speaker showed correspondences with the structure of the tale. No gestures were made during the expository phase or during the episode about a solemn discourse of the chief, but numerous movements of varying amplitude accompanied other parts of the story. Thus, by pantomiming some actions, the speaker not only made the narrative more vivid but also gave indications about the underlying structure, and by attending to gestures, the listener could receive supplementary cues about discourse organization (Calame-Griaule, 1977). The validity of this hypothesis, however, cannot easily be demonstrated, and to our knowledge, no attempt has been made to supply experimental support.

Numerous spoken utterances may be understood only in relation to the context of their occurrence; these mostly involve deictic expressions. Pointing gestures may diminish the ambiguity of incompletely specified references. In the use of computers, human–machine dialogue is facilitated by nonlinguistic devices like the icon of an extended index finger specifying the meaning of adverbs such as *here* and *there* (Reithinger, 1987). Of course, other graphic means may be used for the same purpose. However, a pilot study using a short narrative did not demonstrate close relationships between the performance of pointing gestures and the potential polysemy of the linguistic expression. Indeed, some ambiguities, for example, in the identification of the referent of a personal pronoun, can be resolved by nongestural means. The listener actually processes information from diverse origins, and the comprehension of spoken language results from the integration of lexical semantics, logical or pragmatic inferences, and indications from gestures (Marslen-Wilson, Levy, & Tyler, 1982).

Finally, some gestures may convey meanings as precise words. This is obviously the case with emblems that paraphrase utterances such as "I do not know" or "May I ask a question?" Illustrative gestures that cannot be understood outside a verbal context may, nevertheless, modify the meaning of the speech to which they relate. Following Efron, Ekman (1977) distinguished among these gestures eight categories devoted to specific functions. "Batons are movements which accent a particular word. Underliners emphasize a phrase, a clause, a sentence, or a group of sentences. Ideographs sketch the path or direction of thought. Kineto-graphs depict a bodily action or a nonhuman action. Pictographs draw the shape of the referent in the air. Rhythmics depict the rhythm or pacing of an event. Spatials depict spatial relationships. Deictics point to a referent." Other similar categories can be added: Some gestures express temporal or logical relationships; others express "modalities" of discourse, namely, the propositional attitudes of the subject toward the truth value of the utterance; and still others relate to anaphoric relationships. Some of these illustrative gestures are simply redundant with regard to the spoken message, but in other cases they may add information. Thus, full understanding would require integration of verbal and gestural meaning. In the following sections, we will examine how gestures and speech interact in discourse comprehension. First, hypotheses will be formulated about the underlying mechanisms, and then, the empirical evidence will be reviewed.

Working hypotheses about functions of gestures in speech comprehension

Semantic processes

If a listener is presented verbal and gestural information, does the nonverbal part of the message influence comprehension of the spoken language? And, reciprocally, does speech comprehension modify the gesture meaning? Answers to these questions depend on assumptions about the processes by which discourse is understood and by which gestures are recognized. From the viewpoint of cognitive psychology, the task the listener faces is a complex one that involves several components, some specific to one modality and others more general. Speech comprehension relies on categorical perception of acoustical signals resulting in a phonological representation, in word recognition, in syntactic parsing, and in inferences about meaning from knowledge of the world in order to process ambiguity resulting from homophony, elliptic or anaphoric expressions, double entendre, and so on. Thus, speech comprehension requires multiple abilities that remain partially unspecified. Even if not analogous, gesture comprehension also implies several operations. It may be compared to other kinds of visual processing like object recognition, which suggests that access to meaning results from feature extraction and integration and from recognition of an invariant structure that does not depend on the viewer's perspective or on other peculiarities of execution.

How can these visual, auditory, and more abstract processes be combined? The earliest operations on the input are necessarily modality specific. Moreover, it is not readily apparent how the information from gestures influences linguistic processing if, by definition, phonemes, words, and sentences refer only to verbal units. Late operations, however, when meaning is accessed from different sources, may not depend on the modality, and the interpretation of the message may integrate information conveyed by speech and the nonverbal context. This general view can be qualified in several ways.

One question concerns the organization of the component that codes for meaning. Things and events can be referred to by different means. For instance, the verbal expression "an ascending curve" may also be represented by a gesture or a picture. How can the equivalence of these signals be decided? One answer would be to conceive a single abstract conceptual representation accessed by different routes. A defining characteristic of that semantic system would be a capacity to integrate information across modalities. However, it is not certain that words and gestures refer to the same aspects of the referent, and thus information from different sources would not necessarily be identical. A modality effect might thus be observed in semantic processing, especially if the response requested from the subject relates to modality-specific aspects. Another solution is to assume separate but connected networks in which verbal, gestural, and pictorial meanings are coded. Specific semantic systems may be distinguished if somewhat different features are extracted from gestures, words, and pictures. This suggestion is illustrated by a study in which the subjects had to decide whether two phrases describing actions, for instance, "to polish the car" and "to wipe the blackboard," involved the same gesture. The response time was found to be shorter when the subjects were instructed to imagine the movement in the interval between the two sentences than when they had to repeat the sentence. This result suggests a modality-specific memory for action (Zimmer & Engelkamp, 1985; see also Engelkamp & Zimmer, 1989).

Other discussions concern the relationships between the presemantic processes involved in a complex task. Almost everybody agrees with the notion of multiple interactions within or between the semantic system or systems. The meaning of a referential gesture might thus be integrated when the full understanding of the message is demonstrated by the response of the subject. Controversies arise from the assumption of earlier interactions. According to "modularist" views, autonomous components would be specialized to process features of a specific input, for instance, a mental lexicon recognizing words from a phonological code or a syntactic parser recognizing grammatical functions. Other components could recognize gestures from visual input. Different modules cannot interact outside a sequence of discrete stages in which the output of a process constitutes the input for the next one. Alternatively, "connectionist" models admit two-way associations or feedback in such a way that top–down interactions become possible. Furthermore, different processes would progressively release output in such a way that no strict sequential order is followed. Instead of "early" and "late" stages, rapid and slow processes may be distinguished by the time needed to reach stability. With these connections, gestural input could influence speech processing before the completion of the semantic analysis.

Finally, there is the problem raised by the specification of the procedures by which speech and gestures are understood. There might be, first, a direct and rather automatic activation of meaning so that information from the input would be sufficient for comprehension. From another perspective, however, typical of pragmatics, grasping the intention of the speaker does not reduce to accessing literal meaning, and second-order operations integrating semantics and other sources of knowledge are also required. The issue is illustrated by a study on the comprehension of deictic expressions. Demonstrative pronouns or pointing gestures often leave the referent underspecified, so inferences from linguistic and perceptual evidence, along with community membership, are needed for full understanding. If a photograph of the president of the United States with a visitor is shown and the question "You know who this man is, don't you?" is asked, most people assume that the reference is to the president, and few would ask "Which one?" The case is different with the same photograph and the question "Do you have any idea at all who this man is?" (H. H. Clark, Schreuder, & Buttrick, 1983).

Nonsemantic interactions between gestures and speech

Gestures might influence verbal comprehension without conveying meaning by themselves. Therefore, movements other than symbolic or representational gestures may facilitate or impair the processing of spoken language. Various studies in cognitive psychology permit one to speculate in this direction.

Intersensory facilitation in reaction time. In decision tasks such as moving a lever in one direction if a sound is localized on the right and in another direction if it comes from the left, the response time is shorter when the sound is accompanied by a flash displayed on the center of a screen. This intersensory facilitation may be interpreted in several ways. One hypothesis refers to "energy summation." It is assumed that a combination of two sources of energy leads to earlier stimulus identification and thus more rapid response times. This hypothesis was not supported in an experiment where the effect of accessory stimulation was not found to interact with the intensity of the stimulus to be processed. Another hypothesis suggests that facilitation results from response preparation analogous to the influence of a warning signal that, in itself, gives no indication of the correct response (see, e.g., Posner, Nissen, & Klein, 1976; Radeau & Bertelson, 1987; Schmidt, Gielen, & Van den Heuvel, 1984).

It remains to be demonstrated whether speech-related movements influence language processing in similar ways and to identify the "response" elicited in the listener by the auditory signal, analogous to the lever move in the spatial-decision task. If facilitation mainly concerns response preparation or programming, the relevance of these studies might be reduced in natural conditions of speech processing in which no overt oral or manual reaction is required.

Lipreading. Other examples of the influence of visual information on spoken language processing are provided by studies on lipreading. Hearing-impaired subjects are not the only ones to be helped by attention to mouth movements: lipreading also influences normal subjects listening to an intact message (i.e., nondegraded and without added noise). For instance, there is the McGurk effect, which is the illusion of perceiving a phoneme that does not correspond to the auditory signal or to the shape of the mouth uttering the sound but to a combination of these two pieces of information (for instance, many subjects reported hearing the syllable /da/ when the sound /ba/ paired with the picture of a mouth pronouncing /ga/ was presented). However, this result was not observed when words instead of syllables were presented (Easton & Basala, 1982; MacDonald & McGurk, 1978; for reviews, see Campbell, 1989; Massaro, 1987, 1989; Summerfield, 1987).

Viewing the speaker also exerts other influences. In a speech-shadowing task (repetition with minimal delay), a higher number of words were correctly reproduced when the subject could see the mouth of the speaker, especially if the text was difficult to understand (presented in a nonnative language or related to philosophical matters). In a serial recall task, presentation of pictures of mouths uttering words yielded results comparable with those from hearing words. Primacy and recency effects (i.e., advantage of the first and the last words of a list over the central items) were similar with spoken words, mouthed words, and manual signs arbitrarily associated with words. After auditory presentation, similar "suffix" effects (i.e., suppression of the recency advantage) were noted when a spoken word or a mouthed word was added to the list to be recalled. These experiments were aimed at ruling out interpretations assuming a "phonological auditory store" to account for results in verbal memory tasks (see, e.g., Campbell & Dodd, 1980; Campbell, Dodd, & Brasher, 1983; Greene & Crowder, 1984; Reisberg, McLean, & Goldfield, 1987; Turner et al., 1987).

One wonders, from such a perspective, whether hand movements can provide similar information as mouth movements. Like lipreading, attending to manual gestures could probably influence perception of speech rate (K. P. Green, 1987). Some gestures might also be spontaneously associated with words and produce the same effects as those experimentally demonstrated by Campbell et al. (1983), who trained subjects to match hand signs and words. It is unlikely, however, that phonemic discrimination could be as facilitated by these gestures as it is by labial cues.

L. A. Thompson and Massaro (1986) devised one of the few experiments where the influence of gestures on auditory comprehension was studied from considerations about the role of lipreading. Five-year-old children and adult subjects were presented synthetized speech that corresponded to the syllable /ba/, the syllable /da/, or various intermediate sounds a human speaker cannot reliably produce. It was explained that the so-called speaker was referring either to a "ball" or to a "doll." The task was to identify the referent. In one condition, the sound was accompanied by a pointing gesture of the speaker to a ball or a doll. In the control condition only the audio recording was presented. The decisions of young and adult subjects were found to be influenced by the gesture to a large extent. The authors proposed a model for categorical perception of speech sounds combining two sources of information, one auditory and one visual (manual or facial). Of course, this model only concerns referential gestures that provide evidence for one or another response choice (selecting /ba/ or /da/).

Processing intonation. Gestural production relates to prosody when, for instance, the maximal amplitude of an arm extension during a gesture corresponds to a loudness peak. One can imagine, therefore, that on the receptive level also, gestures play a role similar to prosody by expressing emphasis (Bolinger, 1983). Several studies have examined the influence of prosody on speech comprehension. Intonation, together with other linguistic devices like the use of adverbs or cleft sentences, may underscore the semantic focus of an utterance. In a phoneme-monitoring task and in a task involving pressing a key as soon as a sentence is understood, response times were found to be shorter when stress was assigned to the part of the utterance that conveyed new information. These effects of prosody were generally interpreted as bearing on the latest processes of speech comprehension or response preparation instead of on word recognition itself (e.g., Bock & Mazzella, 1983; Cutler & Fodor, 1979; Cutler & Foss, 1977; Grosjean & Gee, 1987).

Might gestures exert a similar influence on speech processing? To answer this question, Bull and Connelly (1985) presented a video recording of a conversation with the sound off. The subjects were instructed to identify body movements expressing emphasis. They noted very diverse gestures of the head and hands as potential stress signals. However, these results did not demonstrate that gestures actually serve this function, because in the devised procedure, the subjects responded only on the basis of nonverbal signals. The role of some eyebrow movements in accentuating a word or a part of a sentence in association with intonation was also suggested by studies at the expressive level, but it has still to be shown at the receptive level (Walker & Trimboli, 1983; see also Ekman, 1979).

Two other pilot studies compared the functions of gestures and prosody in speech comprehension and revealed the methodological problems of such attempts (Feyereisen, unpublished). In the first experiment, video recordings of utterances were presented with their transcript. In some sentences, the subject or the object noun phrases were emphasized by the use of a cleft construction; in other sentences, emphasis was indicated by intonation, by a gesture made by the speaking actress, or by a combination of these cues. The subjects were instructed to underline in the transcript the parts felt to be the most "important." Gestures were found to influence responses to the same extent as intonation and cleft constructions. The procedure, however, had shortcomings. It is possible that sentences uttered by the actress with the instruction to perform a gesture on a specified word had acoustical properties that influenced the subjects' responses. Thus, the control of presenting the material in the auditory modality only is necessary.

In the second experiment, similar sentences were presented in such a context that one part of the sentence conveyed new information and another part old information. Emphasis generally concerns new information, and thus, sentences in which new information is stressed appear most appropriate. In this respect, do gestures influence sentence processing in the same way as prosody? From 120 target sentences 240 short dialogues were constructed that were preceded by two different contexts, one priming the subject, the other the object. For instance, the target sentence "The cat is watching a mouse" once followed the context "The dog is not watching a mouse" and once the context "The cat is not watching a bird." The subject or the object of the target sentences was emphasized by the use of a cleft construction, intonation, or gesture. Thus, for half of the dialogues, the emphasis corresponded to new information, and for the other half, to the old. The subjects had to rate the appropriateness of the target sentence. The results for the gestural variable were ambiguous. Gestures that accompanied the subject noun phrase did not influence judgments, but when gestures accompanied the object noun phrase, the sentence was rated less appropriate when the context primed that object than if the object was new. As with the first experiment, possible mediation of acoustic or linguistic factors should be controlled by the presentation of auditory and written versions of the material.

Conclusions

From these different propositions, it appears that gestures may affect speech comprehension in several ways. Thus, a diversity of processes underlying responses to gestures related to spoken language should be considered. However, before we analyze mechanisms, we must demonstrate that gestures do, indeed, exert influences. Experimental evidence is scarce in comparison with studies on interactions between gestures and speech at the expressive level. Nevertheless, several questions may be raised: Does the listener pay attention to gestures to facilitate speech understanding or does the listener focus on the verbal components of the message to avoid distraction? If gestures are processed, what components of the system also involved in speech comprehension do they concern?

Experimental data

Assessing what other people understand from a message and knowing how they compute meaning from auditory or visual sources are among the most difficult issues psychology has addressed. The only way to establish that words and gestures signify in the same way for different persons is to observe overt behavior and infer mental representations from that behavior. Different procedures have been devised to elicit observable responses from gestural or verbal input and to examine the possible influence of nonverbal context on speech comprehension. One approach is to gather indirect evidence by considering the consequences of the elimination of visual cues (see also section 3.2). Thus, the first question to be raised is whether gestures play any role in referential communication. The answer is not obvious. For some authors, like Rimé (1983), indeed, the weight of nonverbal signals in information transmission has been overestimated in studies on nonverbal communication, and body movements are thought mainly to help the speaker formulate thought into words instead of being directed toward influencing the listener (see also Rimé & Schiaratura, 1991).

Without gestures: elimination of visual cues and speech
comprehension

Everybody knows that speech can be understood even when the speaker is not seen. Furthermore, experimental analysis of the influence of communication systems on the turn-taking system and on impression formation has suggested that visual cues play only a minor role in communication (e.g., Short et al., 1976; Williams, 1977). Some of these studies also considered interactions between gestures and speech. These studies deserve more attention. Do the speakers modify their behavior in sound-only conditions when gestures are useless? Are auditory records of speech less well understood than audiovisual ones?

Rimé (1983) has argued that the primary function of gestures is not to illustrate or modify spoken utterances. He noted that speakers still used gestures when conversing from behind a screen. If the behavior was controlled in order to manage the best conditions for receiving the message, these gestures would be suppressed. Adaptation to the characteristics of the listener is known to be fundamental in shaping verbal production: Words, syntactic constructions, and intonation are selected in relation to assumptions about the mental state of the listener (being a child, a person using a foreign language, or simply a familiar partner having certain beliefs and knowledge). Gestural behavior should display the same adaptation to the listener, and when it becomes superfluous, it should be inhibited and replaced by linguistic devices, or when reliable as a mode of communication, it should be activated, as with foreigners, for example. However, such a hypothesis relies on the assumption that the speaker can control gestural activity. If the programming of movement characteristics and the release of gestures depend on automatic processes, their inhibition in sound-only conditions is unlikely. The observation that in these conditions, speakers reduce but do not suppress hand gesturing is probably related to a subtle balance of automatic and controlled processes in gesture production (Cohen, 1977; Cohen & Harrison, 1973; Lickiss & Wellens, 1978; Rimé, 1982).

Another kind of analysis concerns the content of speech addressed to an invisible partner. If gestures play a role in referential communication, verbal utterances should be modified to compensate for the elimination of visual information. However, the number of uttered words was not found to increase when visual feedback was suppressed or when the speaker was forced to inhibit gestures. Rimé (1982) also noted a similar use of adverbs expressing emphasis whatever the condition, but the possibility of changes in other aspects of speech relating to emphasis was not investigated (Graham & Heywood, 1975; Krauss et al., 1977; Rimé, 1982; Rimé et al., 1984; Siegman & Reynolds, 1983a, 1983b).

One may see the limitations of these attempts: Showing that gestures exert little influence in communication would require the consideration of a wealth of indices in tedious speech content analyses to draw the conclusion that among the dependent variables that were taken into account in statistics, none allows the null hypothesis to be rejected.

A more direct approach to the study of gestural communication is to compare speech comprehension in different visual conditions. The same text was presented in sound-only condition and in two audiovisual conditions: intact video recording or with the facial cues used in lipreading masked. To assess comprehension, factual questions were asked and the response had to be selected from six propositions. To avoid ceiling effects in such a task, which is usually performed flawlessly even without access to the speaker's gestures, speech processing was made more difficult by the addition of different amounts of noise to the signal. The two variables, mode of presentation and signal-to-noise ratio, influenced performance interactively. As expected, facilitation by visual cues was inversely related to the signal-to-noise ratio. Moreover, the advantage of audiovisual presentation was superior when the questions concerned the action (verb) or the agent (subject) rather than the purpose, recipient, location, or qualifier, which suggests specificity of conveyed information (Rogers, 1978, 1979).

A similar result was observed in a study in which the subjects had to guess a defined but unnamed object (actually, a fishing rod). The responses were faster when the speaker performed an illustrative gesture, but no similar advantage of audiovisual presentation occurred with the two other, easier, items. More experiments are required that better control task difficulty and the relationship between the gesture and the speech content across a larger set of stimuli (Riseborough, 1981). These findings also contradict the still mentioned advantage of written (i.e., verbal) over audiovisual (i.e., verbal plus nonverbal) presentation in the comprehension of difficult texts (Chaiken & Eagly, 1976). Finally, when response time is the dependent variable, the temporal distribution of input is critical, but it was not controlled in Riseborough's study.

A specific influence of gestures on the comprehension of spatial relationships was demonstrated in an experiment devised by Graham and Argyle (1975). The task for the speaker was to describe drawings selected as easy or difficult to translate into words (corresponding to short or long utterances), and the task for the audience was to reproduce these drawings. In one condition, the speakers had to maintain a folded-arm posture, and in another, gestures were allowed (the number and form of the gestures actually performed were not reported). The dependent variable was the judged similarity between the original and the copy. Drawings resulting from the gestured condition were rated better, and the effect interacted with codability of the drawing. As analysis of the discourses produced in the two conditions showed very few differences, the advantage taken by the listeners in the gestured condition likely resulted from the illustrative quality of hand movements (Graham & Heywood, 1975). Graham and Argyle (1975) obtained similar results with British and Italian subjects in spite of the assumed greater experiences of the latter in gestural communication. However, the expected cross-cultural difference did emerge in a comparable study in which the Italian and Anglo-Saxon listeners had to delay drawing reproduction until completion of the speaker's message (Walker & Nazmi, 1979).

Without speech: the referential function of illustrative and deictic gestures

The communication value of gestures may also be studied by their associations to words or pictures in matching tasks. However, such a procedure can only be used with representational gestures and not with batonic gestures. Furthermore, it draws the subject's attention to the movement, removes gestures from their context, and requires explicit responses. Therefore, processes different from those by which speech-related gestures are spontaneously understood are probably involved. Gesture comprehension might, nevertheless, be compared to spoken-word comprehension, and the influence of combined cues examined in special populations like beginners in foreign-language learning, hearing-impaired individuals, young children, and aphasics (see sections 5.3 and 6.3).

Can gestures be understood without a verbal context? What meaning do they convey? Are they specialized in the transmission of information about spatial or dynamic features? Very few studies have attempted to answer these questions relative to the number of those that have examined the comprehension of symbolic gestures. From such a perspective, studies on sign transparency may also be mentioned, because subjects who do not know sign languages process manual signs as if they were spontaneous gestures (see sections 1.1 and 1.2, and especially Bellugi & Klima, 1976; Berger & Popelka, 1971; Calbris, 1980; Daniloff et al., 1983; Kumin & Lazar, 1974; Michael & Willis, 1968; Morris et al., 1979).

Feyereisen, Van de Wiele, and Dubois (1988) conducted one of the few available systematic studies on the meaning of speech-related gestures. From the video recordings of two university lecturers, 60 segments were selected, half with a gesture considered "representational," half with a "batonic" gesture. In the first two experiments, untrained subjects were instructed to distinguish these gesture categories either with the sound on or with the sound off. If gestures are considered representational by their visual characteristics only, no differences would emerge between the two conditions. If, on the contrary, *representational* means "related to speech content," the task should be difficult, and responses should be near chance level in the visual-only condition (lipreading remained possible). The results did not support these extreme hypotheses. In the visual-and-sound condition, speech significantly influenced gesture classification, but in the visual-only condition, the performances were above chance level. Moreover, even in the visual-and-sound condition and in spite of a preexperimental selection of gestures as either representational or batonic, several gestures were considered representational by some subjects and batonic by others. By their quality, gestures may thus fall in different places on a continuum from batonic to representational (or in a two-dimensional space where gestures may relate to the meaning of an utterance and to its phonetic realization). A second experiment with similar material was inspired by the study of Bellugi and Klima (1976) on the transparency of the signs of the American Sign Language. Selected gestures were presented without sound, and the subjects were asked to choose the proposition that the gesture illustrated out of three presented. One proposition was the actual utterance that the gesture accompanied, another was a "plausible" interpretation made previously by several subjects who had to guess the meaning of the isolated gesture, and the last was an idiosyncratic answer of the same origin. The results related to the extent the gesture was considered representational in the first experiments, but selection of the actual utterance was the most frequent for only some of these representational gestures. It was concluded that speech-related gestures convey imprecise meaning and that intermediate performances exist between explicit pantomime and a rough sketch presenting a single or a few features of the referent.

Interactions of verbal and gestural information in speech comprehension and memory

Being able to repeat a spoken utterance, to answer questions about it, and to perform the action it describes are some ways by which listeners show comprehension. However, it is difficult to demonstrate whether gestures influence these tasks under normal conditions of speech perception when performances reach ceiling levels. Moreover, the elicited processes involve a working-memory component to store the target utterances until response execution. It would, therefore, be useful to find other measures of comprehension and to examine the influence of gestures on recognition or recall of verbal material.

Comprehension time. The psychology of language has devised original methods to study comprehension. Speech understanding may not only be characterized by accuracy but also by temporal parameters: Auditory and gestural input is not instantaneous but distributed in time, and the activation of meaning units or responses is delayed. Tasks like phoneme monitoring or speech shadowing have been proposed to investigate comprehension in real time (on-line processing). Other tasks like lexical decisions or judgments of truth, meaningfulness, or plausibility, which also have response time as the dependent variable, consider events whose duration is often less than 1 sec. In some of these studies, the length of time necessary to integrate pictorial and verbal information was also analyzed.

These methods have not yet been used to assess the possible role of gestures in verbal comprehension. However, experiments by Klatzky and co-workers (1987, 1989) show their feasibility. In the first stage, pictures of hand configurations were shown that corresponded to the action of touching or grasping with the full hand or one index finger, that is, to "palm," to "poke," to "clench," and to "pinch." The subjects were asked to name objects for which each action was appropriate. In the second stage, other subjects were trained to associate these movements with two verbal labels: "touch" or "grasp" and "finger" or "hand." Finally, these subjects had to decide whether presented phrases like "to cut with a knife" or "to close a nail" were sensible or nonsensical. These sentences were constructed from the results of the first investigation. Each sentence was primed by one or two words displayed 750 msec before the onset of the target sentence. The prime gave either full information about the described action (e.g., "touch"–"finger") or partial information (prehensility or size) or no information ("blank"). The responses to sensible sentences were faster when two words cued the action, whereas the responses after only one cue did not differ from those following no information. Using shorter intervals between the primes and the target sentences – 250 and 500 msec – and substituting icons for verbal cues yielded the same results. No facilitation occurred in other subjects who, during the learning phase, were trained to make purely verbal associations, for instance, to associate the word *poke* with the cues "touch"–"finger," which suggests involvement of motor imagery. One may predict similar facilitation effects from presentation of actual gestures instead of verbal associations even if the timing of these cues is more difficult to control (Klatzky, McCloskey, Doherty, Pellegrino, & Smith, 1987; Klatzky, Pellegrino, McCloskey, & Doherty, 1989).

Gestural context and verbal memory. The hypothesis may also be proposed that gestures, like any event that is contiguous to a spoken utterance, can influence the utterance's recognition or recall. This hypothesis may receive different formulations according to the theoretical framework within which it is proposed. Indeed, the psychological study of the diverse effects of past events on observed behavior cannot be captured in an undefined structure called memory, but several aspects have to be distinguished. Thus, how could the gestures of a speaker affect the processing of the memory trace left by the utterance in the listener?

A first answer to this question is to consider that attention during stimulus presentation influences subsequent response. More particularly, the alertness of the organism and its ability to select relevant information would be critical in processing a complex input like a spoken sentence accompanied by gestures and embedded in a natural context. Close synchrony between gestures and speech should facilitate attention, and artificial asynchrony in an edited videotape should be distracting. Experimental results supported the second part of this proposition only. The absence or presence of synchronized gestures did not influence recall of a spoken message, but asynchrony impaired it. Subjects also felt more distracted during asynchronous presentation (Woodall & Burgoon, 1981).

Some gestures that illustrate aspects of meaning of a spoken utterance could play a role similar to that of pictorial information in text processing. Free recall of a list of verbs and cued recall of words belonging to a short story were better when illustrative gestures accompanied presentation of the verbal material (Riseborough, 1981, exps. 2 and 3). These experimental results should be discussed in relation to models of picture processing in memory and semantic-decision tasks.

Finally, Woodall and Folger (1981, 1985) examined the influence of gestured presentation on the recall of verbal information from the perspective of studies on "episodic memory" that show that performance in a memory task depends on the similarity of context in the learning and the testing phases. The authors proposed cued recall tasks. In the learning phase, the video recording of a conversation was presented, and after a delay, the film was shown again, without sound, to subjects instructed to recall the verbal content. Two variables were controlled during learning in a 3-by-3 between-subjects design: mode of presentation (no gesture, representational gestures, or batonic gestures) and encoding strategy (listening to the conversation, associating gestures and co-occurrent utterances, and creating images to associate gestures and speech). The subjects in the no-gesture conditions were instructed to pay attention to all nonverbal signals. Recall was found superior when representational gestures were presented during learning even if the instructions did not mention them. Encoding strategy did not influence performance and did not interact with the gesture effect. Notwithstanding the theoretical interest of such an observation, its significance remains limited by the rarity of situations in which verbal material has to be recalled from gestural cues.

Conclusions

An evaluation of this review of the comprehension of speech-related gestures might emphasize the discrepancy between the wealth of hypotheses and the paucity of experimental results. We have tried here to construct a framework for future studies. It is suggested that a better understanding of the role of gesture in discourse processing can be hoped for from a fuller integration of still-separate domains of inquiry concerning either the comprehension and memory of verbal and pictorial information or the simple, but still unanswered, question of whether gestures influence speech reception.

4.3. Concluding remarks

The study of the interactions between gestures and speech from a cognitive perspective is clearly in its beginnings. Diverse components have been distinguished in relation to input and output processing and to gestural and verbal modalities. Within each of the sectors so defined, "peripheral" modality-specific processes are assumed to be linked to a "central" amodal component. Such an information-processing architecture may imply a sequential organization of stages, but this idea is probably false and has been criticized by McNeill (1987b, 1989). Nevertheless, even by adopting alternative connectionist views and assuming multiple associations between processing layers, the task of proposing theoretically separable components cannot be avoided (the empirical demonstration of separations is another matter). It is difficult to assume direct connections between visual–gestural or auditory–spoken input and conceptual nodes associated within a "semantic network" because according to experimental conditions, relationships between gestures and speech were found to be sometimes facilitative and sometimes competitive. Thus, multiple intermediate components like feature or phoneme detectors in object or word recognition have to be hypothesized in such a way that activation may spread along some links and inhibition may occur along others. Similarly, on the expressive level, one supposes that "ideas" are connected to articulatory and manual movements through the mediation of "hidden" units (see current perspectives on speech production or motor control). Together with experimental analysis, observations from developmental psychology and neuropsychology may be used to delineate the functioning of such a human information processor.

5. Developmental perspectives

To an extent, all the questions we have examined so far have inspired studies on the development of verbal and nonverbal behavior. Like language, symbolic gestures and social rules have to be acquired from exposure to the uses of a community. Facility in nonverbal communication develops into adulthood in relation to various other social skills (Feldman, White, & Lobato, 1982; Mayo & LaFrance, 1978). Human ethology is highly concerned with the functional analysis of expressive movements in children and especially with the study of attachment in mother–infant interactions (Hinde, 1983). From a similar perspective, it was hypothesized that the quality of a social bond depended on sensitivity and reactivity to signals, mostly nonverbal, that are exchanged during communication. It was also suggested that preverbal interactions play an important role in the regulation of emotional arousal: Adults would have to provide optimum stimulation and, therefore, to adapt to the infant's state so expressed by motor activity, head orientation, facial and vocal expression, etc. (Campos, Barrett, Lamb, Goldsmith, & Stenberg, 1983). All these aspects of the development of emotional and gestural behavior cannot be exhaustively reviewed in a single chapter, and here we will focus on the more specific question of the relationships between gestures and speech during ontogeny.

The problems in this domain somewhat resemble those about the origin of gestures and speech in the phylogeny of the human species. Homology between the two fields of inquiry can be seen without assuming that ontogeny "recapitulates" phylogeny. On the one hand, one may wonder how, during hominization, language emerged from archaic forms of communication relying on motor, social, and cognitive competences that also exist in nonhuman primates. On the other hand, the question is raised of how infants develop the ability to speak while they acquire motor control, social skills, and knowledge of the world. In both cases, similar discussions arise from the opposition of two points of view, which assume either continuity or discontinuity between verbal and nonverbal behavior. Is there, in early communication, a smooth transition from gestures to the first words, or do linguistic devices develop separately? According to one hypothesis, language may be acquired on the basis of achievements in other domains. This general proposition can be specified in two directions that focus either on cognitive development assessed by nonverbal behavior or on social competence displayed in preverbal communication. According to the alternative view, language acquisition would rely on specific processes that can be distinguished from those that control gestural behavior (Bates, Benigni, Bretherton, Camaioni, & Volterra, 1977; Bates, O'Connell, & Shore, 1987).

Most studies on the relationship of gestures and speech during ontogeny were set up to show either that language depends on cognitive or social development or that it depends on an autonomous system. However, one might reasonably suppose the correct answer to the question of how children acquire language is not to accept one hypothesis and reject the others but to try to delineate their respective domains of relevance by considering their empirical support. Let us begin with the suggestion that gestures and speech relate to the level of cognitive development reached by infants and, more particularly, to the general capacity to use symbols.

5.1. Early symbols

Symbolic function: unitary or manifold?

According to Piaget, the slow emergence of language depends on the evolution of intelligence that may be observed in the sensorimotor activity of the subject, mostly in imitation and play behavior. Thus, the first words appear when a more general semiotic function is built. Around 1 year of age, infants understand that signs, be they vocal or gestural, substitute for things in order to represent them. Later, a general capacity of combining several signs, either manual or verbal, develops in several modalities (Piaget, 1946/1951; see also Inhelder, Lézine, Sinclair, & Stambak, 1972; McCune-Nicolich, 1981; Shore, O'Connell, & Bates, 1984).

Numerous observations of nonverbal behavior have been guided by this notion. Piaget, in particular, based his assessment of stages in cognitive development on gestural cues like gaze orientation or expressive movements of infants. Well-known works like *The Origins of Intelli-*

gence in Children (1936), *The Child's Construction of Reality* (1937), and *Play, Dreams, and Imitation in Childhood* (1946) may be read again beneficially with selective attention to these aspects. By way of illustration, excerpts of *The Origins of Intelligence* may be quoted. Among the first acquired adaptations in visual behavior, Piaget stressed the active role of gaze:

> Observation 35. – There is generalizing assimilation, not only with respect to the successive objects which the child sees, but also in connection with the successive positions which the subject assumes in order to look. The acquisition of the "alternate" glance may be cited in this connection. . . . During the third month, the emergence of the following behavior pattern may be observed: the glance compares, so to speak, two distinct objects while alternately examining them. (1936/1952, p. 69)

Observations 34, 99, and 150 may also be mentioned in this context. Laughter, smiles, and frightened expressions may be indications of a new organization of schemata, as shown by the acquisition of so-called secondary circular reactions:

> Observation 106. – In the evening of 0;3 (13) Laurent by chance strikes the chain while sucking his fingers: he grasps it and slowly displaces it while looking at the rattles. He then begins to swing it very gently which produces a slight movement of the hanging rattles and as yet faint sound inside them. Laurent then definitely increases by degrees his own movements: he shakes the chain more and more vigourously and laughs uproariously at the result obtained. – On seeing the child's expression it is impossible not to deem this graduation intentional. (P. 185)

See also observations 98, 109, and 110.

> Observation 102. – . . . Jacqueline, too, at 0;9 (5), shakes while holding a celluloid rattle in the form of a parrot which she has just been given. She smiles when the noise is slight, is anxious when it is too loud and knows very well how to graduate the phenomenon. She progressively increases the noise until she is too frightened and then returns to the soft sounds. (Pp. 166–167)

Mouth opening in front of a box may be interpreted as the beginning of representation of actions:

> Observation 180. – . . . Lucienne, by opening her mouth thus expresses, or even reflects her desire to enlarge the opening of the box. . . . Also it is probable that the act of opening her mouth in

front of the slit to be enlarged implies some underlying idea of efficacy. (P. 338)

Even though Piaget's interpretations of these observations may now sometimes seem premature, they indicate that facial expressions relate not only to emotion but also to representation and that, when emotional, they relate to a level of cognitive development that allows some emotions to be experienced.

McNeill (1975, 1979) more recently presented an analogous conception. For him, language acquisition relates to gestural development because the early mental representations are built from sensorimotor schemata. These cognitive structures link and integrate actions, objects, events, and states. In the infant, action schemata constitute the matrix of a true propositional language in which the semantic relationships that underlie verbal utterance are first conceived. This suggestion, very plausible in its generality, may orient research in several directions.

First, in the study of Greenfield and Smith (1976), the vocal and gestural behavior of children in their second year of age is described to show the progressive elaboration of semantic functions. Hand movements that are associated with the initial utterances may substitute for still-absent terms for actions, agents, objects, or characteristics like location. The child who begins to speak combines single words with gestures related to some aspects of the physical or social environment. Accordingly, these early vocalizations cannot be understood without the nonverbal context. At this stage, protowords are uttered in the frame of an action, for instance, the syllable /te/ emitted while giving an object during an exchange game. Plausible paraphrases might be "I give you this" or "Look at this," that is, multipart sentences. Such observations do not imply privileged connections between the verbal and gestural domains. It is simply stated that early utterances depend closely on the context and that any meaning results from the relationship that is made between the semantic content of a sentence and the actual state of the world in which the action is unfolding.

In another direction, one may suppose that the production of verbal utterances depends on the formation of concepts. A level of cognitive development, as demonstrated by nonverbal behavior, must be reached to use words and syntactic devices. For instance, emitting a noun that refers to the agent of an action would result from an underlying notion of causality, whose acquisition is also demonstrated by gestures. A child who wishes a switch to be turned on may utter a sound, point to the object, grasp an adult's clothes, and, finally, integrate the word *Mommy* in a nonverbal sequence that demonstrates the understanding of the adult as a causative agent (Olswang & Carpenter, 1982). However, it remains difficult from such observations to establish tight links between conceptual representations and their expressions in the vocal or gestural modalities. One knows, indeed, that one of the most difficult problems in the study of language development is raised by the mapping of a child's concepts onto adult thought. Children use words in more restricted senses than do adults or with an enlarged extension, and this might also be the case with the conditions of gesture production. Thus, words and gestures in children's behavior likely express the acquisition of some concepts, like the notion of permanent object or causality, but these concepts are not necessarily identical with those formed in adulthood after long development.

Finally, McNeill (1975) proposed the phrase *semiotic extension* to describe the development of mental representations that begin with sensorimotor schemata and later include formal operations. Young and adult speakers use figurative expressions of action as metaphors for abstract processes. Thus, a meaning constructed from concrete manipulations extends to other domains. Mathematicians, for example, use a wealth of images and speak of "extraction of the square root" or of "inversion of a matrix." From such a conception, progress in language acquisition does not result in the disappearance of gestures but rather in changes of their forms and functions. Thus, gestures performed by adults while speaking would represent vestiges of the sensorimotor stage of early cognitive development. They would not constitute simple embellishments but would relate to the very nature of thinking (see chap. 4 for a discussion).

These different ways of considering relationships between gestures and speech within cognitive development contrast with a conception of language acquisition as the result of specific processes. For other authors, indeed, several symbolic processes should be distinguished. Play, drawing, pantomimes, and speech would rely on partially autonomous systems. Symbolic function should not be considered unitary but built from separate components that may interact during some developmental phases. Thus, according to Werner and Kaplan (1963), deictic gestures and early vocalizations simultaneously emerge as "twinned" referential devices, and they later progressively differentiate. Gestures remain related to a primitive mode of communication, whereas oral expression allows greater "distanciation" from the external world and, therefore, reference to more diverse elements. Parallelly, different "fields of knowledge" may be considered to evolve asynchronously during ontogeny. Bates and co-workers (1979), for instance, propose a notion of "local homologies" instead of a syncretic and unitary system of representations. By this term, they mean that separate systems may relate in different ways according to the proposed task and the selected measure or to the child's age. Similarly, Gopnik and Meltzoff (1986) assume specific and multiple connections between cognitive development and language acquisition rather than global characterization in terms of stages (see also Meltzoff, 1988).

Empirical evidence that may be used to disentangle alternative conceptions is very diverse. Since the early works of Piaget, several studies have been devoted to imitation, symbolic play, or concept formation in relation to language acquisition. Research on the development of perceptual, motor, and cognitive competence in infancy also refers, by definition, to nonverbal behavior. From that body of literature, representative studies dealing more particularly with the gestural mode of representation may be presented.

The development of vocal and manual naming

When children produce single-word utterances, they are already endowed with a diversified gestural repertoire. Some routines, like sending a kiss, waving good-bye, or blowing on food to mean "it's hot," are used during social interactions. Moreover, some actions performed out of context, like pretending to stir in an empty cup or holding the receiver of a toy telephone to the ear, display quasi-linguistic properties. Like names, they designate known objects and may be used by shared convention in referential communication. The term *manual name* has been proposed for these gestural performances (Bates, Bretherton, Shore, & McNew, 1983).

How does this behavior relate to language acquisition? At least three different kinds of evolution may be hypothesized: (*i*) simultaneity and coordination in the development of gestural and vocal repertoires, (*ii*) asynchrony and anteriority of gestures over corresponding words, and (*iii*) replacement of gestural symbols by words. Finally, the null hypothesis of an absence of relationships between the gestural and verbal domains may also be considered.

Some observations suggest that the occurrence of the first lexical items closely relates to the development of gestures. Bates and co-workers (1979) have computed correlations between several verbal and nonverbal measures in a sample of 25 children observed at 9 and 13 months of age. Their results indicated that different gestural complexes have to be distinguished, for example, "communicative" pointing gestures that are performed in a social context and associated with gazing toward the partner, and noncommunicative gestures or pointing to oneself. Both kinds of gestures correlated with the number of words produced or understood, and the correlations increased from 9 to 13 months of age. Thus, the replacement hypothesis was not supported for this age-group, and the acquisition of vocabulary would extend the capacity of communication rather than substitute one mode for another.

Qualitative analyses also showed connections between gestures and speech during development. Vocal and gestural emissions often referred to the same domains of reality: animals, food, or toys. Around 1 year of age, children often have only one sign, either gestural or vocal, for one referent. The two modes of communication are integrated and complement each other (Acredolo & Goodwyn, 1985, 1988; Bates, Benigni, Bretherton, Camaioni, & Volterra, 1979; Bates, Thal, Whitesell, Fenson, & Oakes, 1989).

The notion of a single symbolic system controlling gestural and vocal performances must be qualified, however. First, there is the magnitude of the observed correlations. A coefficient of .50 between the number of words and gestures produced is certainly significantly different from zero but it is also less than 1.00. Furthermore, Bates and co-workers (1979) observed higher correlations between verbal measures than between verbal and gestural measures. Some degree of specificity of two related symbolic systems is thus suggested.

A second element of discussion concerns the age of the children who were observed. Frequency of use of gestural and vocal symbols correlated until a particular level of development, but when the children mastered about 50 items of vocabulary, no new symbolic gestures were acquired. Linguistic progress, of course, continued. From 10 to 21 months of age, the proportion of purely gestural performances decreases and that of purely verbal utterances increases. These observations of children older than those studied by Bates et al. support the replacement hypothesis (Acredolo & Goodwyn, 1988; Zinober & Martlew, 1985).

The third, still more important remark bears on the respective role of the child and the adult partner in symbol use. Gestural conventions most often result from appropriate, stereotyped, and consistent reactions to signals performed by children within established routines. From 9 to 15 months of age, children address more gestures to their mothers than to a peer. In the latter situation, they perform only gestures previously used in interactions with their mothers. Symbolic gestures generally occur during shared activities involving objects and not in relation to objects only or persons only. Thus, it is difficult to determine precisely, in the smooth transition from interaction rituals to innovative use of symbols, when children realize that a sign may substitute for a thing (Bakeman & Adamson, 1986; Martinsen & Smith, 1989).

Finally, Bates et al. (1983) stress two characteristics by which the use of gestures differs from the use of corresponding words. First, with reference to the notion of "symbolic distanciation" proposed by Werner and Kaplan (1963), gestures seem relatively more context dependent than words, even if the early utterances also relate to a definite context. Second, symbolic gestures fulfill a different function in communication during social interactions. For instance, children were never observed pretending to drink from an empty glass in order to ask for orange juice. From such a point of view, different kinds of gestural uses have to be distinguished along physical and social dimensions (presence versus absence of objects referred to and addressed versus solitary activity).

Imitation in the vocal and gestural modalities

Imitation refers to the control of behavior by templates that may be taken from others or formed by the subject from his or her own behavior or from inanimate objects. Functionally, it may be defined as a process by which conformity with a model is achieved. Even if the outcome is not just a copy but involves transformations, it is still guided by the model. This mechanism plays an obvious role in the ontogeny of communication behavior. In this way, children acquire the largest part of their gestural and verbal repertoire. Moreover, "invented" representational gestures often derive their meaning from their iconicity, that is, a relation of similarity by which the hand movement captures an aspect of the referent. However, even if one limits the discussion to the process of immediate imitation, little is known about the psychological conditions underlying the copying of a model. As already emphasized by Guillaume (1926), a central issue is the problem of creativity in imitation. How are the first, imperfect attempts progressively corrected to result in conformity with the model, and how is that conformity acknowledged? A dual process can be assumed. First, assimilation of the model into one's own behavior and then checking of similarity between the copy and the original and correction of casual errors. In this latter control, imitation differs from simple motor mimicry, in which several persons behave in the same way.

Another, related question raised about imitation is how the subject can code in motor programs what has been perceived visually or auditorily. Several hypotheses may be examined. Some deal with relatively automatic processes like those involved in contagion of yawning or in motor mimicry, for instance, when a caregiver opens his or her mouth while feeding a baby. Others imply that symbolic representations underlie motor control. This would be the case when children adopt the behavior of a character in a television program. Observational learning in animals or early imitation in infancy probably relies on different processes.

Early imitation

The capacity of neonates to imitate movements such as mouth opening or tongue protrusion now seems established, but problems remain in the interpretation of the phenomenon. First, that imitation might depend on still-unknown individual variables or on minor changes in experimental procedures, for instance, the duration of the model presentation, the size of the stimulus, or the infant's vigilance. Sharper control of these factors could account for some discrepant results (Fontaine, 1984b; Hayes & Watson, 1981; Koepke, Hamm, Legerstee, & Russell, 1983; McKenzie & Over, 1983; Meltzoff & Moore, 1983, 1989; Vinter, 1985a, 1985b).

It has also appeared that some models, for instance, tongue protrusion, were more easily reproduced than others, like expressions of joy or surprise. Neonates also more willingly imitated facial than manual gestures. Moreover, moving stimuli, for example, alternate opening and closing of the hand, were more often imitated than static forms. Stimulation by the model might thus possess arousing properties and elicit the most available response in the infant's repertoire without true imitation of the model by the subject. Nevertheless, in frequent cases, the model is more efficient than any other stimulus to trigger the response (Fontaine, 1984a; Jacobson, 1979; Kaitz, Meschulach-Sarfaty, Auerbach, & Eidelman, 1988; Vinter, 1986).

Finally, there are problems concerning evolution with age during infancy. The capacity for imitation decreases until 6 months of age and appears again around 12 months of age. Thus, early imitation may depend on other mechanisms than those underlying later imitation (Abravanel & Sigafoos, 1984; Field, Goldstein, Vega-Lahr, & Porter, 1986; Fontaine, 1984a; Heimann, Nelson, & Schaller, 1989; Lewis & Sullivan, 1985).

Manual and vocal imitation compared in 1-year-old children

Imitation likely does not depend on a unitary function, as suggested by studies on the development of imitation beyond 1 year of age.

Converging evidence concerns the influence exerted by the presence of objects on model reproduction. Even if *gesture* refers here to somewhat different behavior, modality effects observed in this context are worth consideration. Between 10 and 16 months of age, children imitate more easily toy manipulation than meaningful gestures and more easily meaningful than meaningless movements. Around the same age, the rate of correct imitation of sounds has been found to be comparable to that of meaningful gestures. Similarly, between 8 and 20 months of age, greater success in imitating movements with objects was observed than in imitating body postures or sounds. When, with children around 14 months of age, gestural model and verbal support were combined, imitation performance varied in relation to the children's word comprehension level, as one might expect. However, children of different levels performed similarly in a control condition when a neutral, uninformative comment was supplied. Thus, low-comprehension children were not influenced by linguistic information but they were nevertheless able to imitate symbolic gestures. Later, at 20 months of age, vocabulary size correlated with the capacity to repeat words but not with the capacity to imitate object manipulation. Furthermore, these modality effects were found to interact with age in longitudinal studies. More gestural models were imitated than vocal models at 13 months of age while the reverse was observed at 20 months of age. Mean length of utterances correlated with the capacity to combine several items in gestural sequences at 20 months of age, but no longer at 28 months of age. Indeed, grammatical constructions in older children relied on distinctions between parts of speech, a variable that has no analogue in the gestural modality. Finally, in a sample of late talkers, the ability to imitate single actions with objects was found to dissociate from the ability to combine several items within a sequence: as compared to age-matched controls, late talkers performed worse in the former task but not in the latter. All these observations support the conception of "local homologies" between distinct subdomains better than the hypothesis of a single capacity in symbolic processing (Bates et al., 1989; Bates, Bretherton, Snyder, Shore, & Volterra, 1980; Bretherton et al., 1981; Masur, 1987; Masur & Ritz, 1984; Rodgon & Kurdek, 1977; Shore et al., 1984; Thal & Bates, 1988).

However, an alternative explanation of discrepancies between gestural and verbal development during ontogeny remains compatible with the assumption of a shared underlying mechanism. Décalages between gestural and verbal behavior may be interpreted from a "complexity" hypothesis according to which evolving organisms process the less demanding material earlier in infancy and later in old age. Thus, for instance, imitation of actions with objects might be more successful than imitation of gestures, not because different systems are involved, but because the objects provide cues for movement recall. Similarly, symbol manipulation might be easier in the gestural than in the vocal modality either because hand movements are related more to the context or because their motor execution is simpler. Different factors that concern lexical development, semantic memory, and motor control must be considered in the explanation of, for example, why normal and mentally retarded children learn sign languages earlier or better than spoken languages (Abrahamsen, Cavallo, & McCluer, 1985; Meier & Newport, 1990).

The study of congenitally deaf-mute children allows one to assess the complexity hypothesis, because they acquire language in the gestural modality. If gestures occur earlier in ontogeny because they are easier to process, deaf-mute children should differ from hearing children by, for example, imitating linguistic signs as soon as other gestures.

Gestures and acquisition of sign language

Deaf-mutes, like hearing children, use gestures in their engagement with persons and objects. They develop a manual system of communication either spontaneously from object manipulation or by imitating adult models (Feldman, Goldin-Meadow, & Gleitman, 1978; Goldin-Meadow, 1979, 1982, 1985).

Thus, there is a greater similarity between their prelinguistic gestural behavior and their use of a sign language than is the case with hearing children acquiring a spoken language, and deaf-mute children should not encounter some of the difficulties met by hearing children in the transition from prelinguistic gestural behavior to verbal behavior. From such a perspective, Petitto (1987) studied the acquisition of the pronouns *I* and *you*, which, in American Sign Language (ASL), are, respectively, represented by a pointing gesture toward the signer's chest and toward the addressee's chest. In hearing children, these pronouns are acquired later than other words, and some confusion occurs during the first utterances because children use the same form to refer to themselves as that used by their partners to address them. Similar mistakes in referring to oneself by means of the second-person pronoun were casually observed in two deaf-mute children before 2 years of age. Moreover, these children, who, up to 1 year of age, frequently had used pointing gestures toward persons and objects reduced the frequency of pointing gestures toward persons between 12 and 13 months of age. Pointing to objects did not follow a similar trend. Such an evolution was interpreted as indicating transition from the prelinguistic to the linguistic use of the pointing gesture. The two phases were separated by a period during which the production of forms that belong to both the linguistic and the gestural system was inhibited.

Other differences in gestural behavior between deaf and hearing children suggest discontinuity between linguistic and nonlinguistic modes of representation. Sign languages possess a syntax deaf children acquire progressively, probably at the same age as hearing children in their spoken language (thus, sign language advantage mainly concerns the vocabulary, not the syntax). However, hearing children very rarely combine two gestures in a complex proposition, for instance, by extending the hand in a begging gesture and then pointing to the requested object. When gestures are combined with vocal utterances, the two signals most often convey the same meaning. Gestures of hearing children lack the property of words of belonging to grammatical categories. Finally, comprehension of gestures does not follow a common pattern in language acquisition. Spoken words are usually understood before being produced. However, when an experimenter performed a gesture belonging to a child's repertoire with the instruction to point to the picture of the object referred to, neither hearing nor deaf children could fulfill the task before 30 months of age. Thus, children produce gestures they do not understand when made by other people (Caselli & Volterra, 1990; Goldin-Meadow & Morford, 1985; Meier & Newport, 1990; Petitto, 1988; Volterra & Caselli, 1986).

Conclusions

The hypothesis of a cognitive foundation of language acquisition has not received unambiguous support from studies on symbolic gesturing. To some extent, problems arise from the diversity of phenomena considered under the label "gesture." According to the meaning given to the term, different kinds of relationships may be conceived. Some observations concern symbolic processes involving object manipulations, others pointing, and still others interaction rituals between children and familiar partners. All these movements are characterized by being performed in the presence of the referent or in a defined context. Thus, they differ from the gestures made by older children to accompany spoken utterances relating to a distant referent and from later achievements in language acquisition.

This is not to conclude the full autonomy of gestures and speech. On the contrary, the notion of local homology allows one to consider continuity and discontinuity between verbal and nonverbal communication. On the one hand, some specialization of the different systems may be assumed in relation to distinct properties of the referent, like visual or functional features for depictive gestures and taxonomic relationships for words. Modality effects are thus likely in situations where these aspects are relevant. On the other hand, enhancements in one domain may be transferred to another, and thus, some capacities developed in gestural behavior, like using signals to reach some end by means of other persons, isolating an object from its surroundings, or stressing one of its properties, may facilitate similar performances in verbal behavior. Accordingly, studies on prelinguistic communication may describe gestural antecedents of some language uses.

5.2. Language acquisition and preverbal social interactions

Continuity or discontinuity?

It is banal to state that language is a social activity and that children begin to speak during interactions with speaking adults. A less trivial endeavor is to search for the processes by which linguistic devices appear within such exchanges.

From a pragmatic perspective, one may consider that during the first year, before speech, infants develop their ability to form intentions to communicate. There would be continuity between nonverbal and verbal means to reach a goal. Indeed, empirical criteria for intentionality are not easy to formulate, as shown by related discussions about "purposes" in animal behavior in the 1930s. But sometimes, by repeating their message or crying because they are not understood, infants show expectation of a definite outcome. In another direction, however, one may stress the diversity of the components involved in communication and the heterochrony of their development. A behavior that manifests with the same appearance might serve different functions during ontogeny or be already present without being functional. A parallel can be drawn with the development of a different complex behavior such as walking, which displays discontinuities, as probably does language. Bipedal locomotion relies on several acquisitions that are not necessarily simultaneous: muscular force to sustain body weight, postural equilibrium, limb coordination, long-distance vision. Some components are inborn, like the early reflex walking, which disappears if untrained. Some others develop with experience or maturation. Previously separate processes are integrated later in a different structure. This kind of evolution can also be demonstrated in the development of communication, which also involves multiple competences (Fogel, 1985; Fogel & Thelen, 1987; Golinkoff, 1983, 1986; Harding, 1982; Shatz, 1983).

Origins of conversation in preverbal interactions

At birth, an infant is endowed with a repertoire of vocal, facial, and bodily signals that elicit responses from caregivers. Communicative gestures may be assumed to derive from these movements. Reciprocally, in the presence of infants, adults behave in such a way as to release reactions like smiles or vocalizations or to stop expressions of fussiness. By touch, voice, and facial movements, a mother often tries to attract her infant's attention, to regulate its arousal level, and to increase reactivity. By imitating the infants' movements more frequently than infants imitate their mothers, mothers enable the construction of a shared code. Thus, infants can learn precociously that their own behavior is followed by predictable effects on surroundings. They demonstrate a capacity to detect regularities in the environment, as already shown by the sensitivity of newborns to conditioning. The ability to anticipate the consequences of actions and familiarity with situations are assumed critical in the development of communication. For instance, infants may show distress in experimental conditions in which the mother is instructed to keep her face immobile. Furthermore, adults willingly attribute meaning to infants' signals emitted during interactions, and thus, contingent responses can become intentional expressions (see, e.g., Brazelton, Koslowski, & Main, 1974; Cohn & Elmore, 1988; Field, Vega-Lahr, Scafidi, & Goldstein, 1986; Fogel, 1981; Pawlby, 1977; Stern, 1974; Stern, Hofer, Haft, & Dore, 1985; Trevarthen, 1977, 1979; Tronick & Cohn, 1989).

In the context of the preceding chapters, special attention may be given to studies that, from such a viewpoint, concern infants' manual activity. Trevarthen (1977) suggested that as early as the age of 8 to 12 weeks, hand and finger movements are synchronized with prespeech movements, namely, small facial movements like tongue protrusion and lip contraction, which are interpreted by the mother as attempts to talk. These facial movements, which are usually produced without concurrent vocalization, are accompanied by hand, foot, or trunk movements. Among these, hand and arm movements, especially hand waving, finger pointing, and fingertip clasping, are very finely synchronized with prespeech movements within a window of 0.1 sec. Thus, there seems to be an innate basis for the coordination of manual and oral movements, even if the relationship can later be shaped by cultural influences, and the coactivation of gestures and speech that was discussed in chapter 4 may be deeply rooted in ontogeny.

A study on a larger scale was conducted with 28 infants, 9 to 15 weeks old, by Fogel & Hannan (1985). Four hand movements were distinguished: spreading, pointing, curling, and grasping. Gaze behavior, facial behavior, and vocalization were also recorded. Some coordination between hand movements and other activities was demonstrated; for instance, right-hand curling, but not right-hand spreading, occurred significantly more often during vocalization than in silence. Sequential analysis also revealed associations between pointing and mouthing or vocalization. However, some of these relationships could be due to variations in the state of arousal, the influence of which on the behavior of very young infants is known. Nonetheless, even if the precise coordination between hand and speech movements remains to be demonstrated, it is suggested that gestural movements appearing later in life have precursors in early manual activity and that some primitive mechanisms may explain their coordination with speech movements. First nonfunctional, these gestures would progressively be used in communication.

Contingencies, interactional synchrony, and behavioral dialogue

Consistent reactions to the behavior of each other has been called metaphorically "dialogue" or "protoconversation." In one sense, only formal similarity is stressed between successions of on–off phases in vocal or gestural behavior, but sometimes it is also assumed that important aspects of language use, such as perception of turn-taking signals or the distinction between subject and object, develop in prelinguistic interactions (Beebe, Stern, & Jaffe, 1979; Beebe, Jaffe, Feldstein, Mays, & Alson, 1985; Freedle & Lewis, 1977; Jaffe, Stern, & Peery, 1973; Mayer & Tronick, 1985).

Mother–infant interactions may be analyzed in different ways according to the chosen settings, mostly play or feeding situations, and observation codes. One procedure is to record discrete states that may be described in binary terms: gaze contact or avoidance, vocalization or silence, movement or rest. Other studies deal with continuous variables that are derived from a set of behavioral indices assumed to relate to a single motivation. For instance, states of "avoidance," "engagement," etc., are defined from several cues like head and eye orientation and facial or vocal expression. In this case, different signals are considered equivalent, and no attempt is made to distinguish among modalities of expression (e.g., Als, Tronick, & Brazelton, 1979; Bakeman & Adamson, 1984; Tronick, Als, & Brazelton, 1980). Such a procedure reduces the number of data to be processed, but the rationale for grouping signals in a small number of dimensions may be questioned (Fogel, 1988). In developmental studies as elsewhere, changes in the selection of behavioral indices often lead to different conclusions. For instance, the orienting of newborns toward a human voice was demonstrated by a measure of mouth asymmetry, but direction of the first head move did not show discrimination (Alegria & Noirot, 1978; Noirot, 1983).

However, the regularity of early interactions is shown whatever the procedure. During meals, the state of the mother, who may either actively stimulate the baby or remain quiet while bottle-feeding or breast-feeding, relates to the state of the infant, who may either suck or pause. Furthermore, these states are not randomly distributed in time but occur in "runs," that is, strings of similar states (Alberts, Kalverboer, & Hopkins, 1983; Bakeman & Brown, 1977; Kaye, 1977; Stevenson, Roach, VerHoeve, & Leavitt, 1990).

In mothers and infants at play, behavior may be organized according to compensatory reactions, when, for instance, infants avoid approaching mothers, or from matching reactions in imitation or reciprocity when they look attentively toward an expressive face. During development, the same movement, such as gaze averting, may first be involved in compensatory and then in reciprocal reactions. Thus, newborns were observed to turn the head away when an adult was facing them, but 3-month-old infants preferred to look at their mothers when the mothers were oriented toward them. Likewise, the rated pleasantness of vocal reactions to eye contact with relatives was found to increase during the first 6 months of age. Special attention has been paid to the influence of the mother's vocalizations on the infant's vocal and motor behavior. In the first months, coaction is observed before turn alternation, so duetting precedes dialogue (e.g., Anderson, Vietze, & Dokecki, 1977; Cohn & Tronick, 1987; Elias, Broerse, Hayes, & Jackson, 1984; Fogel, 1982; Fogel, Toda, & Kawai, 1988; Ginsburg & Kilbourne, 1988; Kaye & Fogel, 1980; Keller & Schölmerich, 1987; Keller, Schölmerich, & Eibl-Eibesfeldt, 1988; Messer & Vietze,1984; Peery, 1980; Rutter & Durkin, 1987; Stern, Jaffe, Beebe, & Bennett, 1975; for a review, see Cappella, 1981).

From such a perspective, the infant's motor activity that accompanies its mother's vocalizations needs to be more precisely assessed. In this respect, a specific hypothesis was proposed by Condon and Sander (1974), according to whom infants', like adults', body movements synchronize during speech listening with a segmental organization of the speaker's utterance. In frame-by-frame analysis of sound film, the onset of movement of different body parts of the listener was found to coincide with phonic articulation. In this way, the infant precociously shows "involvement" in conversation (see also Condon, 1977). However, the first reports on this phenomenon did not give many details on the scoring procedure, and more recent analyses have questioned the hypothesis (Dowd & Tronick, 1986). As noted earlier, it does not seem possible to identify the beginning of a movement from visual analysis with an accuracy greater than about 125 msec, that is, a "window" of 3 frames in a film made at the speed of 24 frames per second (McDowall, 1987a, 1978c). Moreover, psycholinguists tell us that phoneme localization in the acoustic speech flow raises considerable problems. The same signal may convey several phonemes simultaneously, and thus, for the syllable /ba/, it is impossible to establish when the sound /b/ ends and the sound /a/ begins. Accordingly, Dowd and Tronick (1986) observed the movements performed by infants at 2 and 10 weeks of age during the presentation of a recorded spoken message, and they selected periods of emission of the first vowel in a stressed syllable. The motor behavior of infants did not differ at that moment or shortly before or after it. One can thus conclude that the results of observations by Condon and Sander were based on artifacts. When synchrony is defined on a larger time scale, it might be noted that the frequency of simultaneous movement by adults and infants is higher during vocal exchanges than during silent periods. However, this result might depend only on chance if both partners produce more movements during vocalization phases than during silence (Austin & Peery, 1983).

Respective contributions of adults and infants to dialogue

If social influence may clearly be demonstrated in prelinguistic interactions, true reciprocity implies mutual adaptation to the behavior of the partner. The question is thus raised as to whether mothers and infants play similar roles in early dialogues. Is the relationship symmetrical? In the case of a behavior that is interpreted as a break of contact, such as gaze avoidance or turning away the head, infants seem to take the initiative more often, but in other cases, adults look more responsive than infants. Contingencies in nonverbal dialogue may thus depend on an adaptation of the adult to the infant and not the inverse.

Several statistical procedures have been proposed to identify the relative contributions of each partner in an interaction. Time-series analyses face the problem of isolating the part of variance explained by interaction and the part explained by temporal regularities within each sequence in two parallel sequences that correspond, respectively, to the infant's and its partner's behavior. Indeed, before analyzing interaction, departures from randomness that result from fluctuations in the probability of occurrence of an event have first to be removed. The influence of adult on infant and of infant on adult may then be compared (Gottman & Ringland, 1981; Sackett, 1987; Thomas & Martin, 1976; Wampold, 1984; for illustrations, see also Cohn & Tronick, 1988; Stevenson et al., 1990; Symons & Moran, 1987).

The issue of directionality of effects in social interactions has also been dealt with in other ways. Hinde and Herrmann (1977) defined derived measures from simple frequencies in mother and infant behavior. These indices concerned the analysis of approach and avoidance movements, but they may be generalized to other situations where the initiatives taken by each partner may be compared. Murray and Trevarthen (1986) had mothers interacting with their babies via a closed-circuit television system. At one moment, the direct signal was imperceptibly replaced by a recorded signal, and thus the behavior of the subjects was no longer contingent on that of the partner. Speech content was found to be influenced by the experimental condition: More questions, expansions, and repetitions were produced in direct exchanges, and more negative comments and calls to attention were noted in the delayed condition. Thus, an active role of the infant is demonstrated, but with the chosen dependent measure, only the mother's adaptation to the infant's behavior could be analyzed.

A probably simpler method consists of controlling for contingencies by comparing actual to fictitious sequences that result from inversion of two parts in the record. Such an operation does not modify the frequency or the duration of a target behavior such as gaze orientation toward the partner, but it should selectively eliminate effects due to interaction. By using this procedure, Messer and Vietze (1988) found that probabilities of transitions between states like "mutual eye contact" and "mother's gaze toward the infant" did not differ in real and sham sequences and, thus, that the contingencies did not depend on mutual adaptation but were chance products.

Pragmatic analysis of preverbal communication

Under the hypothesis of continuity, communicative competence evolves within interactions between infants and their caregivers that anticipate later language uses. Thus, some functions of speech may be fulfilled in early stages by nonverbal means: referencing by pointing or looking at objects, requesting by arm extension, protesting by head turning away, motor agitation, or crying, fiction by pretend play. Similarly, nonverbal exchanges would exhibit formal properties that would facilitate acquisition of analogous linguistic structures. For instance, systematics for turn taking may apply before actual conversations are held: In games like peek-a-boo or in exchanging objects, infants may learn role reversibility, rule recursivity, and task segmentation. By these structured activities, a framework for further verbal exchanges is built (Bruner, 1975a, 1975b, 1977; Chalkley, 1982; Dore, 1974; Halliday, 1975; Ninio & Bruner, 1978; Ratner & Bruner, 1978).

A critical step toward language acquisition would be the capacity to use communication in order to reach some objective. Accordingly, Bates, Camaioni, and Volterra (1975) have analyzed preverbal interactions from a pragmatic perspective on "speech acts." Three phases were distinguished concerning perlocution, illocution, and locution. In the perlocutionary phase, infants simply influence the partner by gesture or another action but without being able to control this effect. Examples were provided in the previous section. In the illocutionary phase, specialized manual, facial, or vocal signals are intentionally used to elicit expected reactions, like receiving physical contact by raising arms or attracting attention by pointing gestures (referential functions will specifically be examined in the next section). Early vocalizations were also analyzed from such a perspective. The first uttered sounds gain meaning only through appropriate responses by familiar persons. From their context of occurrence, a linguistic signification is inferred. For instance, a syllable beginning with /m/ and accompanied by a reaching gesture may be understood as a request for help in order to get something. Finally, the locutionary phase is characterized by language use that substitutes for nonverbal means. A smooth transition is observed through a period in which verbal and nonverbal signals are combined and vocal emissions progressively differentiated (Carpenter, Mastergeorge, & Coggins, 1983; Carter, 1975, 1979).

The distinction between perlocutionary and illocutionary phases corresponds to that made by Trevarthen and co-workers between primary and secondary intersubjectivity. Early communication relies on more or less automatic reactions to signals sent by the partner. From reciprocal adaptation, the infant begins to perceive other persons as a source of autonomous activity. For instance, gaze is directed toward the mother when a game is interrupted, which, according to Trevarthen, indicates that the mother is considered a causative agent. At the same time, from 8 to 12 months of age, the proportion of interactions involving both a social partner and object manipulation increases and that of purely social or purely manipulative interactions decreases. Thus, the period of appearance of the first words coincides with the integration of social and physical domains and the coordination of activities that had been dissociated (Trevarthen, 1979, 1980; Trevarthen & Hubley, 1978).

Referring by gaze and pointing gestures

The development of reference illustrates the transition from the illocutionary to the locutionary phase, or from communication to language. Discovery of word meaning depends on the ability to relate semantic representation to defined aspects of the environment. Thus, the capacity to attract attention to objects or features is a prerequisite for lexical development. Several nonverbal means may be used to fulfill such a function. One longitudinal study of a child during its second year showed changes in deictic behavior. First, a specific vocal utterance, /da/, was associated with a pointing gesture to designate a spatial location. Then, the vocal schema differentiated into /di/ and /da/ used in different contexts, and gesture became optional (Carter, 1978a, 1978b).

The use of pointing gestures in communication is clearly established by 14 months of age. It closely follows comprehension of the same movement. These gestures are generally accompanied by vocal utterances and gazes toward the partner. Thus, a social function is inferred and the continuity between pointing and early naming assumed. From 12 to 16 months of age, about 70% of deictic expressions combine the oral and the gestural modality. Beyond this age, progress in differentiation of phonologically related forms makes the gesture unnecessary. As emphasized by E. V. Clark (1978), the spoken words *here* and *there* offer the advantage over gestures by enabling contrasts between points on the same vector. In the transition to linguistic expression, special attention was paid to the moment when, by 15 months of age, infants become able to indicate by gaze and hand movement two different directions, one toward the partner, the other toward the referent. This performance rather than simple pointing would mark the appearance of the first words (Lempers, 1979; Lempers, Flavell, & Flavell, 1977; Leung & Rheingold, 1981; Lock, Young, Service, & Chandler, 1990; Masur, 1983; Murphy, 1978).

Relationships between pointing with the index finger and reaching with the open palm remain open to discussion. For some authors, like Vygotsky (1956/1962), the former gesture derives from the latter. An infant trying to get an object would first reach and then would solicit help from an adult by simply pointing. Both forms would relate to requests. However, for others, the two movements appear early in distinct forms and already serve different functions by 1 year of age. Only reaching is a request, whereas pointing is more similar to naming or, according to Werner and Kaplan (1963), to the contemplation of an object whose possession is not necessarily desired. In this context, a similar discussion about the gestures of apes may be cited. For some authors, these learned responses have been reinforced and simply serve to obtain a material reward, but for others they demonstrate social understanding or symbolic processing (see chap. 2). Differences between reaching and pointing are also observed in the course of development and in responses by adults, who casually give what is asked for or comment. The transition from pointing to naming may thus be shaped by reactions of caregivers, who, with infants of 9 to 18 months of age, more often answer verbally to pointing than to reaching or holding objects. Infants, too, accompany pointing more often than other gestures with vocalizations. These observations demonstrate a specialization of this gesture for reference, a continuity between gestural and verbal means to designate objects, and an influence of the adult partner that may be determinant (Hannan, 1982, 1987; Lempert & Kinsbourne, 1985; Leung & Rheingold, 1981; Lock, 1980; Masur, 1982; Nelson, 1987; Savage-Rumbaugh et al., 1983; Seidenberg & Petitto, 1987).

Thus, one is led to emphasize a fundamental characteristic of infant–adult interactions of displaying a discrepancy between the actual competence of the infant and the expectations shown by adult behavior. Attentive caregivers interpret early vocalizations as speaking attempts, and they give meaning to gestures and respond accordingly. In this way, they perhaps anticipate an infant's capacity but surely enable the formation of a framework for communication. It might be excessive to attribute intentions to early expressive movements, and purposiveness might exist only in the eyes of the adult, who sometimes must confess inability to guess what an infant's gestures "mean." But by providing consistent answers, adults enable the infant to develop instruments for communication in structured interactions (Fogel & Thelen, 1987; Packer, 1983).

Thus, the notion of conversation to refer to prelinguistic exchanges seems to serve mainly as a metaphor; strictly speaking, it should not be used before the first spoken utterances. A discontinuity between pointing and naming or between nonverbal and verbal means of referencing may be considered. The movement of extending the index finger was observed as early as 3 months, at which age a capacity to establish reference is not assumed. It may be distinguished reliably from other movements, such as hand opening or finger curling. Thus, early manual activity does not reduce to undifferentiated motor arousal. However, adults generally do not pay attention to these movements, and pointing does not seem to be integrated into a visuospatial analysis of the environment. Like the first vocal emissions, they seem to be merely orienting reactions instead of social signals used to draw the attention of other persons to some particular object. With older infants, however, adults react to these movements as if they were intentional. Still later, vocal or gestural attention-directing devices are considered attempts to name, and help in that direction is provided. Thus, in communication, forms may anticipate functions, as is the case with many anatomical structures during ontogeny. Furthermore, in behavioral development, functions seem to be acquired by exercise during social exchanges (Edwards & Goodwin, 1985; Hannan, 1982, 1987; Hannan & Fogel, 1987; Legerstee, Corter, & Kienapple, 1990; Lempert & Kinsbourne, 1985).

In summary, there are arguments for continuity and for discontinuity between pointing and naming. The discussion, however, seems to rely heavily on the chosen time scale: Over the first 2 years of age, language becomes distinct from preverbal communication, whereas during "microgenesis," gestures and speech are integrated, for instance, in episodes in which words are added to the infant's vocabulary by adult verbal responses to children's gestures. One may thus follow Shatz's (1987) suggestion that gestures do not belong to the linguistic system but allow its development. As a general rule, infants have to use what they know to learn more. Gestures, in particular, enable them to elicit verbal utterances from adults and, thus, to obtain the material that is necessary for the acquisition of a native language and to associate word meaning with environmental features.

5.3. The nonverbal input in first verbal exchanges

Until now, this chapter has been focused on gestures made by infants. Another problem is to assess the influence of the nonverbal behavior of other persons on language acquisition. Studies on this topic may be distinguished according to investigators' assessment of two criteria. The first criterion is whether the emphasis is put on the infant's disposition to learn or on environmental factors to account for interindividual or cross-cultural differences. The second is the exclusive consideration of linguistic variables versus the inclusion of nonverbal factors such as adults' gestures performed while speaking to infants (Hoff-Ginsberg & Shatz, 1982). If language acquisition relies on mechanisms that are not restricted to verbal behavior, the comprehension of gestures may facilitate the processing of analogous utterances such as "look" or "there." And, if the infant is endowed with inborn language acquisition devices, it might discover phonological, lexical, or syntactic principles of language organization from the provided sample of spoken utterances without being influenced by an extralinguistic context. It is likely that the two hypotheses address different components of the language-comprehension process.

Joint attention

Exchange of symbols in communication relies on the ability of the partners to share referents. There are different ways to establish this common ground, which is necessary for agreement on word or gesture meaning. At least in Western societies, adults devote a great deal of effort to teaching verbal responses to infants. They use diverse means to elicit vocalizations, and they modify intonation and select lexical items and sentence forms according to the age of the addressee. Furthermore, utterances are spoken in close connection to the nonverbal context. Thus, during play with her infant, a mother tries to attract its attention by leaning forward, tilting her head, and emitting various sounds. She speaks about ongoing, instead of past, actions. She mentions objects she holds or points to and, when introducing another topic, uses lengthy pauses or changes her manual activity. Thus, she attempts in several ways to simplify the infant's task of understanding what is being spoken about (Adamson & Bakeman, 1984; Garnica, 1978; Halliday & Leslie, 1986; Harris, Jones, & Grant, 1983; Harris, Jones, Brookes, & Grant, 1986; Messer, 1978, 1981, 1983; Rocissano & Yatchmink, 1984).

One of the first opportunities for an infant to manifest comprehension of referential gestures is the moment when it can look toward a location in the direction of its mother's gaze. In the study of Scaife and Bruner (1975), only a third of the 2- and 4-month-old infants responded to a visual fixation by their mother of a location to her left or her right, but all the 1-year-old infants followed her gaze direction. In other studies, contingencies in the behavior of both the partners were analyzed, and during the first year of an infant's life, the mother was found to follow the infant's gaze direction more often than the inverse. Moreover, while sitting beside the infant, she modified her own posture by leaning and looking at her infant's face to monitor its visual behavior. Thus, mothers seemed to play the main role in the achievement of joint attention, and the actual ability of infants to understand this kind of deictic gesture seemed to remain limited. For instance, in face-to-face conditions, most infants can follow their mothers' gaze direction toward a location in their own visual field by orienting to the left or to the right, but the behavior of looking backward when mothers fixated on a point behind the infant was only observed at 18 months of age (G. Butterworth & Cochran, 1980; Collis, 1977, 1979; Collis & Schaffer, 1975).

Comprehension of deictic gestures by young children

Pointing gestures, by themselves or in association with spoken utterances, could provide the infant clearer and fuller indications to the referent than gaze orientation, an unspecific gesture, or a purely verbal message whose understanding requires linguistic competence. After 9 months of age, an infant is able to look at an object pointed to if the infant is sitting on one side of the mother and the object is located on the other. Only at 14 months of age are they able to look at designated objects in front or beside them. If the experimenter asks the infant to show one of two objects, better results are obtained with holding gestures than with pointing. Thus, comprehension of deixis remains incomplete until 18 months of age (Lempers, 1979; MacNamara, 1977; Murphy & Messer, 1977).

However, beyond this age, deictic gestures may facilitate spoken language processing. By 3 years of age, when contrasts between the meanings of *this* and *that* or *here* and *there* are not yet clearly established, pointing gestures with utterances involving these words enhance performance in a task of object placement. The influence of gesture was also demonstrated in the task in which children had to decide whether the speaker was referring to a ball or to a doll (see section 4.2). The speaker pointed to one of these objects, and some of his utterances were made ambiguous by using sounds that varied from /ba/ to /da/ (Tfouni & Klatzky, 1983; L. A. Thompson & Massaro, 1986).

Pointing gestures can play several roles according to the context, can be used with different utterances, and, thus, can be understood in various ways. For instance, the function of pointing gestures when adults are telling stories from illustrated books changes with age. With younger children, from 9 to 14 months, mothers name the pictures pointed to, whereas with older children of 20 and 24 months, the same gesture is used with an interrogative sentence to elicit naming (Murphy, 1978).

The influence of gestural cues on language acquisition

One may reasonably assume that adult gestural behavior facilitates the mapping of word meaning on states of the world in early phases of language acquisition. However, the empirical evidence remains inconclusive. In one study, mothers were observed to perform more gestures when they reformulated spoken utterances misunderstood by children. Fewer comprehension errors occurred with these gestured sentences than with previous verbal commands. However, the positive influence of adult gestures was expressed mainly in the nonverbal behavior of children. For instance, when the question "What says meow?" was asked with or without a pointing gesture toward a cat, 16- and 18-month-old children responded more appropriately in the gestured condition when looking, pointing, or manipulating behavior was scored, but no differences occurred in their verbal behavior. Actually, pointing or holding gestures mainly serve to attract the infant's attention in order to trigger an intended action. Infants more willingly oriented toward the mother when she performed gestures, but compliance to verbal instructions was not increased in the gestured conditions. A subtle integration of verbal and nonverbal components of the message would be achieved: to elicit interest by pointing gestures or unspecific utterances like "look," onomatopoeia, or interjections and to shape action by demonstrating object use or by giving explicit verbal instructions (Allen & Shatz, 1983; Bates, Bretherton, Beeghly-Smith, & McNew, 1982; Schaffer & Crook, 1980; Schaffer, Hepburn, & Collis, 1983; Schnur & Shatz, 1984; Shatz, 1982, 1983)

However, the influence of this interplay between verbal and nonverbal behavior of an adult on the strictly verbal comprehension of an infant remains to be demonstrated. The first problem arises when gestural performances of mothers are analyzed according to the age of the addressed children. If gestures are intended to facilitate comprehension in early phases of language acquisition, their frequency should decrease as the child's verbal competence increases. Such a trend was observed in studies comparing mothers' behavior toward 1- and 3-year-old children but not in those done with 10- and 18-month-old infants. While telling stories to 30- and 54-month-old children, mothers even performed fewer gestures with younger children. Because mothers' gestural behavior likely relates to some characteristics of discourse held with listeners of different ages, the form and content of the utterances should be examined to interpret these results. One must also consider that older children still have to learn new words and formal aspects of language use (Garnica, 1978; Gutman & Turnure, 1979; Schaffer et al., 1983; Schnur & Shatz, 1984).

A more serious problem for the hypothesis is that the relationships between gestures and sentence structures are too loose to facilitate the understanding of spoken utterances. The same gesture may accompany a reference or a request, and different verbal forms may be used in each of these cases. Moreover, a single gesture often relates to a multiword sentence. For instance, a mother may say "Can you put the people in the holes?" while pointing to the set of corresponding toys. This gesture may be used to infer the general scope of the utterance but not to access the meaning of each of the constituents (Shatz, 1982). These remarks are relevant to the larger issue of the development of the semantic system in children. How do concepts derived from individual experience become integrated into a shared body of knowledge? Gestures performed by adults while speaking to children might be of little help in such an evolution.

Conclusions

Beyond the likelihood of adult nonverbal behavior influencing language acquisition by children, the relevant gestural variables still have to be identified. Furthermore, long-term effects of mother–infant interactions on linguistic competence may be interpreted in several ways (Bates et al., 1982). Some methodological problems in the study of early communication also have to be underlined. For reasons that concern the sociology of science more than a research rationale, cross-sectional studies are more numerous than longitudinal ones. Moreover, many observations do not warrant high reliability, because low interobserver agreement was achieved or because no control of this sort was provided (Brinker & Goldbart, 1981). It is sometimes difficult to identify the way behavior is scored because categories are not defined or context described with enough precision. One knows that the term *gesture* may refer to various phenomena: demonstrating object use, pointing to an object, describing some of its features. If it is focused on cognitive development, manipulatory activity and symbolic play are considered gestures, but from other perspectives, one must distinguish movements that are made while touching or handling objects, those that are made while only looking at objects from a distance, and those that evoke objects in their absence. Thus, to some extent, the gestures considered in this chapter differ from the speech-related gestures studied in the other sections.

Finally, difficulties arise from the generality of a hypothesis concerning relationship between gestures and speech. As a complex behavior, language use has several components that may develop asynchronously. Relevance from a pragmatic point of view, semantic and syntactic structure, and phonetic realization imply different kinds of spoken or gestured input even if, of course, the diverse components of the verbal behavior remain related. Thus, hypotheses concerning interactions of verbal and nonverbal behavior during development have to be specified in reference to a model allowing for both continuity and discontinuity, or specificity and cross-modality transfers.

5.4. Development of gestural behavior beyond infancy

Coevolution or replacement?

In the preceding sections, the development of gestures was examined in the early phases of language acquisition. However, communicative behavior evolves throughout one's life. At present, the question will be raised whether in later phases of development, when a larger vocabulary and more complex syntactic structures have been learned, there are changes in gesture appearance, usage, and frequency. McNeill (1985), for instance, proposed that the successive emergence of different kinds of gestures – deictic, iconic, and beats – related to the appearance of the first spoken symbols, the progressive decontextualization of the expressed meanings, and the attainment of the text coding stage, respectively. Another hypothesis, however, suggests that when gestures are combined with the first acquired words, their function changes. Children would rely more and more on the verbal mode of communication; gestures would be replaced and emerge later in different forms with other functions. Few studies are available that are relevant to these propositions. Furthermore, older children are often observed in experimental settings, whereas infants' gestural behavior is generally assessed during natural interactions with familiar caregivers. Because gestural behavior is influenced by the conditions of elicitation, the results obtained with different procedures may be compared only with caution.

Spontaneous production of gestures by children

There are some indications in the single-case study of Carter (1978b) that at the end of the second year of age, gestures became optional and were relegated to a supportive role. However, studies on larger samples have rather suggested independence between the two domains: Language development would be associated with neither an increase nor a decrease in gesture production. Dobrich and Scarborough (1984) found no differences in form and frequency of pointing gestures between two groups of 2-year-old children characterized by high and low mean length of utterances, respectively. In a pilot study with three children producing verbal directives, no global trend for a reduction of gestural production was observed, but in another study, children from 2 to 4 years of age used fewer gestures and more verbal imperatives in pretending to ask for an object from a doll (Read and Cherry, 1978; Wilkinson & Rembold, 1981). When the adult experimenter pretended to misunderstand a verbal or a gestural request during play with children of 17 to 24 months of age, very few reformulations of the message were observed. Children most often persisted in repeating the same behavior or abandoned it, independent of their level of linguistic development (Wilcox & Howse, 1982).

Beyond 4 years old, it seems clearer that gesture production continues to increase. During conversations about a cartoon movie, the total number of gestures produced by subjects from 4 to 18 years of age increased (Jancovic, Devoe, & Wiener, 1975). In the same age range, Van Meel (1982) also observed a general increase in gesture production by older children in a word-definition task. However, another study suggested discontinuity in development. A U-shaped distribution of gesture frequency was observed in comparing 6-, 8-, and 10-year-old children explaining the rules of a game to an adult experimenter, but no difference appeared in the total number of adequate rules formulated (Evans & Rubin, 1979). More information should be collected about possible "dips" in the evolution of gestural behavior around 3 to 4 or 8 to 9 years of age. Language developments paralleling these modifications in gesture use have not yet been extensively analyzed. Consideration should also be paid to the observation that while speaking, blind-born adolescents do not perform gestures other than self-touching movements, which suggests that development of gestural behavior might depend on specific features of visual experience (Blass, Freedman, & Steingart, 1974).

Other analyses dealt with the development of the communicative function of gestures. The proportion of representational gestures or of pantomimes decreases with age, and that of batonic gestures, which appear around 4 years of age, increases until adulthood. McNeill (1986) carefully described iconic gestures performed during the narration of a cartoon movie and compared them with the gestures of adult subjects in the same circumstances. The children used a larger space and sometimes mimed action instead of representing it. Differences also occurred in the temporal association of gestures and speech, the children's gestures relating to shorter segments of the utterance (Elmslie & Brooke, 1982; Freedman, Van Meel, Barroso, & Bucci, 1986; Jancovic et al., 1975; Van Meel, 1982).

The study of gestural behavior is of particular interest when it reveals aspects of cognitive processes in children. For instance, it has been noted that when children explain the rules of a game, inadequate verbalizations were sometimes clarified by accompanying gestures (Evans & Rubin, 1979). Thus, there is a lack of association between verbal and gestural expressions of some concepts. In Piagetian conservation tasks, too, children may produce gestures that are discordant with the given verbal explanations (Church & Goldin-Meadow, 1986). Discrepancies result from contradictory or, more often, complementary information given gesturally but not verbally. For example, when water is transferred from a wide to a narrow glass, children around 6 years of age may say that the quantity has been modified, because the dimensions of the containers differ, and simultaneously show, by a pouring gesture, an understanding of reversibility. Children were classified as (*i*) nonconservers, partial conservers, and conservers, and (*ii*) "discordant" or "concordant" on the basis of this kind of relationship between gesture and speech. Discordant children were more inconsistent in verbal explanations within and across conservation tasks. In a subsequent session bearing on partial conservers, the discordant children were found to benefit more from instructions or from demonstrations by the experimenter than the concordant children. It was concluded that the discordant children manifested an actual comprehension of conservation although they were unable to integrate it into their verbal explanations and that their gestural behavior showed a higher level of reasoning than their verbal behavior.

Moreover, gestural demonstration might facilitate the linguistic representation of some cognitive processes. One of the clearest examples concerns the acquisition of the concept of number and of the corresponding lexicon in counting tasks. Fuson (1988) suggested that a difficulty hindering development was the matching of a spatial array (the series of objects to be counted) with the temporal structure of a sequence of digits. Nonverbal behavior, be it successive pointing gestures, finger extensions, or gaze fixations, is both spatially and temporally organized. By 4 years of age, children commit fewer errors in counting if gestures are allowed than if they have to stay immobile. Experimental conditions have no influence on younger children, who may make errors even when using gestures, or on older children, who perform flawlessly without hand gesturing (Saxe & Kaplan, 1981). These observations give insightful extensions to the discussion on symbolic development presented in the first section of this chapter. Children use number words before a full understanding of their meaning, which may be enriched into adulthood, whereas the evolution of gestural processes may be completed sooner. Thus, motor, linguistic, and conceptual development may show asynchrony, assuming, of course, that verbal and gestural behavior express a way of thinking.

Gesture use during referential communication

In several studies on referential communication, that is, experimental tasks in which subjects have to lead the partner to identify what they are speaking about, the puzzling use of inappropriate forms by young children has been described, and it was suggested that the ability to produce adequate messages involves more than the mere acquisition of the necessary expressive means (see, e.g., Dickson, 1981, for a review).

Pointing gestures, for instance, may be more or less appropriate due to the confusion that is possible from the context of their use. By 4 years of age, children still point to designate a distant object surrounded by other objects, but by 9 years of age, children, like adults, prefer to name it. No age difference was observed in a condition when the target object was near and misunderstanding less probable (Pechman & Deutsch, 1982). Likewise, Alegria (1981) showed increased reliance on gestures in older deaf children trained in oral language; the gestural mode was found to be the most efficient by these subjects when possible confusion between the referents made the task difficult. Taking into account the partner's perspective may also be demonstrated in cross-cultural communication. Bilingual children gestured more and reduced their verbalization less than monolingual children while conversing with a puppet speaking an unknown language; they probably had learned by experience that people speaking foreign languages could understand them, especially if some gestures accompanied speech (Marcon, 1986).

The development of gestural representations

Representation using gestures likely differs from spontaneous gestures observed during communication. Tasks that require symbolic gestures to be performed at the verbal instruction of an experimenter allow experimenters to assess a competence that is not displayed in other tasks. In this way, the repertoire of conventional gestures that may be produced was found to be acquired later than the ability to comprehend these gestures. The influence of cultural or educational variables was also demonstrated (Hoots, McAndrew, & François, 1989; Kumin & Lazar, 1974; Michael & Willis, 1968).

As far as the ability to pantomime the use of familiar objects is concerned, continued development was observed beyond the age at which semiotic function was first acquired. Children who are asked to create gestural symbols must confront several problems that are solved only progressively. Difficulties have been described in isolating the medium (i.e., selecting the relevant body segments), in detaching gesture from the referent (younger but not older children sometimes use "the body part as object," such as opening the palms to refer to a newspaper instead of pantomiming the holding position), and in motor organization (notably, when the two hands must coordinate to produce asymmetric configurations). For instance, in an unpublished pilot study, de Lannoy and Aebischer presented, one at a time, common objects like a glass, an ashtray, and a key to children from 6 to 13 years old and asked them to "explain what they see without speaking" to an adult who could not see the object. In the second condition, drawings were presented, and in the third, three familiar games had to be described, still without speech. Developmental trends concerned, first, the body part selected for the gestural performance. Whereas the younger children used only one hand or even one finger, the older used either these means or two-handed movements and even the upper part of the body in the referential activity. The younger children often evoked the shape of the object, the contour of the picture, or some elements of the game, like a ball, by drawing in the air with the hand or the finger, whereas the older children pantomimed the prehension or the use of the items. The gestures of the younger children were also more difficult to understand by the adult experimenter. However, the results varied with the object, the picture, and the game considered. For instance, gestures about a paintbrush more often illustrated action with the object than gestures about a shoehorn, which was evoked by its shape. Thus, representational gestures that rely not only on motor memory but also on perceptual factors develop in relation to properties of the referent. Moreover, these observations support the suggestion of Werner and Kaplan of a progressive decentration during development. In their gestural as in their verbal behavior, children are first guided by their own point of view and later become able to take into account the perspective of the partner and, thus, to be better understood (see also Barten, 1979; Galifret-Granjon, 1974; Jackson, 1974; Overton & Jackson, 1973).

Does the development of subtle conceptual distinctions between related meanings that may be represented nonverbally, such as denying or forbidding, influence gestural behavior? In the gestural modality, negation may be expressed by head movements, a part of the body on which attention is focused during conversations, but other gestures may also be used with the same purpose. According to Collett and Contarello

(1987), a finger shake simply transposes to the hand the lateral head shake for "no," which is acquired much earlier (see, e.g., Pea, 1980). However, at least in northern Europe, two related gestures can be distinguished, a lateral shake for denial and a sagital shake for forbidding even if the two notions, which can both be expressed by the same word, *no*, are difficult to define in logic and in psychology. In an unpublished pilot study, de Lannoy, Monini, and Meyer studied the development of the behavior expressing negation or prohibition from 6 to 12 years of age. Children were asked several questions that should elicit either answers in relation to a criterion of truth (for instance, the experimenter held a sheet of paper and asked "Is the sheet on the table?") or answers in reference to rules of conduct (for instance, "Is it permissible to cross the road when the light is red?"). Nonverbal responses were requested. In another condition, children had to explain to people who did not speak their language some situations also involving prohibition. In order to deny, young children mostly used a lateral head shake. By 9 years of age, they performed a lateral finger shake in the same proportion as the head movement. Beyond that age, they again showed preference for head shaking. To express forbidding, younger children used head and finger movements indiscriminately. From 7 to 9 years of age and beyond, finger movements predominated, and 10-year-old children also performed other hand gestures.

In a further experiment, de Lannoy and Monini (unpublished) constructed a model of several roads leading to a house. Obstacles of different kinds – a fence, a wild animal, a red light, and a policeman – hindered passage on all the roads except one. Children had to explain first verbally, then by gestures, to foreigners which road could or could not be followed and why. From 7 years on, children used lateral index-finger movement to mean "One cannot take this way." This gesture and head movements were performed at all ages, and expressions of denial or prohibition did not differ. Inconclusive results from these observations may have been due to the ambiguity of the verbal expression – "to can" often means "to be able to" and "to have permission to" – or to the ambiguity of the situation because children were not in a position to forbid but simply to give advice or simply to indicate the presence of a physical or normative obstacle to which they sometimes pointed. Nonetheless, from 6 to 12 years of age, verbal and nonverbal expression of negation and prohibition continued to evolve, and new gestures appeared, probably in relation to cognitive development. In this respect, the use and meaning of gestures are not independent of social and linguistic competence.

6. Gestures and speech in neuropsychology and psychopathology

Neuropsychology, at first, was mainly concerned with the description of the neural mechanisms underlying behavior. From this point of view, researchers hoped to identify the anatomical structures on which gestures and speech depend. The results of that research could potentially provide strong arguments for the association of gestures and speech in phylogeny and ontogeny if the same neural structures were involved or for their dissociation if modality-specific mechanisms were identified. However, attempts to localize human mental functions turned out to be premature because of the temporal or spatial resolution of available imaging techniques and the advancement of models of the neural implementation of complex activities. Nonetheless, as far as the issue of association or dissociation is concerned, data from neuropsychology and psychopathology can be fruitfully exploited even without a precise knowledge of the functioning of underlying neural substrata. Dissociations that result from selective impairments or lateral differences may be described, and thus the separability of underlying mechanisms may be indirectly demonstrated before the mechanisms themselves are actually identified. The literature on the relationships between gestures and speech in neuropsychology and psychopathology can be reviewed from such a perspective (see Feyereisen, 1988, 1991, for further developments).

6.1. Introduction: on drawing inferences from pathology and lateral differences

A good deal of information has been gathered about the loci and the anatomy of cerebral structures in which lesions disrupt visual-gestural or auditory-vocal processing. Several left-hemisphere sites are involved in the production of symbolic gestures, and similarly, the comprehension of pantomimic gestures is disrupted by very different left-hemisphere lesions (Ferro, Martins, Mariano, & Castro-Caldas, 1983; Heilman, Rothi, & Kertesz, 1983; Varney & Damasio, 1987; Varney, Damasio, & Adler, 1989).

This diversity of localization is a function of the present knowledge of the brain mechanisms of motor control and visual perception. The precise localization of brain functions cannot be achieved if the behavioral categories are too large. Global terms like *gesture production* or *gesture recognition* cover a diversity of processes, so they are not useful for understanding the brain code. Only rough inter- or intrahemispheric distinctions may be made, and the neural organization remains poorly described. Moreover, it may be that some structures are involved in multiple types of processing, and thus one must wait to see if the assumption of a one-to-one correspondence between elementary psychological input–output functions and neuronal activity is realistic or whether more distributed organizations (many-to-many correspondences) have to be described.

Neuropsychology may pursue a more reasonable objective by contributing, together with other psychological approaches, to the description of the architecture of the underlying behavior and to the identification of the multiple components involved in gestural and verbal processes. The information-processing models proposed in cognitive psychology and discussions on developmental continuity and discontinuity provide starting points for a taxonomic analysis of mental functions. Two kinds of methods may be used to show dissociations. First, the observation of brain-damaged subjects may reveal selective impairments of processes that are closely related in normal functioning and, thus, support the models that distinguish these processes. Second, several procedures have been devised to compare left and right hemispheres in normal subjects, with dissociations being shown by finding Task × Hemisphere interactions. In both cases, by comparing patients or studying laterality effects, the interest is in showing that the same lesion or the same treatment has different effects on different processes rather than in localizing functions in the left–right or the anterior–posterior dimension.

From such a perspective, single-case studies become the preferred paradigm in research with brain-damaged subjects. When neuropsychology sought localizations, large groups of subjects were used in order to compare the consequences of right- and left-hemisphere anterior and posterior lesions. These data are relevant in the assessment of general probabilistic propositions such as the claim that impairments of symbolic-gesture comprehension more likely follow left-hemisphere damage than right-hemisphere damage. However, group studies are inadequate when a finer description of the cerebral architecture is attempted, largely because of the heterogeneity of the pathological population (Caramazza, 1986; Caramazza & Badecker, 1989; McCloskey & Caramazza, 1988).

Consider, for example, whether the comprehension of pantomimes relates to that of nonverbal sounds (Varney, 1982). In a sample of 44 aphasics, performances in two tasks, gesture-to-picture and sound-to-picture matching, were significantly associated. However, 5 subjects behaved normally in processing pantomimes but were impaired in processing sounds, and 4 other subjects showed the reverse dissociation. Likewise, the production and comprehension of symbolic gestures are generally associated in the aphasic population, but there are cases of impaired comprehension without expressive disorders. These results suffice to indicate that identifying objects from gestures and sounds or performing and understanding gestures may be independently impaired by some brain lesions. Thus, attention is focused on cases of dissociation instead of association, and little value is seen in computing contingency indices of performances in heterogeneous groups of brain-damaged subjects.

Nevertheless, methodological problems remain in single-case studies (Shallice, 1988a, chap. 10). The first relates to the possibility of unusual pathologies that could result, for instance, from atypical lateralization of functions. If the majority of interesting but rare cases of apraxia without aphasia that demonstrate independence of some gestural and verbal processes had antecedents of left-handedness, the conclusions drawn on that basis could hardly be generalized. Another problem is ruling out alternative accounts of dissociations in terms of task demands. For example, some aphasics can pantomime the function of an object they cannot name. Such data could be evidence for functional independence of two communicative modalities. However, another explanation may be simply that one task, gesturing, is easier than another, naming. The single processor underlying speech and gestures would only show impairment in the most demanding conditions (assumed to be the verbal ones) because the most complex processes are also the most prone to disruption by brain lesions. Thus, in order to demonstrate a separation of verbal and gestural communication processes, it is necessary to find subjects who are impaired in the gestural task without a language deficit. In this way, the description of the reverse dissociation, or the analysis of task requirements in normal subjects, rules out an interpretation in terms of processing demands. If this demonstration cannot be made, a single component will be assumed and its functioning described to account for the observed impairment. Aphasics have been shown, for instance, to be able to learn to perform some gestures more easily than others and to be more impaired in understanding emblems than pantomimes. It is unlikely that specific brain areas code different kinds of gestures (Amer-Ind, American Sign Language [ASL], pantomimes, etc.) or that patients with inverse performances can be found (Coelho & Duffy, 1986; Daniloff, Fritelli, Buckingham, Hoffman, & Daniloff, 1986; Daniloff, Noll, Fristoe, & Lloyd, 1982; Davis, Artes, & Hoops, 1979; Feyereisen, Barter, Goossens, & Clerebaut, 1988).

Another method used in neuropsychology to disentangle mental processes relies on the observation of lateral differences in normal subjects. On the expressive level, the comparison of hand performances is straightforward. If Task A gives an advantage to the right hand and Task B to the left, it is concluded that different processes are involved. For example, if most right-handed subjects use principally the right hand in speech-related gestures but show no hand preference in body touching, one may suppose that the two kinds of gestures rely on different mechanisms (Kimura, 1973). On the receptive level, the comparison concerns performances when input reaches one hemisphere before the other in divided visual field studies. However, like the results of single-case studies, dissociations demonstrated in these ways are difficult to interpret when an alternative account in terms of task difficulty is possible, for instance, when ceiling levels of processing are reached (Hellige, 1983; see Dunn & Kirsner, 1988, for a related discussion).

6.2. Verbal and gestural communication

Are verbal and gestural behavior independent? Left-hemisphere superiority in verbal tasks has been known since the earliest descriptions of aphasia, and in the first half of the 20th century, the role of the right hemisphere was described in the visuospatial or attentional processing of nonverbal material. Accordingly, lateral differences in normal subjects were first interpreted as functions of the verbal or nonverbal nature of the task. Nevertheless, the issue of hemispheric specialization remains disputed. The question arose whether cerebral asymmetries relate to the specificity of language processing, such as, for example, to the unilateral representation of phonology and syntax in the left, verbal hemisphere, or whether the verbal/nonverbal dichotomy is only a consequence of more fundamental specializations. Three explanations challenged the specificity of left-hemisphere linguistic competence and the verbal/nonverbal distinction. It was suggested that the left-hemisphere superiority results from the asymmetry of symbolic functioning, motor control, or analytic versus holistic processing. Until recently, these three explanations constituted the main framework for the analysis of lateral differences and the study of the gestural behavior of left-hemisphere-damaged aphasic subjects (Christopoulou & Bonvillian, 1985; Feyereisen & Seron, 1982; Peterson & Kirshner, 1981).

Symbol processing

The asymbolia hypothesis

Language may be viewed as just one manifestation of the symbolic function, which includes the use of representational gestures. Accordingly, it was suggested as early as 1870, when Finkelnburg introduced the notion of "asymbolia," that language disorders observed after left-hemisphere damage are only some of the many impairments of symbolic functioning that can arise (R. J. Duffy & Liles, 1979). Neuropsychology now has specific terms for these nonverbal disorders on the expressive and receptive levels. However, the idea remains that left-hemisphere specialization is not restricted to verbal processes but also concerns the use of nonverbal symbols (see, e.g., Bates et al., 1983; Kendon, 1983).

Difficulties in making the conventional gestures called emblems and in pantomiming objects are well established in the population of left-hemisphere-damaged subjects. The problems cannot be explained by impairments in understanding verbal instructions only, because they remain in imitation tasks or may arise in the absence of auditory comprehension disorders. Furthermore, performances in demonstrating object use are generally better in conditions where actual objects are manipulated. Thus, the impairment is less likely to be located on the motor execution level than in response selection. In this context, the "body part as object" response was often interpreted as a regression to an early stage of gestural representation in which the subject does not distance himself or herself from the object (see section 5.4). However, Ska and Nespoulous (1987) showed that such behavior was not typical of the brain-damaged population (see also R. J. Duffy & J. R. Duffy, 1989). Similarly, on the receptive level, aphasic subjects are, statistically speaking, more impaired than control subjects in gesture-to-picture matching tasks, the most frequent error being the confusion of visually and semantically related objects like a nail and a screw. Partial comprehension is thus demonstrated (J. R. Duffy & Watkins, 1984; Varney & Benton, 1982). But, although the existence of disorders in gesture processing after left-hemisphere damage is not disputed, the problem of identifying the impaired mechanism remains. A central assumption of the asymbolia hypothesis is the association of deficits on the receptive and expressive levels. Some subjects conform to this construct, but others show more specific impairments, and thus, the hypothesis would be true only for a part of the population (e.g., R. J. Duffy & Buck, 1979; R. J. Duffy & J. R. Duffy, 1981; Gainotti & Lemmo, 1976; Rothi, Heilman, & Watson, 1985; Rothi, Mack, & Heilman, 1986; for reviews, see De Renzi, 1985; Feyereisen, 1988; Roy, 1982).

The hypothesis of a central communication disorder

Very similar to the asymbolia hypothesis is the assumption of a central communication system that relies on the description of parallel changes in verbal and nonverbal behavior after left-hemisphere lesions in more interactive situations like interviews or referential communication tasks. It is suggested that the more or less spontaneous gestures performed by aphasics do not depend on a separate nonverbal communication system but rather originate with words in a single computational stage (McNeill, 1985; see also R. J. Duffy & J. R. Duffy, 1990; R. J. Duffy, J. R. Duffy, & Mercaitis, 1984; Glosser & Wiener, 1990; Glosser, Wiener, & Kaplan, 1986, 1988; McNeill et al., 1990).

Empirical support for this position was found in a study that described parallels in gestures and speech of four aphasic subjects (Cicone, Wapner, Foldi, Zurif, & Gardner, 1979). Two subjects with a speech rate (number of words per minute) below normal made fewer gestures than the two subjects with word-finding difficulties but a normal speech tempo. However, this result was contradicted by other studies in which the rate of gesture production did not relate to speech fluency. Furthermore, contrary conclusions were also reached when other indices like gesture-to-word ratio or mean length of utterance were used to assess gestural and verbal performance, and there are the difficulties of computing such indices from aphasic speech (Feyereisen, 1983; LeMay, David, & Thomas, 1988; L. Smith 1987a, 1987b).

The study by Cicone et al. (1979) also showed a relation between the information value of gestures and that of speech. The two nonfluent aphasics had difficulties in using function words. They produced a kind of "telegraphic" speech, and the majority of their gestures (80%) were informative. The two other subjects used few content words, and their empty speech was accompanied by nonrepresentational gestures (but still in the same proportion [about 50%] as in normal production). The results are somewhat difficult to interpret because the reason why aphasics sometimes can and sometimes cannot compensate for word-finding difficulties by gesturing remains unknown (Behrmann & Penn, 1984; Feyereisen, Barter, et al., 1988; Herrmann, Reichle, Lucius-Hoene, Wallesch, & Johannsen-Horbach, 1988).

The discrepancies between observations seem mainly due to inter-individual variability in such unconstrained communication situations. Normal people often speak without gesturing even though they have the capacity to make gestures. One set of questions concerns the cognitive conditions for being able to find adequate nonverbal substitutes for un-available word forms (as most aphasics sometimes do); another concerns the pragmatic reasons for performing gestures in conversation. The hypothesis of a general communication disorder should also be rejected on the basis of the pragmatic appropriateness of aphasic behavior in interactive situations (Foldi, Cicone, & Gardner, 1983; Prutting & Kirchner, 1987).

Motor control

Speech and gestures may also be considered skilled motor perfor-mances, and a general inability to control movement sequencing would result in verbal and nonverbal deficits. Thus, an alternative to the asymbolia hypothesis is to interpret the association of verbal and ges-tural disorders in aphasia as a result of left-hemisphere dominance in the temporal organization of sequential movements (Kimura, 1976).

Motor impairments after unilateral left-hemisphere damage

The main argument in support of the hypothesis of a motor deficit was that copying meaningless hand movements is as impaired as imitat-ing symbolic gestures (see also De Renzi, Motti, & Nichelli, 1980; Lehmkuhl, Poeck, & Willmes, 1983). The processes underlying behavior were not precisely described in that context, and several hypotheses have been proposed to identify the nature of the disorder: control of rapid changes in the speech apparatus or in hand positions (Kimura, 1982), activation of visuokinetic formulae in the memory for static posi-tions as well as for movement sequences (Jason, 1983, 1985; Rothi & Heilman, 1984), and the preparation or execution of movements without visual feedback (Haaland, Harrington, & Yeo, 1987). These hypotheses address various aspects of motor control, and all might be supported by appropriate case studies if lesions have different consequences accord-ing to their locations and the subjects (Hécaen, 1978; Heilman, Rothi, & Valenstein, 1982).

Lateral differences in normal subjects

A motor-control hypothesis has also been proposed to account for lateral differences in gesture production by normal subjects (see reviews in Feyereisen, 1986; L. J. Harris, 1989). Left-hemisphere involvement in gesture production has been assumed from the right-hand preference of right-handers. In self-touching gestures, no consistent asymmetry has been observed, the preferences changing according to the task being performed concurrently, and thus it has been suggested that these two kinds of movements rely on different cerebral mechanisms (Dalby, Gibson, Grossi, & Schneider, 1980; Hatta & Dimond, 1984; Ingram, 1975; Kimura, 1973; Ruggieri, Celli, & Crescenzi, 1982; Sousa-Poza et al., 1979).

However, several interpretations of lateral differences in gestural performance remain plausible. First, Kimura (1976) related right-hand preference to right-hand ability and to left-hemisphere motor competence. Flexion–extension and pronation–supination components of gestures spontaneously performed during conversations were recorded, and the right-hand movements were found to be more complex than those of the left hand; that is, right-hand gestures involved more changes (Kimura & Humphrys, 1981). Moreover, hand choice was not influenced by the conversation topic, which was assumed to influence hemispheric activation. When subjects had to describe their daily activity (neutral condition), to comment on a favorite book (verbal condition), and to explain the way to reach a given place (spatial condition), lateral differences did not differ, but it must be noted that the three tasks involved verbalization (Lavergne & Kimura, 1987).

Second, Kinsbourne (1986) has suggested explaining manual preference in gesturing in the same way as lateral eye movements. Left-hemisphere involvement in verbal tasks would induce biases in favor of using the right hand and looking to the right, whereas right-hemisphere involvement in visuospatial tasks would have the opposite effect. When the hand movements were analyzed in block manipulations during problem solving, manual preference interacted with the nature of the problems, verbal in tasks like solving crossword puzzles and nonverbal in tasks like putting together jigsaw puzzles (Hampson & Kimura, 1984). The interpretation of lateral eye movements is still disputed, and no clear conclusion emerges from this abundant literature (Ehrlichman & Weinberger, 1978; Hiscock, 1986). However, the motor complexity of eye movements to the right and to the left should not differ, so other variables are expected to influence the lateral bias. Asymmetry in mouth opening has also been analyzed in this context. Lateral differences have been shown to vary with task and subject characteristics. The aperture may vary as a function of the activation of the contralateral hemisphere, but some data also support the alternative interpretation of a left-hemisphere superiority in the control of verbal and nonverbal oral movements (Goodale, 1988; Graves, 1983; Graves, Goodglass, & Landis, 1982; Graves, Landis, & Simpson, 1985; Hager & Van Gelder, 1985; Wolf & Goodale, 1987; Wyler, Graves, & Landis, 1987).

Finally, manual preference in the performance of gestures may be due to different uses of the two hands in the manipulation of objects. These preferences do not relate to efficiency of performance (in other words, a certain hand is not always chosen because of its higher efficiency). Thus, it is unlikely that complexity in motor control is the sole factor determining hand choice in this case and, more generally, in the explanation of handedness (Annett, 1985; Fennell, 1986; M. J. Morgan & McManus, 1988).

Similar discussions arise about the development of hand preference in gestural behavior. Although a large body of data has been gathered on laterality in reaching and in object manipulation by infants, only a few observations concern gestures that relate to vocal or verbal activity (G. Young, Segalowitz, Corter, & Trehub, 1983). In a pilot study, Trevarthen (1986) interpreted the right bias in expressive hand movements of newborns as indicative of the innateness of asymmetry in motor control, but a more systematic analysis yielded ambiguous evidence (Fogel & Hannan, 1985). Furthermore, the nature of the bias – perceptual versus motor or antecedent versus subsequent to language lateralization – remains disputed. Clearer conclusions do not follow from the observation of a right-hand preference in pointing gestures in infants (A. W. Young, Lock, & Service, 1985).

In summary, studies on hemispheric differences in motor control have been successful in dismissing a verbal/nonverbal dichotomy for the explanation of cerebral asymmetry and in questioning the asymbolia hypothesis. However, the critical variables accounting for motor impairments after left-hemisphere damage and for hand preference and dexterity in right-handers have still to be isolated.

Analytic versus holistic perceptual processes

The verbal/nonverbal dichotomy in describing cerebral asymmetry can also be criticized as far as perceptual processes are concerned. In normal subjects, lateral differences in the visual, auditory, or tactile modalities did not relate to the verbal or symbolic nature of the input. Some visual processing of linguistic information may give rise to a right-hemisphere advantage or to the absence of a laterality effect. This is the case with Japanese ideographs and with gestures of the ASL (Poizner & Battison, 1980). Inversely, some experimental conditions favor the left hemisphere in processing nonverbal information. Left-hemisphere-damaged subjects are impaired in recognizing meaningless shapes and in nonverbal comprehension tasks, and some right-hemisphere contribution to linguistic processing is recognized. Accordingly, it has been suggested that the verbal/nonverbal dichotomy be abandoned and, instead, that the left hemisphere specializes in the analytic processing mode, and the right hemisphere in the holistic (Bradshaw & Nettleton, 1981). Nonverbal receptive disorders in aphasics, as assessed, for instance, in gesture-to-picture matching tasks, might basically relate to this contribution of the left hemisphere to perceptual processing or to analytic conceptual processing rather than simply to symbol use. For example, aphasic subjects have been found to be impaired in the comprehension of emotional cues, which are more natural signs than symbolic gestures or pantomimes (for a review, see Feyereisen, 1989).

However, the analytic/holistic distinction has drawn criticism. First, it has been noted that the processes for which one hemisphere is advantaged are very diverse, and thus it is meaningless to look for a single label to describe multidimensional performances (Bertelson, 1982). The circularity of the argument has also been pointed out. As no external criterion allows for an a priori distinction between analytic and holistic processes, there is a tendency to call a task holistic when a right-hemisphere advantage is observed and analytic when the inverse result is found (Sergent, 1983). The alternative interpretation of Sergent (1983) is that lateral differences depend on physical properties (luminance, spatial frequency, etc.) of the input in relation to task demands (discrimination, identification, etc.). Another solution is to call holistic the processing of structural or configurational properties and analytic the processing of local information (Morais, 1982). The behavior of brain-damaged patients and lateral differences in processing gestural signals have not yet been studied from these perspectives.

Conclusions

Many brain lesions cause simultaneous verbal and nonverbal impairments. Moreover, lateral differences have been observed across a wide range of mental tasks and do not reduce to a verbal/nonverbal dichotomy. Many confounding variables have been identified: Verbal behavior, like some aspects of nonverbal behavior, is also symbolic and sequentially organized and relies on analytic processes. Thus, the brain structures that are believed to specifically underlie linguistic functions might also serve for nonverbal behavior and relate to more general purposes: communication, motor control, or fine-grained perceptual processes.

At the same time, however, specific disorders have been described in different domains of cognitive processing, and neuropsychology has moved toward the identification of separable components in mental functioning (Ellis & Young, 1988). A central assumption guiding such research is that perceptual phenomena elicit responses via specialized devices. From such a perspective, speech is special, as are visually presented objects, spatial locations, and, perhaps, gestures. Generalizations like those favored by hypotheses of central deficits become untenable.

Specificity of linguistic processing is suggested by observations of the effects of brain damage on sign language. Six deaf subjects who had suffered strokes were proposed for thorough neuropsychological examination (Poizner, Klima, & Bellugi, 1987). One left-brain-damaged subject, who was aphasic for sign language, scored flawlessly in performing gestures on command (but no control was provided for the relative difficulty of the different types of task). The right-brain-damaged subjects, who showed impairments in nonverbal spatial processing, could still use the spatial devices by which ASL codes verb agreement and pronominal reference. Thus, dissociations between verbal and nonverbal performances were demonstrated within the same gestural modality.

Similarly, lateral differences in signing by deaf subjects have been explained by assuming that the left-hemisphere specialization in linguistic processing does not change with the used modality, oral or manual. Two experimental tasks, sign fluency and shadowing, were performed successively with both hands by left- and right-handed deaf subjects. The resulting group-by-hand interactions showed that, in the two groups, the preferred hand was more efficient (Vaid, Bellugi, & Poizner, 1989).

These observations, however, remain compatible with the original motor hypothesis of Kimura (1976; see also Kimura, 1988). It would be interesting in this context if dissociations of linguistic processing and skilled manual performances could be demonstrated in left-handers whose language was controlled by the left hemisphere. (Different patterns of lateralization exist in the left-handed population: left dominance for language, as in right-handers, more bilateral representation of language, or right dominance. There is no good method, however, for assessing language lateralization reliably in healthy subjects, and moreover, handedness itself may vary with task demand; see, e.g., Healey, Liederman, & Geschwind, 1986; Salmaso & Longoni, 1985; Steenhuis & Bryden, 1989; Todor & Smiley, 1985; for reviews, see Annett, 1985; Fennell, 1986.)

6.3. The fractionation of functions in gestural and verbal processing

Although the specificity of gestural processes has not yet been firmly demonstrated, the evolution of the cognitive neuropsychology of language, motor control, and visual perception invites the abandonment of unspecific labels – aphasia, apraxia, visual agnosia, etc. – and encourages the attempt to identify the underlying elementary operations. Studies of word-finding difficulties, for example, show that the inability to give an object its name may result from impairments of different kinds, and consequently, aphasic subjects who display such a symptom may or may not be able to repeat words or point to named pictures or perform gestures that correspond to the name. Thus, explanations for aphasia definitely discount the hypotheses of asymbolia, motor control, and analytic processing that are still used in the study of relationships between gestures and speech. How can one reduce such a discrepancy between the two fields of research?

A provisional model

Information-processing models provide a framework for a taxonomic analysis of mental functions. These models have been developed mainly with regard to word, face, and object recognition and may be expanded to account for gesture production and comprehension. Several processes are distinguished: stimulus identification from perceptual analysis, response selection, and response programming (see chap. 4). For instance, it is assumed that a task like confrontation naming involves different, partially parallel processes: first, a visual analysis leading to a structural description of the item to be named independently of some peculiarities of the input; second, a semantic description leading to the selection of a lexical entry; and third, a phonological description addressing the articulatory programs. Likewise, pantomiming object use on verbal request results from spoken-word recognition, action planning from a mental image of the object, and specification of motor parameters. Some independent variables may selectively affect one of these processes. Similarly, brain lesions may disturb one operation while sparing the others. Thus, there is converging evidence for the distinctions drawn from experimental analysis of normal subjects.

The question of the relationships between gestures and speech may be raised from such an information-processing perspective. Modality specificity is assumed for input and output components, and modality independence for central processing. Sense organs code information in different forms, and these signals are assumed to address specific recognition devices. In the visual modality, for instance, there would be specialized processing units for written words, objects, mouth shapes in lipreading, hand gestures, etc. (see, e.g., Perrett et al., 1989). According to the input modality, different kinds of information are available from these processes. For example, phonological information is more readily extracted from written words than from pictures, so oral-naming responses are faster or more accurate for the former than for the latter. Inversely, some functional or affective features might be more easily activated from nonverbal than from verbal input.

The question then arises as to whether the central "semantic" component is really amodal or whether it is still shaped by some modality-specific properties. If so, verbal and nonverbal (visual or motor) long-term memories should be distinguished (Shallice, 1988a, 1988b). Some responses may also bypass this central stage and be said to be automatic. This could be the case with spontaneous gestures made while speaking, which would be outside awareness and attentional control. A similar hypothesis was proposed by Riddoch and Humphreys (1987) about a case of optic aphasia, that is, a specific inability to name objects from visual analysis, whereas the abilities to name objects from tactile exploration and from an aurally presented definition were spared. This subject demonstrated object recognition by pantomiming its use and by correct discrimination between real objects and composites drawn from two different objects. Such a dissociation between verbal and gestural performances might be accounted for by assuming that a deficit in accessing semantic information from vision has been compensated for by a capacity to bypass this semantic processing by using direct links between object recognition and motor programming. Shallice (1988b) criticized this hypothesis because pantomime does not provide unambiguous evidence of object recognition and because some partial information about the object may suffice to perform the action but not to find its name. For instance, how can one be certain from the gesture of using an axe that it is not confused with a hammer? Because the distinction between the two rival hypotheses – direct connections between input and output processing versus subdivisions within the semantic system – relies heavily on the way the assumed underlying operations are specified, it is not easy to disentangle them by experimental analysis.

This information-processing model assumes the possibility of selective impairment of gesture production without language disorders. However, little support for this hypothesis has been reported in neuropsychological literature when care was taken to equate the difficulty of verbal and motor tasks. Indeed, aphasia without apraxia is far more frequent than the reverse dissociation. Impairments of spontaneous gestures made while speaking have never been clearly identified, and many aphasics can compensate for word-finding difficulties by using gestures. Nonaphasic pathologies in which some "inexpressivity" is described remain to be studied from such a perspective (right-hemisphere damages, frontal lesions, Parkinson's disease, etc.).

As far as gesture comprehension is concerned, the specificity of gestural processing is suggested by two cases reported by Rothi et al. (1986). These left-hemisphere-damaged subjects were impaired in discriminating and comprehending gestures, but their auditory comprehension and gesture imitation were within the normal range. Thus, the receptive disorders did not result from impairment of visual analysis or semantic processing. The nature of these nonverbal comprehension deficits, however, is difficult to specify with the present state of knowledge about gesture perception because gestural impairments can be identified only in comparison with normal functioning (see chap. 4).

Gesture production

Such an information-processing model predicts that gestures and speech may dissociate in some cases of aphasia and associate in others according to the nature of the impairment. Different hypotheses may be proposed to explain why some aphasics can produce gestures in relation to pictures they cannot name. First, information extracted from a picture may be used to program a gesture but not to activate the phonological store. Second, a response may be more difficult to select in the verbal modality, and motor programs for gestures may be less demanding than those for words, for instance, because there are more words than plans for action. Third, the impairment may be restricted to an inability to access the phonological word form from visual or semantic information (see, e.g., the cases described by B. Butterworth, Swallow, & Grimston, 1981; and by Nespoulous, 1979).

These hypotheses are difficult to test in poorly constrained tasks like interviewing or elicited narratives. To assess the quality of verbal and gestural performances, some information is needed about the input given to the subjects and their communicative intent. It is easier to establish what the subjects have in their minds if they are requested to refer to visually presented items, to answer yes–no questions, to repeat words, or to recall gestures than if they are simply chatting to allow the experimenter to record spontaneous speech. A second difficulty due to lack of constraints concerns the process of response selection. Several skills are required to compensate for a word-finding inability by using gestures. First, the word search must be abandoned and the performance of a gestural analog decided upon. Then distinctive functional or visual features must be found that can shape the movement to evoke the referent. Indeed, spontaneous gestures are not coded as are signs of manual language, and thus some innovation is needed. Finally, the relevant motor program has to be activated. Thus, performance depends on strategic choices as well as on true gestural capacity, so observing that an aphasic does not gesture in some circumstances does not mean that he or she is unable to perform appropriate gestures. Finally, problems exist in scoring procedures. There is no clear definition of what impaired gestures resemble because any movement may be called gesture (whereas a phonemic string does not necessarily constitute a word). "Errors" in performance cannot be identified, and at first sight, most gestures by aphasic subjects seem quite normal. Therefore, the use of neuropsychological data to demonstrate specificity of impairments is limited.

To some extent, some of these problems become less critical in experimental situations where subjects are requested to perform gestures or to produce words in relation to defined targets. Obviously, however, this gain in control over variables must be paid for by a loss in spontaneity of behavior. An aphasic woman suffering from naming and auditory comprehension deficits but with an intact capacity for repetition was studied from such a perspective (Feyereisen, Bouchat, Déry, & Ruiz, 1990). In the first part, a single set of pictures was used to elicit naming and gesturing by instructing the subject "to get another person who does not see the picture to guess what it means." The proportion of correct responses was the same in the two modalities, and a significant association between performances was found across items. In the second part, comprehension of spoken words and pictures was examined with yes–no questions ("Is it an X?"), and gestures were elicited from auditory information ("How do you represent an X?"). Her gestural performance was similar to that observed with pictures, but it did not significantly relate to question answering. These results support the hypothesis of association between verbal and gestural behavior in a patient suffering from defective semantic processing, and they do not support the hypothesis of a direct link between visual object recognition and motor programming. Of course, different results may be obtained with aphasic patients presenting different pathologies.

The influence of gestural context on auditory comprehension

Only two studies have experimentally examined the clinical intuition that gestural cues facilitate auditory comprehension in aphasia beyond the frequent observation that imitation of action is less impaired than execution of verbal commands. Venus and Canter (1987) studied a group of 16 subjects with comprehension disorders. They did not find different performances in matching pictures to spoken words and to words accompanied by gestures. These results are not conclusive, however, because of the heterogeneity of the aphasic population. By accepting the null hypothesis of an absence of effect, one runs the risk of missing possible facilitative effects of the gestural context in specific cases. From the model presented above, facilitation may be expected in subjects with defective recognition of spoken words without a semantic disorder but not in subjects with defective gesture recognition or with conceptual impairments. A critical feature could be a better comprehension of written words than of spoken words because these subjects usually understand gestures (Varney, 1978).

In the other study, greater attention was paid to the description of comprehension disorders in the individual aphasic subjects (Feyereisen & Hazan, unpublished study). A group of 16 subjects was given pretests to examine phonological discrimination in words and nonwords, word recognition, and semantic-relatedness judgments. It was hypothesized that gestures facilitate comprehension in the case of defective phonological processing but not in the case of semantic disorders. Thus, a critical observation for the hypothesis concerned the use of gestural cues by subjects with pure word deafness (impaired auditory comprehension with correct understanding of written material). However, this pathology is very infrequent, and no case of dissociation between written and auditory comprehension was present in the group. It remained possible, however, that the disorders of the subjects showing impaired comprehension resulted from defective access to semantic information from word recognition with spared access from nonverbal input. Indeed, the pictorial context was sometimes found to facilitate sentence comprehension in cases of aphasia. To evaluate such a hypothesis, a word-to-picture matching task was devised, and three conditions were compared: The target words were presented in isolation, with a gesture, or with a verbal qualification. Of the three subjects who made numerous errors in the verbal condition, two performed better when a gestural cue was added, but one showed similar impairment. Verbal qualification did not improve performances to the same extent. However, subject characteristics accounting for differences in facilitation by context were not identified.

Other pathologies: dementia, schizophrenia, depression, and developmental disorders

It should be possible to analyze from a similar perspective relationships between gestures and speech in other pathologies that affect language. More particularly, several mental disorders seem to concern a central level of processing, so different patterns of association or dissociation than those shown by focal brain damage may be demonstrated.

Senile dementia of the Alzheimer type

Some subjects suffering from senile dementia of the Alzheimer type display language impairments in naming tasks that may be compared to aphasias resulting from left-hemisphere lesions. These disturbances are often interpreted as resulting from defective semantic processing rather than from phonological impairment. Indeed, in early stages of the illness, patients are usually able to read aloud or repeat words they cannot produce from pictures. Disorders also affect the gestural modality in standard testing of apraxia or in assessment of pantomime comprehension. These performances may be interpreted either as the consequences of a general impairment of the cognitive structure by which words, objects, and gestures relate or as the conjunction of multiple modality-specific disorders. Moreover, the occurrence of more spontaneous gestures performed while speaking remains to be assessed in mild forms of senile dementia in which some aspects of conversational competence are spared as well as in normal, aging subjects who may suffer from temporary word-finding difficulties. Residual nonverbal communication in more severe cases in which the people no longer speak is beginning to be studied (de Ajuriaguerra, Richard, Rodriguez, & Tissot, 1966; de Lannoy, Cedraschi, & Roessli, 1989; Kempler, 1988; Rapcsak, Croswell, & Rubens, 1989).

Thought and language disorders in schizophrenia

The behavior of schizophrenic patients may also be analyzed from the perspective of thought and language disorders that characterize some forms of the illness. One knows that the diagnosis of schizophrenia may cover very different pathologies. Some patients present "positive" signs like incoherent discourse, use of neologisms, or socially inappropriate utterances, and others are characterized by "negative" signs such as a lack of responsiveness or impoverished language. Furthermore, these symptoms may occur in acute or chronic stages, change with environmental conditions, or be modified by pharmacological treatment. Very few systematic studies have analyzed gestural behavior in relation to these language characteristics in controlled conditions. Nonetheless, Freedman and co-workers have observed the nonverbal behavior of 16 chronic schizophrenic subjects who had symptoms of either opposition or withdrawal and were free of medication (no control group was included). Correlations between gesture–word ratio and measures of language complexity did not reach significance, but self-touching behavior differentiated the two types of patients. As no prediction can be made about relationships between varieties of self-touching and speech-production mechanisms, the results might depend on other, unknown characteristics of the patients. In another study bearing on 10 bilingual Spanish–English schizophrenics, the pattern of correlations between the rate of gestures and symptoms assessed from interview changed with the language used. No clear indication of modification of gestural behavior in relation to thought or language disorders emerged from these observations, but the issue should be revisited in the light of the study of cognitive processing in schizophrenic subjects (Grand, Freedman, Steingart, & Buchwald, 1975; Grand et al., 1977; Steingart, Grand, Margolis, Freedman, & Buchwald, 1976).

Affective disorders

The nonverbal behavior of psychiatric patients has most often been assessed in relation to diagnosis of affective disorders. Gaze orientation and facial expressions, for instance, were interpreted either as signs of specific impairments of social conduct or as cues of anxiety (for a review, see de Lannoy & Feyereisen, 1988). A decrease in frequency of head gestures and an increase in self-touching gestures or stereotypies have also been observed from such a perspective (e.g., Fisch, Frey, & Hirsbrunner, 1983; Fossi, Faravelli, & Paoli, 1984; I. H. Jones & Pansa, 1979;

see section 2.2). Thus, effects of this nonverbal behavior in turn-taking regulation, impression management, or referential activity may be expected. However, the results of such studies are often difficult to interpret because of a lack of control of confounding variables or because general conclusions are drawn from selected behavior in selected environments. For instance, visual behavior may change with conversation topics. Accordingly, gaze avoidance during a psychiatric interview may well be the normal reaction in disclosing personal matters (Rutter, 1977; Rutter & O'Brien, 1980). Because the behavior of the clinician changes in relation to the nonverbal expression of the patient, the influence of the social interaction must also be considered (Altorfer, 1989; Fairbanks, McGuire, & Harris, 1982; see also section 3.1). Positive or negative correlations between discourse variables and some aspects of nonverbal behavior do not suffice to demonstrate either association or dissociation of gestures and speech. Illustrative are the cases of depression in which symptoms may be assessed not only from self-report but also from unelicited verbal and nonverbal cues. For example, a given description reads as follows: "Depression can be seen in the face through decreased brow raises, downward gaze and decreased eye contact. Depressives are likely to show decreased speech illustration and gesticulation, a downward slant of the head, slumped posture, briefer responses and engage in fewer activities" (Kupfer, Maser, Blehar, & Miller, 1987, p. 13). A monotonous tone of voice and reduced speech loudness have also been described (e.g., Gotlib, 1982; Scherer, 1979). Thus, some common motivation to perform gestures, to modulate prosody, and to initiate verbal exchanges is suggested. Systematic analyses of nonverbal behavior in depression, however, do not always confirm the clinical intuition, in part because of the extent of individual variability of normal and pathological behavior and in part because facial expression, gestures, and speech may change independently during recovery (Ellgring, 1989).

Developmental disorders: autism and Down's syndrome

Some clearer indications of dissociations have been provided by the study of nonverbal behavior in cases of developmental disorders. Particularly, the comparison of autistic and Down's syndrome children suggests that some specific processes involved in the use of speech and gestures may be selectively impaired by pathology. During free play with caregivers, Down's syndrome infants often take the initiative in the social interaction but rarely use gestures to request help from adults. This behavior was interpreted in relation to the low level of arousal displayed by these infants in other circumstances, that is, as the consequence of a reduced motivation to explore the environment and to manipulate objects. In contrast, autistic children do not differ from normal, control children in using request gestures but display a specific deficit in achieving joint attention and in pointing to direct the gaze of other people toward some aspect of the environment. They cannot be considered globally impaired in verbal and nonverbal communication, but instead, they show a specific deficit in the referential use of pointing gestures in relation to an inability to represent what other people may have in mind. Baron-Cohen (1989) has demonstrated a dissociation between two conditions of gesture use by showing that autistic children can understand and perform "protoimperative" pointing (compliance with experimenter's requests or the subject's attempts to obtain an object) but not "protodeclarative" pointing (looking in the pointed direction or directing the attention of another person toward inaccessible objects like cars or airplanes). To some extent, this disorder may dissociate from language delay. For instance, the case was reported of a child who showed normal lexical and syntactic development but who did not respond adequately to the parents' messages, did not point to objects, and did not imitate other persons (Attwood, Frith, & Hermelin, 1988; Blank, Gessner, & Esposito, 1979; Loveland & Landry, 1986; Mundy, Sigman, Ungerer, & Sherman, 1986, 1987; Mundy, Sigman, Kasari, & Yirmiya, 1988; Sigman, Mundy, Sherman, & Ungerer, 1986; Wetherby, 1986).

These diverse pathologies indicate that gestural as well as verbal performances depend on multiple cognitive processes and also on motivational or emotional factors. The study of selective impairments allows one to identify the aspects by which gestures and speech associate and dissociate.

Conclusions

A tentative model has been proposed to distinguish between input and output processes and to search for the possibility of different patterns of relations between gestures and speech. The distinctions drawn, however, represent only preliminary stages, and enhancements must be made. First, a better description of the assumed operations is needed. If, for instance, there are special plans for manual and oral action, what kinds of input–output transfer are realized to result in motor execution? To what extent are gestural and verbal performances influenced by impairments in perceptual or motor processing or by more central semantic impairments? Second, the nature of the relations between the different processes should be identified (see section 4.3). Does the system function on the basis of representations and rules using "if . . . then" instructions, or can it be described as the propagation of activation along a set of excitatory and inhibitory connections? May discrete stages be identified or is information continuously processed until a threshold for a response decision is reached? Third, more consideration must be given to the issue of automaticity and control in verbal and nonverbal expression. The psychology of nonverbal communication has most often described behavior such as affective reactions, motor mimicry, and spontaneous gestures to which subjects often pay no attention. The cognitive approach also assumes some autonomous modules processing information without awareness. Inversely, experimental neuropsychology has most often devised situations in which subjects had to perform gestures on request or to match pantomimes to pictures. A cross-fertilization of these different domains of inquiry would reveal promising perspectives.

References

Abele, A. (1986). Functions of gaze in social interaction: Communication and monitoring. *Journal of Nonverbal Behavior, 10,* 83–101.

Abrahamsen, A., Cavallo, M. M., & McCluer, J. A. (1985). Is the sign advantage a robust phenomenon? From gesture to language in two modalities. *Merrill-Palmer Quarterly, 31,* 177–209.

Abramovitch, R., & Grusec, J. E. (1978). Peer imitation in natural setting. *Child Development, 49,* 60–65.

Abravanel, E., & Sigafoos, A. D. (1984). Exploring the presence of imitation during early infancy. *Child Development, 55,* 381–392.

Acredolo, L. P., & Goodwyn, S. W. (1985). Symbolic gesturing in language development: A case study. *Human Development, 28,* 40–49.

Acredolo, L. P., & Goodwyn, S. W. (1988). Symbolic gesturing in normal infants. *Child Development, 59,* 450–466.

Adamson, L. B., & Bakeman, R. (1984). Mothers' communicative acts: Changes during infancy. *Infant Behavior and Development, 7,* 467–478.

Alberts, E., Kalverboer, A. F., & Hopkins, B. (1983). Mother–infant dialogue in the first days of life: An observational study during breast feeding. *Journal of Child Psychology and Psychiatry, 24,* 145–161.

Alegria, J. (1981). The development of referential communication in deaf and hearing children: Competence and style. *International Journal of Behavioral Development, 4,* 295–312.

Alegria, J. & Noirot, E. (1978). Neonate orientation behaviour towards human voice. *International Journal of Behavioral Development, 1,* 291–312.

Allen D. E., & Guy, R. F. (1977). Ocular breaks and verbal output. *Sociometry, 40,* 90–96.

Allen, R., & Shatz, M. (1983). "What says meow?" The role of context and linguistic experience in very young children's responses to what-questions. *Journal of Child Language, 10,* 321–335.

Allott, R. (1989). *The motor theory of language origin.* Lewes: Book Guild.

Als, H., Tronick, E., & Brazelton, T. B. (1979). Analysis of face-to-face interaction in infant–adult dyads. In M. E. Lamb, S. J. Suomi, & G. R. Stephenson (Eds.), *Social interaction analysis: methodological issues* (pp. 33–76). Madison: University of Wisconsin Press.

Altmann, S. A. (1967). The structure of primate social communication. In S. A. Altmann (Ed.), *Social communication among primates* (pp. 325–362). Chicago: University of Chicago Press.

Altorfer, A. (1989). Verbale und nichtverbale Verhaltensweisen von Depressiven als "aktives Verhalten" zur Interaktionssteuerung. *Schweitzerische Zeitschrift für Psychologie, 48,* 99–111.

Ancelin-Schützenberger, A., & Geffroy, Y. (1979). The body and the group: The new bodily therapies. In S. Weitz (Ed.), *Nonverbal communication: Readings with commentary* (2nd ed., pp. 207–219). New York: Oxford University Press.

Anderson, B. J., Vietze, P., & Dokecki, P. R. (1977). Reciprocity in vocal interactions of mothers and infants. *Child Development, 48,* 1676–1681.

Anderson, F. J., & Willis, F. N. (1976). Glancing at others in preschool children in relation to dominance. *Psychological Record, 26,* 467–472.

Andrew, R. J. (1972). The information potentially available in mammal display. In R. A. Hinde (Ed.), *Nonverbal communication* (pp. 179–206). Cambridge: Cambridge University Press.

Annett, M. (1985). *Left, right, hand, and brain: The right-shift theory.* London and Hillsdale, NJ: Lawrence Erlbaum.

Appleton, P. L. (1980). A factor analytic study of behavior groupings in young children. *Ethology and Sociobiology, 1,* 93–97.

Archer, D., & Akert, R. M. (1977). Words and everything else: Verbal and nonverbal cues in social interpretation. *Journal of Personality and Social Psychology, 35,* 443–449.

Argentin, G. (1985). Système gestuel et communication. *Psychologie Française, 30,* 11–23.

Argyle, M. (1988). *Bodily communication* (2nd ed.). London: Methuen.

Argyle, M., Alkema, F., & Gilmour, R. (1972). The communication of friendly and hostile attitudes by verbal and nonverbal signals. *European Journal of Social Psychology, 1,* 395–402.

Argyle, M., & Dean, M. (1965). Eye contact, distance and affiliation. *Sociometry, 28,* 289–304.

Argyle, M., & Graham, J. A. (1976). The Central-Europe experiment: Looking at persons and looking at objects. *Environmental Psychology and Nonverbal Behavior, 1,* 6–16.

Argyle, M., Lalljee, M., & Cook, M. (1968). The effects of visibility on interaction in a dyad. *Human Relations, 21,* 3–17.

Argyle, M., Salter, V., Nicholson, H., Williams, M., & Burgess, P. (1970). The communication of inferior and superior attitudes by verbal and nonverbal signals. *British Journal of Social and Clinical Psychology, 9,* 222–231.

Aries, E. J. (1982). Verbal and nonverbal behavior in single sex and mixed-sex groups: Are traditional sex roles changing? *Psychological Reports, 51,* 127–134.

Asendorpf, J., & Wallbott, H. G. (1982). Contributions of the German "Expression Psychology" to nonverbal communication research. I. Theories and concepts. *Journal of Nonverbal Behavior, 6,* 135–147.

Attwood, A., Frith, U., & Hermelin, B. (1988). The understanding and use of interpersonal gestures by autistic and Down's syndrome children. *Journal of Autism and Developmental Disorders, 18,* 241–257.

Austin, A. M. B., & Peery, J. C. (1983). Analysis of adult–neonate synchrony during speech and nonspeech. *Perceptual and Motor Skills, 57,* 455–459.

Bakeman, R., & Adamson, L. B. (1984). Coordinating attention to people and objects in mother–infant and peer–infant interaction. *Child Development, 55,* 1278–1289.

Bakeman, R., & Adamson, L. B. (1986). Infants' conventionalized acts: Gestures and words with mothers and peers. *Infant Behavior and Development, 9,* 215–230.

Bakeman, R., & Brown, J. V. (1977). Behavioral dialogues: An approach to the assessment of mother–infant interactions. *Child Development, 48,* 195–203.

Baker, M. C., & Cunningham, M. A. (1985). The biology of bird song dialects. *Behavioral and Brain Sciences, 8,* 85–133.

Barash, D. P. (1974). Human ethology: Displacement activities in a dental office. *Psychological Reports, 34,* 947–949.

Barlow, D. H., Hayes, S. C., Nelson, G. O., Steele, D. L., Meeler, M. E., & Mills, J. R. (1979). Sex role motor behavior: A behavioral check list. *Behavioral Assessment, 1,* 119–138.

Baron-Cohen, S. (1989). Perceptual role taking and protodeclarative pointing in autism. *British Journal of Developmental Psychology, 7,* 113–127.

Barroso, F., & Feld, J. K. (1986). Self-touching and attentional processes: The role of task difficulty, selection stage, and sex differences. *Journal of Nonverbal Behavior, 10,* 51–64.

Barroso, F., Freedman, N., & Grand, S. (1980). Self-touching, performance, and attentional processes. *Perceptual and Motor Skills, 50,* 1083–1089.

Barroso, F., Freedman, N., Grand, S., & Van Meel, J. (1978). Evocation of two types of hand movements in information processing. *Journal of Experimental Psychology: Human Perception and Performance, 4,* 321–329.

Barten, S. B. (1979). Development of gesture. In N. R. Smith & M. B. Franklin (Eds.), *Symbolic functioning in childhood* (pp. 139–151). Hillsdale, NJ: Lawrence Erlbaum.

Barthes, R. (1964). Elements de sémiologie. *Communications, 4,* 91–136. (English trans.: *Elements of semiology.* London: Jonathan Cape, 1967)

Bateman, R., Goddard, I., O'Grady, R., Funk, V. A., Mooi, R., Kress, W. J., & Cannell, P. (1990). Speaking of forked tongues: The feasibility of reconciling human phylogeny and the history of language. *Current Anthropology, 31,* 1–24 & 177–183.

Bates, E. (1979). The emergence of symbols: Ontogeny and phylogeny. In W. A. Collins (Ed.), *Children's language and communication: The Minnesota symposia on child psychology* (vol. 12, pp. 121–155). Hillsdale, NJ: Lawrence Erlbaum.

Bates, E., Benigni, L., Bretherton, I., Camaioni, L., & Volterra, V. (1977). From gestures to the first word: On cognitive and social prerequisites. In M. Lewis & L. Rosenblum (Eds.), *Interaction, conversation, and the development of language* (pp. 247–307). New York: Wiley.

Bates, E., Benigni, L., Bretherton, I., Camaioni, L., & Volterra, V. (1979). In E. Bates (Ed.), *The emergence of symbols: Cognition and communication in infancy* (pp. 69–139). New York & London: Academic Press.

Bates, E., Bretherton, I., Beeghly-Smith, M., & McNew, S. (1982). Social bases of language development: A reassessment. *Advances in Child Development and Behavior, 16,* 7–75.

Bates, E., Bretherton, I., Shore, C., & McNew, S. (1983). Names, gestures, and objects: Symbolization in infancy and aphasia. In K. E. Nelson (Ed.), *Children's language* (Vol. 4, pp. 59–123). Hillsdale, NJ: Lawrence Erlbaum.

Bates, E., Bretherton, I., Synder, L., Shore, C., & Volterra, V. (1980). Vocal and gestural symbols at 13 months. *Merrill-Palmer Quarterly, 26,* 407–423.

Bates, E., Camaioni, L., & Volterra, V. (1975). The acquisition of performatives prior to speech. *Merrill-Palmer Quarterly, 21,* 205–226. (Reprinted in E. Ochs & B. B. Schieffelin [Eds.], *Developmental pragmatics* [pp. 111–119]. New York: Academic Press, 1979).

Bates, E., O'Connell, B., & Shore, C. (1987). Language and communication in infancy. In J. Osofsky (Ed.), *Handbook of Infant Development* (2nd ed., pp. 49–203). New York: Wiley.

Bates, E., Thal, D., Whitesell, K., Fenson, L., & Oakes, L. (1989). Integrating language and gesture in infancy. *Developmental Psychology, 25,* 1004–1019.

Bavelas, J. B., Black, A., Chovil, N., Lemery, C. R., & Mullett, J. (1988). Form and function of motor mimicry: Topographic evidence that the primary function is communicative. *Human Communication Research, 14,* 275–299.

Bavelas, J. B., Black, A., Lemery, C. R., & Mullett, J. (1986). "I show how you feel": Motor mimicry as a communicative act. *Journal of Personality and Social Psychology, 50,* 322–329.

Baxter, J. C., Winters, E. P., & Hammer, R. E. (1968). Gestural behavior during a brief interview as a function of cognitive variables. *Journal of Personality and Social Psychology, 8,* 303–307.

Beattie, G. W. (1980a). The role of language production processes in the organization of behaviour in face-to-face interaction. In B. Butterworth (Ed.), *Language production* (Vol. 1, pp. 69–107). New York: Academic Press.

Beattie, G. W. (1980b). The skilled art of conversational interaction: Verbal and nonverbal signals in its regulation and management. In W. T. Singleton, P. Spurgeon, & R. B. Stammers (Eds.), *The analysis of social skills* (pp. 193–211). New York: Plenum Press.

Beattie, G. W. (1981a). A further investigation of the cognitive interference hypothesis of gaze patterns during conversations. *British Journal of Social Psychology, 20,* 243–248.

Beattie, G. W. (1981b). Language and nonverbal communication: The essential synthesis? *Linguistics, 19,* 1165–1183.

Beattie, G. W. (1983). *Talk: An analysis of speech and nonverbal behaviour in conversation.* Milton Keynes, England: Open University Press.

Beattie, G. W., & Beattie, C. A. (1981). Postural congruence in a naturalistic setting. *Semiotica, 35,* 41–55.

Beattie, G. W., Cutler, A., & Pearson, M. (1982). Why is Mrs Thatcher interrupted so often? *Nature, 300,* 744–757.

Beattie, G. W., & Hughes, M. (1987). Planning spontaneous speech and concurrent visual monitoring of a televised face: Is there interference? *Semiotica, 65,* 97–105.

Beebe, B., Jaffe, J., Feldstein, S., Mays, K., & Alson, D. (1985). Interpersonal timing: The application of an adult dialog model to mother–infant vocal and kinesic interactions. In T. M. Field & N. A. Fox (Eds.), *Social perception in infants* (pp. 217–247). Hillsdale, NJ: Ablex.

Beebe, B., Stern, D., & Jaffe, J. (1979). The kinesic rhythm of mother–infant interactions. In A. W. Siegman & S. Feldstein (Eds.), *Of Speech and time* (pp. 23–34). Hillsdale, NJ: Lawrence Erlbaum.

Behrmann, M., & Penn, C. (1984). Non-verbal communication of aphasic patients. *British Journal of Disorders of Communication, 19,* 155–168.

Bekoff, M. (1979). Behavioral acts: Description, classification, ethogram analysis, and measurement. In R. B. Cairns (Ed.), *The analysis of social interactions* (pp. 67–80). Hillsdale, NJ: Lawrence Erlbaum.

Bellugi, U., & Klima, E. S. (1976). Two faces of sign: Iconic and abstract. *Annals of the New York Academy of Sciences, 280,* 514–538.

Berger, K. W., & Popelka, G. R. (1971). Extrafacial gestures in relation to speech reading. *Journal of Communication Disorders, 3,* 302–308.

Bergstrom, K. J., & Hiscock, M. (1988). Factors influencing ocular motility during the performance of cognitive tasks. *Canadian Journal of Psychology, 42,* 1–23.

Berman, H. J., Shulman, A. D., & Marvitt, S. J. (1976). Comparison of multidimensional decoding of affect from audio, video, and audiovideo recording. *Sociometry, 39,* 83–89.

Bernieri, F. J. (1988). Coordinated movement and rapport in teacher–student interactions. *Journal of Nonverbal Behavior, 12,* 120–138.

Bernstein, I. S. (1981). Dominance: The baby and the bathwater. *Behavioral and Brain Sciences, 4,* 419–457.

Bertelson, P. (1982). Lateral differences in normal man and lateralization of brain function. *International Journal of Psychology, 17,* 173–210.

Birdwhistell, R. (1970). *Kinesics and context: Essays on body-motion communication.* Philadelphia: University of Pennsylvania Press.

Bischof, N. (1975). A systems approach toward the functional connections of attachment and fear. *Child Development, 46,* 801–817.

Blanck, P. D., Rosenthal, R., Snodgrass, S. E., DePaulo, B. M., & Zuckerman, M. (1981). Sex differences in eavesdropping on nonverbal cues: Developmental changes. *Journal of Personality and Social Psychology, 41,* 391–396.

Blanck, P. D., Rosenthal, R., Snodgrass, S. E., DePaulo, B. M., & Zuckerman, M. (1982). Longitudinal and cross-sectional age effects in nonverbal decoding skill and style. *Developmental Psychology, 18,* 491–498.

Blank, M., Gessner, M., & Esposito, A. (1979). Language without communication: A case study. *Journal of Child Language, 6,* 329–352.

Blaschke, M., & Ettlinger, G. (1987). Pointing as an act of social communication by monkeys. *Animal Behaviour, 35,* 1520–1523.

Blass, T., Freedman, N., & Steingart, I. (1974). Body movement and verbal encoding in the congenitally blind. *Perceptual and Motor Skills, 39,* 279–283.

Blurton-Jones, N. G. (1972). Categories of child–child interactions. In N. Blurton-Jones (Ed.), *Ethological studies of child behaviour* (pp. 97–127). Cambridge: Cambridge University Press.

Blurton-Jones, N. G., Ferreira, M. C. R., Brown, M. F., & Moore, L. (1980). Dimensions of attachment: Comparing a "trait" approach with a functional approach to study children's attachment to their mother. In S. A. Corson & E. O'Leary (Eds.), *Ethology and nonverbal communication in mental health* (pp. 143–165). Oxford: Pergamon.

Blurton-Jones, N. G., & Konner, M. J. (1973). Sex differences in behaviour of London and Bushman children. In R. P. Michael & J. H. Crook (Eds.), *Comparative ecology and behaviour of primates* (pp. 689–750). New York: Academic Press.

Bock, J. K., & Mazzella, J. R. (1983). Intonational marking of given and new information: Some consequences for comprehension. *Memory and Cognition, 11,* 64–76.

Bolinger, D. (1983). Intonation and gesture. *American Speech, 58,* 156–174.

Bond, C. F., Kahler, K. N., & Paolicelli, L. M. (1985). The miscommunication of deception: An adaptative perspective. *Journal of Experimental Social Psychology, 21,* 331–345.

Boomer, D. S. (1963). Speech disturbance and body movement in interviews. *Journal of Nervous and Mental Disease, 136,* 263–267.

Boomer, D. S., & Dittmann, A. T. (1964). Speech rate, filled pause and body movement in interview. *Journal of Nervous and Mental Disease, 139,* 324–327.

Bouhuys, A. L., Beersma, D. G. M., & Van den Hoofdakker, R. H. (1988). Prediction of clinical change by ethological methods. *Acta Psychiatrica Scandinavica, 77*(Suppl. 341), 23–43.

Bouissac, P. (1973). *La mesure des gestes.* The Hague: Mouton.

Bowlby, J. (1969). *Attachment and loss: Vol. 1. Attachment.* London: Hogarth.

Bradshaw, J. L., & Nettleton, N. C. (1981). The nature of hemispheric specialization in man. *Behavioral and Brain Sciences, 4*, 51–91.

Bradshaw, J. L., & Nettleton, N. C. (1982). Language lateralization to the dominant hemisphere: Tool use, gesture and language in hominid evolution. *Current Psychological Reviews, 2*, 171–192.

Brannigan, C. R., & Humphries, D. A. (1972). Human nonverbal behaviour, a means of communication. In N. G. Blurton-Jones (Ed.), *Ethological studies of child behaviour* (pp. 37–64). Cambridge: Cambridge University Press.

Brazelton, T. B., Koslowski, B., & Main, M. (1974). The origins of reciprocity: The early mother–infant interaction. In M. Lewis & L. A. Rosenblum (Eds.), *The effect of the infant on its caregiver* (pp. 49–76). New York: Wiley.

Bretherton, I., Bates, E., McNew, S., Shore, C., Williamson, C., & Beeghly-Smith, M. (1981). Comprehension and production of symbols in infancy: An experimental study. *Developmental Psychology, 17*, 728–736.

Brinker, R. P., & Goldbart, J. (1981). The problem of reliability in the study of early communication skills. *British Journal of Psychology, 72*, 27–41.

Brownell, J. R., & Bakeman, R. (1981). Hitting in toddler–peer interactions. *Child Development, 52*, 1076–1079.

Bruner, J. S. (1975a). From communication to language: A psychological perspective. *Cognition, 3*, 259–287.

Bruner, J. S. (1975b). The ontogenesis of speech acts. *Journal of Child Language, 2*, 1–15.

Bruner, J. S. (1977). Early social interaction and language acquisition. In H. R. Schaffer (Ed.), *Studies in mother–infant interaction* (pp. 271–289). New York: Academic Press.

Brunner, L. J. (1979). Smiles can be back channels. *Journal of Personality and Social Psychology, 37*, 728–734.

Brunswik, E. (1952). The conceptual framework of psychology. *International Encyclopedia of Unified Science* (Vol. 1, p. 10). Chicago: University of Chicago Press.

Bucci, W., & Freedman, N. (1978). Language and hand: The dimension of referential competence. *Journal of Personality, 46*, 594–622.

Buck, R. (1984). *The communication of emotion.* London: Guilford.

Bugenthal, D. E., Kaswan, J. W., Love, L. R., & Fox, M. N. (1970). Child versus adult perception of evaluative messages in verbal, vocal, and visual channels. *Developmental Psychology, 2*, 367–375.

Bull, P. (1978). The interpretation of posture through an alternative methodology to role play. *British Journal of Social and Clinical Psychology, 17*, 1–6.

Bull, P. (1983). *Body movement and interpersonal communication.* New York: Wiley.

Bull, P. (1987). *Posture and gesture.* Oxford: Pergamon.

Bull, P., & Connelly, G. (1985). Body movement and emphasis in speech. *Journal of Nonverbal Behaviour, 9*, 169–187.

Bull, P. E., & Brown, R. (1977). The role of postural change in dyadic conversation. *British Journal of Social and Clinical Psychology, 16*, 29–33.

Buller, D. B., & Aune, R. K. (1987). Nonverbal cues to deception among intimates, friends, and strangers. *Journal of Nonverbal Behavior, 11*, 269–290.

Burgoon, J. K. (1985). The relationship of verbal and nonverbal codes. In B. Dervin & M. J. Voigt (Eds.), *Progress in communication sciences* (Vol. 6, pp. 263–298). Norwood, NJ: Ablex.

Burgoon, J. K., & Koper, R. J. (1984). Nonverbal and relational communication associated with reticence. *Human Communication Research, 10*, 601–626.

Burns, K. L., & Beier, E. G. (1973). Significance of vocal and visual channels in the decoding of emotional meaning. *Journal of Communication, 23*, 118–130.

Butterworth, B., & Beattie, G. (1978). Gesture and silence as indicators of planning in speech. In R. N. Campbell & P. T. Smith (Eds.), *Recent advances in the psychology of language: Formal and experimental approaches* (pp. 347–360). New York: Plenum Press.

Butterworth, B., & Hadar, U. (1989). Gesture, speech, and computational stages: A reply to McNeill. *Psychological Review, 96,* 168–174.

Butterworth, B., Hine, R. R., & Brady, K. D. (1977). Speech and interaction in sound only communication channels. *Semiotica, 20,* 81–99.

Butterworth, B., Swallow, J., & Grimston, M. (1981). Gestures and lexical processes in jargonaphasia. In J. Brown (Ed.), *Jargonaphasia* (pp. 113–124). New York: Academic Press.

Butterworth, G., & Cochran, E. (1980). Towards a mechanism of joint visual attention in human infancy. *International Journal of Behavioral Development, 3,* 253–272.

Calame-Griaule, G. (1977). Pour une étude des gestes narratifs. In G. Calame-Griaule (Ed.), *Langage et cultures africaines: Essais d'ethnolinguistique* (pp. 303–359). Paris: Maspéro.

Calbris, G. (1980). Etude des expressions mimiques conventionnelles françaises dans le cadre d'une communication non verbale. *Semiotica, 29,* 245–346.

Calbris, G. (1981). Etude des expressions mimiques conventionnelles françaises dans le cadre d'une communication non verbale testées sur des hongrois. *Semiotica, 35,* 125–156.

Calbris, G. (1987). Geste et motivation. *Semiotica, 65,* 57–95.

Calbris, G., & Montredon, J. (1986). *Des gestes et des mots pour le dire.* Paris: Clé International.

Campbell, A., & Rushton, J. P. (1978). Bodily communication and personality. *British Journal of Social and Clinical Psychology, 17,* 31–36.

Campbell, R. (1989). Lipreading. In A. W. Young & H. D. Ellis (Eds.), *Handbook of research on face processing* (pp. 187–205). Amsterdam: North-Holland.

Campbell, R., & Dodd, B.(1980). Hearing by eye. *Quarterly Journal of Experimental Psychology, 32,* 85–99.

Campbell, R., Dodd, B., & Brasher, J. (1983). The sources of visual recency: Movement and language in serial recall. *Quarterly Journal of Experimental Psychology, 35A,* 571–587.

Campos, J. J., Barrett, K. C., Lamb, M. E., Goldsmith, H. H., & Stenberg, C. (1983). Socioemotional development. In M. M. Haith & J. J. Campos (Eds.), *Handbook of child psychology: Vol. 2. Infancy and developmental psychobiology* (pp. 783–915). New York: Wiley.

Camras, L. A. (1977). Facial expressions used by children in a conflict situation. *Child Development, 48,* 1431–1435.

Cappella, J. N. (1981). Mutual influence in expressive behavior: Adult–adult and infant–adult dyadic interaction. *Psychological Bulletin, 89,* 101–132.

Cappella, J. N., & Green, J. O. (1984). The effects of distance and individual differences in arousability on nonverbal involvement: A test of discrepancy–arousal theory. *Journal of Nonverbal Behavior, 8,* 259–286.

Cappella, J. N., & Street, R. L., Jr. (1983). A functional approach to the structure of communicative behaviour. In R. L. Street, Jr., & J. N. Cappella (Eds.), *Sequence and pattern in communicative behaviour* (pp. 1–29). London: Arnold.

Caramazza, A. (1986). On drawing inferences about the structure of normal cognitive systems from the analysis of patterns of impaired performance: The case for single patient studies. *Brain and Cognition, 5,* 41–66.

Caramazza, A., & Badecker, W. (1989). Patient classification in neuropsychological research. *Brain and Cognition, 10,* 256–295.

Carpenter, R. L., Mastergeorge, A. M., & Coggins, T. E. (1983). The acquisition of communicative intentions in infants eight to fifteen months of age. *Language and Speech, 26,* 101–116.

Carter, A. L. (1975). The transformation of sensori-motor morphemes into words: A case study of the development of "more" and "mine." *Journal of Child Language, 2,* 233–250.

Carter, A. L. (1978a). The development of systematic vocalizations prior to words: A case study. In N. Waterson & C. Snow (Eds.), *The development of communication* (pp. 127–138). New York: Wiley.

Carter, A. L. (1978b). From sensori-motor vocalization to words: A case study in the evolution of attention directing communication in the second year. In A. Lock (Ed.), *Action, gesture and symbol: The emergence of symbol* (pp. 309–349). New York: Academic Press.

Carter, A. L. (1979). The disappearance schema: A case study of a second year communicative behavior. In E. Ochs & B. B. Schieffelin (Eds.), *Developmental pragmatics* (pp. 131–156). New York: Academic Press.

Cary, M. S. (1978a). Does civil inattention exist in pedestrian passing? *Journal of Personality and Social Psychology, 36,* 1185–1195.

Cary, M. S. (1978b). The role of gaze in the initiation of conversation. *Social Psychology Quarterly, 41,* 269–271.

Cary, M. S. (1979). Gaze and facial display in pedestrian passing. *Semiotica, 28,* 323–326.

Caselli, M. C., & Volterra, V. (1990). From communication to language in hearing and deaf children. In V. Volterra & C. J. Erting (Eds.), *From gesture to language in hearing and deaf children* (pp. 263–277). Berlin: Springer.

Chaiken, S. (1986). Physical appearance and social influence. In C. P. Herman, M. P. Zanna, & E. T. Higgins (Eds.), *Physical appearance, stigma, and social behaviour: The Ontario symposium* (Vol. 3, pp. 143–177). Hillsdale, NJ: Lawrence Erlbaum.

Chaiken, S., & Eagly, A. H. (1976). Communication modality as determinants of message persuasiveness and message comprehensibility. *Journal of Personality and Social Psychology, 34,* 605–614.

Chalkley, M. A. (1982). The emergence of language as a social skill. In S. S. Kuczaj (Ed.), *Language development: Vol. 2. Language, thought and culture* (pp. 75–111). Hillsdale, NJ: Lawrence Erlbaum.

Chance, M. R. A. (1962). An interpretation of some agonistic posture: The role of "cut-off" acts and postures. *Symposia of the Zoological Society of London, 8,* 71–89.

Chance, M. R. A. (1967). Attention structure as the basis of primate rank orders. *Man* (N.S.), *2,* 503–518.

Chang, P., Hammond, G. R. (1987). Mutual interactions between speech and finger movements. *Journal of Motor Behavior, 19,* 265–274.

Cheney, D. L., & Seyfarth, R. M. (1982). How vervet monkeys perceive their grunts: Field playback experiments. *Animal Behaviour, 30,* 739–751.

Cheney, D. L., Seyfarth, R. M., & Smuts, B. (1986). Social relationships and social cognition in nonhuman primates. *Science, 234,* 1361–1366.

Chomsky, N. (1979). Human language and other semiotic systems. *Semiotica, 25,* 31–44. (Reprinted in T. A. Sebeok & J. Umiker-Sebeok [Eds.], *Speaking of apes: A critical anthology of two-way communication with man* [pp. 429–440]. New York: Plenum, 1980)

Christopoulou, C., & Bonvillian, J. D. (1985). Sign language, pantomime, and gestural processing in aphasic persons: A review. *Journal of Communication Disorders, 18,* 1–20.

Church, R. B., & Goldin-Meadow, S. (1986). The mismatch between gesture and speech as an index of transitional knowledge. *Cognition, 23,* 43–71.

Cicone, M., Wapner, W., Foldi, N., Zurif, E., & Gardner, H. (1979). The relation between gesture and language in aphasic communication. *Brain and Language, 8,* 324–349.

Clark, E. V. (1978). From gesture to word. In J. S. Bruner, & A. Carton (Eds.), *Human growth and development* (pp. 85–120). Oxford: Oxford University Press.

Clark, H. H., Schreuder, R., & Buttrick, S. (1983). Common ground and the understanding of demonstrative reference. *Journal of Verbal Learning and Verbal Behaviour, 22,* 245–258.

Coelho, C. A., & Duffy, R. J. (1986). Effects of iconicity, motoric complexity, and linguistic function on sign acquisition in severe aphasia. *Perceptual and Motor Skills, 63,* 519–530.

Cohen, A. A. (1977). The communicative functions of hand illustrators. *Journal of Communications, 27*(4), 54–63.

Cohen, A. A., & Harrison, R. P. (1973). Intentionality in the use of hand illustrators in face-to-face communication situations. *Journal of Personality and Social Psychology, 28,* 276–279.

Cohn, J. F., & Elmore, M. (1988). Effects of contingent changes in mother's affective expression on the organization of behaviour in 3-month-old infants. *Infant Behavior and Development, 11,* 493–505.

Cohn, J. F., & Tronick, E. Z. (1987). Mother–infant face-to-face interaction: The sequence of dyadic states at 3, 6, and 9 months. *Developmental Psychology, 23,* 68–77.

Cohn, J. F., & Tronick, E. Z. (1988). Mother–infant face-to-face interaction: Influence is bidirectional and unrelated to periodic cycles in either partner's behavior. *Developmental Psychology, 24,* 386–392.

Coker, D. A., & Burgoon, J. K. (1987). The nature of conversational involvement and nonverbal encoding patterns. *Human Communication Research, 13,* 463–494.

Collett, P. (1983). Mossi salutations. *Semiotica, 45,* 191–248.

Collett, P., & Chilton, J. (1981). Laterality in negation: Are Jakobson and Vavra right? *Semiotica, 35,* 57–70.

Collett, P., & Contarello, A. (1987). Gesti di assenso e di dissensso. In P. Ricci Bitti (Ed.), *Comunicazione e gestualità* (pp. 69–85). Milan: Angeli.

Collett, P., & Marsch, P. (1974). Patterns of public behaviour: Collision avoidance on a pedestrian crossing. *Semiotica, 12,* 281–299. (Reprinted in A. Kendon [Ed.], *Nonverbal communication, interaction and gesture* [pp. 199–217]. The Hague: Mouton, 1981)

Collis, G. M. (1977). Visual co-orientation and maternal speech. In H. R. Schaffer (Ed.), *Studies in mother–infant interaction* (pp. 355–375). New York: Academic Press.

Collis, G. M. (1979). Describing the structure of social interaction in infancy. In M. Bullowa (Ed.), *Before speech: The beginning of interpersonal communication* (pp. 111–130). Cambridge: Cambridge University Press.

Collis, G. M., & Schaffer, H. R. (1975). Synchronization of visual attention in mother–infant pairs. *Journal of Child Psychology and Psychiatry, 16,* 315–320.

Condon, W. S. (1970). Method of micro-analysis of sound films of behavior. *Behavioral Research Methods and Instrumentation, 2,* 51–54.

Condon, W. S. (1977). A primary phase in the organization of infant responding behaviour. In H. R. Schaffer (Ed.), *Studies in mother–infant interaction* (pp. 153–176). New York: Academic Press.

Condon, W. S., & Ogston, W. D. (1966). Sound film analysis of normal and pathological behavior patterns. *Journal of Nervous and Mental Disease, 143,* 338–347.

Condon, W. S., & Sander, L. W. (1974). Synchrony demonstrated between movements of the neonate and adult speech. *Child Development, 45,* 456–462.

Cook, M. (1980). The relationship between gaze and speech examined afresh with a Mackworth eye-mark camera. In H. W. Deckert & M. Raupach (Eds.), *Temporal variables in speech: Studies in honour of F. Goldman-Eisler* (pp. 153–158). The Hague: Mouton.

Cook, M., & Lalljee, M. G. (1972). Verbal substitutes for visual signals in interaction. *Semiotica, 6,* 212–221.

Cosnier, J. (1982). Communications et langages gestuels. In J. Cosnier, A. Berrendonner, J. Coulon, & C. Orecchioni (Eds.), *Les voies du langage: Communications verbales, gestuelles et animales* (pp. 255–304). Paris: Dunod.

Cosnier, J. (1987). Ethologie du dialogue. In J. Cosnier & C. Kerbrat-Orecchioni, *Décrire la conversation* (pp. 291–315). Lyon: Presses Universitaires de Lyon.

Cosnier, J. (1988). Grands tours et petits tours. In J. Cosnier, N. Gelas, & C. Kerbrat-Orecchioni (Eds.), *Echanges sur la conversation* (pp. 175–184). Paris: C.N.R.S.

Costanzo, M., & Archer, D. (1989). Interpreting the expressive behavior of others: The Interpersonal Perception Task. *Journal of Nonverbal Behavior, 13,* 225–245.

Craig, H. K., & Gallagher, T. M. (1982). Gaze and proximity as turn regulators within three-party and two-party child conversations. *Journal of Speech and Hearing Research, 25,* 65–75.

Craig, H. K., & Washington, J. A. (1986). Children's turn taking behavior: Social-linguistic interactions. *Journal of Pragmatics, 10,* 173–197.

Crosby, F., Promley, S., & Saxe, L. (1980). Recent unobtrusive studies of black and white discrimination and prejudice: A literature review. *Psychological Bulletin, 87,* 546–563.

Cunningham, M. R. (1977). Personality and the structure of nonverbal communication of emotion. *Journal of Personality, 45,* 564–584.

Cutler, A., & Fodor, J. A. (1979). Semantic focus and sentence comprehension. *Cognition, 7,* 49–59.

Cutler, A., & Foss, D. J. (1977). On the role of sentence stress in sentence processing. *Language and Speech, 20,* 1–10.

Dahan, G., & Cosnier, J. (1977). Sémiologie des quasi-linguistiques français. *Psychologie Médicale, 9,* 2053–2072.

Dalby, J. T., Gibson, D., Grossi, V., & Schneider, R. D. (1980). Lateralized hand gesture during speech. *Journal of Motor Behavior, 12,* 292–297.

D'Alessio, M., & Zazzetta, A. (1986). Development of self-touching behavior in childhood. *Perceptual and Motor Skills, 63,* 243–253.

Daly, J. A., Hogg, E., Sacks, D., Smith, M., & Zimring, L. (1983). Sex and relationship affect social self-grooming. *Journal of Nonverbal Behaviour, 7,* 183–189.

Daniloff, J. K., Fritelli, G., Buckingham, H. G., Hoffman, P. R., & Daniloff, R. G. (1986). Amer-Ind versus ASL: Recognition and imitation in aphasic subjects. *Brain and Language, 28,* 95–113.

Daniloff, J. K., Lloyd, L. L., & Fristoe, M. (1983). Amer-Ind transparency. *Journal of Speech and Hearing Disorders, 48,* 103–110.

Daniloff, J. K., Noll, J. D., Fristoe, M., & Lloyd, L. L. (1982). Gesture recognition in patients with aphasia. *Journal of Speech and Hearing Disorders, 47,* 43–49.

Darwin, C. (1881). *The descent of man, and selection in relation to sex* (2nd ed.) London: Murray.

Darwin, C. (1955). *The expression of the emotions in man and animals.* New York: Greenwood Press. (Originally published 1872)

Davis, M., & Weitz, S. (1981). Sex differences in body movements and position.

In C. Mayo & H. N. Henley (Eds.), *Gender and nonverbal behavior* (pp. 81–92). New York: Springer.

Davis, S. A., Artes, R., & Hoops, R. (1979). Verbal expression and expressive pantomime in aphasic patients. In Y. Lebrun & R. Hoops (Eds.), *Problems of aphasia* (pp. 109–123). Lisse: Swets & Zeitlinger.

Dawkins, R. (1976). Hierarchical organisation: A candidate principle for ethology. In P. P. G. Bateson & R. A. Hinde (Eds.), *Growing points in ethology* (pp. 7–54). Cambridge: Cambridge University Press.

de Ajuriaguerra, J., Richard, J., Rodriguez, R., & Tissot, R. (1966). Quelques aspects de la désintégration des praxies idéomotrices dans les démences du grand âge. *Cortex, 2*, 438–662.

De Ghett, V. J. (1978). Hierarchical cluster analysis. In P. W. Colgan (Ed.), *Quantitative ethology* (pp. 115–144). New York: Wiley.

de Lannoy, J.-D., Cedraschi, C., & Roessli, D. (1989). Gestualité et communication non verbale chez des patients atteints de cérébropathie de l'âge avancé. *Archives de Psychologie, 57*, 137–154.

de Lannoy, J.-D., & Feyereisen, P. (1988). Visage et pathologie. In B. Cyrulnik (Ed.), *Le visage, sens et contresens* (pp. 117–130). Paris: Eshel.

Delius, J. D. (1970). Irrelevant behaviour, information processing and arousal homeostasis. *Psychologische Forschung, 33*, 165–188.

De Long, A. J. (1974). Kinesic signals at utterance boundaries in preschool children. *Semiotica, 11*, 43–73. (Reprinted in A. Kendon [Ed.], *Nonverbal communication, interaction, and gesture* [pp. 251–281]. The Hague: Mouton, 1981)

de Meijer, M. (1989). The contribution of general features of body movements to the attribution of emotions. *Journal of Nonverbal Behavior, 13*, 247–268.

Demorest, A., Meyer, C., Phelps, E., Gardner, H., & Winner, E. (1984). Words speak louder than actions: Understanding deliberately false remarks. *Child Development, 55*, 1527–1534.

DePaulo, B. M., & Jordan, A. (1982). Age changes in deceiving and detecting deceit. In R. S. Feldman (Ed.), *Development of nonverbal behavior in children* (pp. 151–180). New York: Springer.

DePaulo, B. M., & Rosenthal, R. (1978). Age changes in nonverbal decoding as a function of increasing amount of information. *Journal of Experimental Child Psychology, 26*, 280–287.

DePaulo, B. M., & Rosenthal, R. (1979). The structure of nonverbal decoding skills. *Journal of Personality, 47*, 506–517.

DePaulo, B. M., & Rosenthal, R. (1982). Measuring the development of sensitivity to nonverbal communication. In C. E. Izard (Ed.), *Measuring emotions in infants and children* (pp. 208–247). Cambridge: Cambridge University Press.

DePaulo, B. M., Rosenthal, R., Eisenstat, R. A., Rogers, P. L., & Finkelstein, S. (1978). Decoding discrepant nonverbal cues. *Journal of Personality and Social Psychology, 36*, 313–323.

DePaulo, B. M., Stone, J. I., & Lassiter, G. D. (1985a). Deceiving and detecting deceit. In B. R. Schlenker (Ed.), *The self and social life* (pp. 323–370). New York: McGraw Hill.

DePaulo, B. M., Stone, J. I., & Lassiter, G. D. (1985b). Telling ingratiating lies: Effects of target sex and target attractiveness on verbal and nonverbal deceptive success. *Journal of Personality and Social Psychology, 48*, 1191–1203.

De Renzi, E. (1985). Methods of limb apraxia examination and their bearing on the interpretation of the disorder. In E. A. Roy (Ed.), *Neuropsychological studies of apraxia and related disorders* (pp. 45–64). Amsterdam: North-Holland.

De Renzi, E., Motti, F., & Nichelli, R. (1980). Imitating gestures: A quantitative approach to ideomotor apraxia. *Archives of Neurology, 37*, 6–10.

deTurck, M. A., & Miller, G. R. (1985). Deception and arousal: Isolating the behavioral correlates of deception. *Human Communication Research, 12,* 181–201.

Deutsch, F. (1949). Thus speaks the body: An analysis of postural behavior. *Transactions of the New York Academy of Sciences,* Series II, 12, 58–62.

de Waal, F. B. M. (1988). The comparative repertoire of captive bonobo (*Pan paniscus*) compared to that of chimpanzees. *Behaviour, 106,* 183–251.

Dickson, W. P. (1981). Referential communication activities in research and in curriculum: A metaanalysis. In W. P. Dickson (Ed.), *Children's oral communication skills* (pp. 189–204). New York: Academic Press.

Diderot, D. (1821). Lettre sur les sourds et muets, à l'usage de ceux qui entendent et qui parlent. In *Philosophie* (Vol. 2, pp. 9–131). Paris: Brière. (Originally published 1751)

Diezinger, F., & Anderson, J. R. (1986). Starting from scratch: A first look at a "displacement activity" in group-living rhesus monkeys. *American Journal of Primatology, 11,* 117–124.

Dimond, S., & Harries, R. (1984). Face touching in monkeys, apes and man: Evolutionary origins and cerebral asymmetry. *Neuropsychologia, 22,* 227–233.

Dingwall, W. O. (1979). The evolution of human communication systems. In H. Whitaker & H. A. Whitaker (Eds.), *Studies in neurolinguistics* (Vol. 4, pp. 1–95). New York: Academic Press.

Dittmann, A. T. (1972). The body movement–speech rhythm relationship as a cue to speech encoding. In A. W. Siegman & B. Pope (Eds.), *Studies in dyadic communication* (pp. 135–151). New York: Pergamon.

Dittmann, A. T., & Llewellyn, L. G. (1968). Relationships between vocalizations and head nods as listener responses. *Journal of Personality and Social Psychology, 9,* 79–84.

Dittmann, A. T., & Llewellyn, L. G. (1969). Body movement and speech rhythm in social conversation. *Journal of Personality and Social Psychology, 11,* 98–106.

Dittmann, A. T., Parloff, M. B., & Boomer, D. S. (1965). Facial and bodily expression: A study of receptivity of emotional cues. *Psychiatry, 28,* 239–244.

Dobrich, W., & Scarborough, H. S. (1984). Form and function in early communication: Language and pointing gestures. *Journal of Experimental Child Psychology, 38,* 475–490.

Dolgin, K. G., & Sabini, J. (1982). Experimental manipulation of a human nonverbal display: The tongue-show affects an observer's willingness to interact. *Animal Behaviour, 30,* 935–936.

Dore, J. (1974). A pragmatic description of early language development. *Journal of Psycholinguistic Research, 3,* 343–350.

Douglas, M. (1973). *Natural symbols: Explorations in cosmology.* Harmondsworth: Penguin Books.

Dovidio, J. F., Brown, C. E., Heltman, K., Ellyson, S. L., & Keating, C. F. (1988). Power displays between women and men in discussions of gender-linked tasks: A multichannel study. *Journal of Personality and Social Psychology, 55,* 580–587.

Dovidio, J. F., & Ellyson, S. L. (1985). Patterns of visual dominance behaviour in humans. In S. L. Ellyson & J. F. Dovidio (Eds.), *Power, dominance, and nonverbal behaviour* (pp. 129–149). Berlin: Springer.

Dovidio, J. F., Ellyson, S. L., Keating, C. F., Heltman, K., & Brown, C. E. (1988). The relationship of social power to visual displays of dominance between men and women. *Journal of Personality and Social Psychology, 54,* 233–242.

Dowd, J. M., & Tronick, E. Z. (1986). Temporal coordination of arm movements in early infancy: Do infants move in synchrony with adult speech? *Child Development, 57,* 762–776.

Dray, N. L., & McNeill, D. (1990). Gestures during discourse: The contextual structuring of thought. In S. L. Tsohatzidas (Ed.), *Meaning and prototypes: Studies in linguistic categorization* (pp. 465–487). New York: Routledge.

Druckman, D., Rozelle, R. M., & Baxter, J. C. (1982). *Nonverbal communication.* London: Sage.

Drummond, H. (1981). The nature and description of behavior patterns. In P. P. G. Bateson & P. H. Klopfer (Eds.), *Perspectives in ethology* (Vol. 4, pp. 1–33). New York: Plenum.

Duffy, J. R., & Watkins, L. B. (1984). The effect of response choice relatedness on pantomime and verbal recognition ability in aphasic patients. *Brain and Language, 21,* 291–306.

Duffy, R. J., & Buck, R. W. (1979). A study of the relationship between propositional (pantomime) and subpropositional (facial expression) extraverbal behaviors in aphasics. *Folia Phoniatrica, 31,* 129–136.

Duffy, R. J., & Duffy, J. R. (1981). Three studies of deficits in pantomimic expression and pantomimic recognition in aphasia. *Journal of Speech and Hearing Research, 24,* 70–84.

Duffy, R. J., & Duffy, J. R. (1989). An investigation of body part as objects (BPO) responses in normal and brain-damaged adults. *Brain and Cognition, 10,* 220–236.

Duffy, R. J., & Duffy, J. R. (1990). The relationship between pantomime expression and recognition in aphasia: The search for causes. In G. R. Hammond (Ed.), *The cerebral control of speech and limb movements* (pp. 417–449). Advances in Psychology, Vol. 70. Amsterdam, New York, Oxford: North-Holland.

Duffy, R. J., Duffy, J. R., & Mercaitis, P. A. (1984). Comparison of the performances of a fluent and a nonfluent aphasic on a pantomimic referential task. *Brain and Language, 21,* 260–273.

Duffy, R. J., & Liles, B. Z. (1979). A translation of Finkelnburg's (1870) lecture on aphasia as "asymbolia" with commentary. *Journal of Speech and Hearing Disorders, 44,* 156–168.

Duncan, S. (1972). Some signals and rules for taking speaking turns in conversation. *Journal of Personality and Social Psychology, 23,* 283–292.

Duncan, S. (1973). Toward a grammar for dyadic conversation. *Semiotica, 9,* 29–46.

Duncan, S., Brunner, L. J., & Fiske, D. W. (1979). Strategy signals in face to face interaction. *Journal of Personality and Social Psychology, 37,* 301–313.

Duncan, S., & Fiske, D. W. (1977). *Face to face interaction research: Methods and theory.* Hillsdale, NJ: Lawrence Erlbaum; London: Wiley.

Duncan, S., Kanki, B. G., Mokros, H., & Fiske, D. W. (1984). Pseudo-unilaterality, simple-rate variables, and other ills to which interaction research is heir. *Journal of Personality and Social Psychology, 46,* 1335–1348.

Duncan, S., & Niederehe, G. (1974). On signalling that it's your turn to speak. *Journal of Experimental Social Psychology, 10,* 234–247.

Dunn, J. C., & Kirsner, K. (1988). Discovering functionally independent mental processes: The principle of reversed association. *Psychological Review, 95,* 91–101.

Easley, S. P., Coelho, A. M., & Taylor, L. L. (1987). Scratching, dominance, tension, and displacement in male baboons. *American Journal of Primatology, 13,* 397–411.

Easton, R. D., & Basala, M. (1982). Perceptual dominance during lipreading. *Perception and Psychophysics, 32,* 562–570.

Eco, U. (1988). *Le signe: Histoire et analyse d'un concept* (J. M. Klinkenberg, Trans.). Brussels: Labor.

Edelman, R. J., Done, G., Easterbrook, J., Evans, J., Foster, T., & Green, M. (1984). Disablement and eye contact. *Perceptual and Motor Skills, 58,* 849–850.

Edelman, R. J., Evans, G., Pegg, I., & Tremain, M. (1983). Responses to physical stigma. *Perceptual and Motor Skills, 57,* 294.

Edelman, R. J., & Hampson, S. E. (1979). Changes in nonverbal behaviour during embarrassment. *British Journal of Clinical and Social Psychology, 18,* 385–390.

Edelman, R. J., & Hampson, S. E. (1981). The recognition of embarrassment. *Personality and Social Psychology Bulletin, 7,* 109–116.

Edinger, J. A., & Patterson, M. L. (1983). Nonverbal involvement and social control. *Psychological Bulletin, 93,* 30–56.

Edwards, D., & Goodwin, R. (1985). The language of shared attention and visual experience: A functional study of early nomination. *Journal of Pragmatics, 9,* 475–493.

Efron, G. (1972). *Gesture, race and culture.* The Hague: Mouton. (Originally published, 1941)

Ehrlichman, H. (1981). From gaze aversion to eye-movement suppression: An investigation of the cognitive interference explanation of gaze patterns during conversation. *British Journal of Social Psychology, 20,* 233–241.

Ehrlichman, H., & Barrett, J. (1983). "Random" saccadic eye movements during verbal-linguistic and visual-imaginal tasks. *Acta Psychologica, 53,* 9–26.

Ehrlichman, H., & Weinberger, A. (1978). Lateral eye movements and hemispheric asymmetry: A critical review. *Psychological Bulletin, 85,* 1080–1101.

Eibl-Eibesfeldt, I. (1972). Similarities and differences between cultures in expressive movements. In R. A. Hinde (Ed.), *Nonverbal communication* (pp. 297–314). Cambridge: Cambridge University Press.

Eibl-Eibesfeldt, I. (1979). Human ethology: Concepts and implications for the sciences of man. *Behavioral and Brain Sciences, 2,* 1–57.

Eibl-Eibesfeldt, I. (1984). *Die Biologie des menschlichen Verhaltens.* Munich: Piper.

Ekman, P. (1977). Biological and cultural contributions to body and facial movements. In J. Blacking (Ed.), *The anthropology of the body* (pp. 39–84). New York: Academic Press.

Ekman, P. (1979). About brows: Emotional and conversational signals. In M. von Cranach, K. Foppa, W. Lepenies, & D. Ploog (Eds.), *Human ethology* (pp. 169–202). Cambridge: Cambridge University Press.

Ekman, P. (1981). Mistakes when deceiving. *Annals of the New York Academy of Sciences, 364,* 268–278.

Ekman, P. (Ed.) (1982). *Emotion and the human face* (2nd ed.). Cambridge: Cambridge University Press.

Ekman, P. (1985). *Telling lies.* New York: W. W. Norton.

Ekman, P., & Friesen, W. V. (1967). Head and body cues in the judgements of emotions: A reformulation. *Perceptual and Motor Skills, 24,* 711–724.

Ekman, P., & Friesen, W. V. (1969). The repertoire of nonverbal behavior: Categories, origins, usage, and coding. *Semiotica, 1,* 49–98. (Reprinted in A. Kendon [Ed.], *Nonverbal communication, interaction, and gesture* [pp. 57–105]. The Hague: Mouton, 1981)

Ekman, P., & Friesen, W. V. (1972). Hand movements. *Journal of Communication, 22,* 353–374.

Ekman, P., & Friesen, W. V. (1974a). Detecting deception from the body or face. *Journal of Personality and Social Psychology, 29,* 288–298.

Ekman, P., & Friesen, W. V. (1974b). Nonverbal behavior and psychotherapy. In R. J. Friedman & M. M. Katz (Eds.), *The psychology of depression* (pp. 203–224). New York: Wiley.

Ekman, P., Friesen, W. V., & O'Sullivan, M. (1988). Smiles when lying. *Journal of Personality and Social Psychology, 24,* 414–420.

Ekman, P., Friesen, W. V., O'Sullivan, M., & Scherer, K. (1980). Relative importance of face, body and speech in judgments of personality and affect. *Journal of Personality and Social Psychology, 38,* 270–277.

Elias, G., Broerse, J., Hayes, A., & Jackson, K. (1984). Comments on the use of conversational features in studies of vocalization behaviours of mothers and infants. *International Journal of Behavioral Development, 7,* 177–191.

Ellgring, H. (1989). *Nonverbal communication in depression.* Cambridge: Cambridge University Press.

Ellis, A. W., & Young, A. W. (1988). *Human cognitive neuropsychology.* Hillsdale, NJ: Lawrence Erlbaum.

Ellyson, S. L., & Dovidio, J. F. (1985). Power, dominance, and nonverbal behavior: Basic concepts and issues. In S. L. Ellyson & J. F. Dovidio (Eds.), *Power, dominance, and nonverbal behavior* (pp. 1–27). New York: Springer.

Elmslie, T. J., & Brooke, J. D. (1982). Communicative gestures of the hand and arm when 4-year-old sons and their mothers interact. *Journal of Experimental Child Psychology, 34,* 151–155.

Engelkamp, J., & Zimmer, H. D. (1989). Memory for action events: A new field of research. *Psychological Research, 51,* 153–157.

Erikson, F. (1979). Talking down: Some cultural sources of miscommunication in interracial interviews. In A. Wolfgang (Ed.), *Nonverbal behavior, applications and cultural implications* (pp. 99–126). New York: Academic Press.

Evans, M. A., & Rubin, K. H. (1979). Hand gestures as a communicative mode in school-aged children. *Journal of Genetic Psychology, 135,* 189–196.

Fairbanks, L. A., McGuire, M. T., & Harris, C. J. (1982). Nonverbal interaction of patients and therapists during psychiatric interviews. *Journal of Abnormal Psychology, 91,* 109–119.

Feldman, H., Goldin-Meadow, S., & Gleitman, L. (1978). Beyond Herodotus: The creation of language by linguistically deprived deaf children. In A. Lock (Ed.), *Action, gesture, and symbol: The emergence of language* (pp. 351–413). New York: Academic Press.

Feldman, M., & Thayer, S. (1980). A comparison of three measures of nonverbal decoding ability. *Journal of Social Psychology, 112,* 91–97.

Feldman, R. S., White, J. B., & Lobato, D. (1982). Social skills and nonverbal behavior. In R. S. Feldman (Ed.), *Development of nonverbal behavior in children* (pp. 259–278). New York: Springer.

Feldstein, S., & Welkowitz, J. (1978). A chronography of conversation: In defense of an objective approach. In A. W. Siegman & S. Feldstein (Eds.), *Nonverbal behavior and communication* (pp. 329–378). Hillsdale, NJ: Lawrence Erlbaum.

Fennell, E. B. (1986). Handedness in neuropsychological research. In H. J. Hannay (Ed.), *Experimental techniques in human neuropsychology* (pp. 15–44). New York: Oxford University Press.

Fentress, J. C., Stilwell, F. P. (1973). Grammar of movement sequence in inbred mice. *Nature, 244,* 52–53.

Ferro, J. M., Martins, I. P., Mariano, G., & Castro-Caldas, A. (1983). CT scan correlates of gesture recognition. *Journal of Neurology, Neurosurgery, and Psychiatry, 46,* 943–952.

Feyereisen, P. (1977). Note sur la description des comportements d'auto-contact chez des sujets humains. *Psychologie Médicale, 9,* 2147–2161.

Feyereisen, P. (1982). Temporal distribution of co-verbal hand movements. *Ethology and Sociobiology, 3,* 1–9.

Feyereisen, P. (1983). Manual activity during speaking in aphasic subjects. *International Journal of Psychology, 18,* 545–556.

Feyereisen, P. (1986). Lateral differences in gesture production. In J. L. Nespoulous, P. Perron, & A. R. Lecours (Eds.), *The biological foundation of gesture: Motor and semiotic aspects* (pp. 77–94). Hillsdale, NJ: Lawrence Erlbaum.

Feyereisen, P. (1987). Gestures and speech, interactions and separations: A reply to McNeill (1985). *Psychological Review, 94,* 493–498.

Feyereisen, P. (1988). Nonverbal communication. In F. C. Rose, R. Whurr, & M. A. Wyke (Eds.), *Aphasia* (pp. 46–81). London: Whurr.

Feyereisen, P. (1989). What can be learned from lateral differences in emotional processing? In G. Gainotti & C. Caltagirone (Eds.), *Emotions and the dual brain* (pp. 119–144). New York: Springer.

Feyereisen, P. (1991). Brain pathology, lateralization, and nonverbal behavior. In R. S. Feldman & B. Rimé (Eds.), *Fundamentals of nonverbal behavior* (pp. 31–70). Cambridge: Cambridge University Press.

Feyereisen, P., Barter, D., Goossens, M., & Clerebaut, N. (1988). Gestures and speech in referential communication by aphasic subjects: Channel use and efficiency. *Aphasiology, 2,* 21–32.

Feyereisen, P., & Blondiau, C. (1978). Comportements de toilettage et activation chez le rat blanc. *Behaviour, 65,* 99–114.

Feyereisen, P., Bouchat, M. P., Déry, D., & Ruiz, M. (1990). The concomitance of speech and manual gesture in aphasic subjects. In G. R. Hammond (Ed.), *The cerebral control of speech and limb movements* (pp. 279–301). Advances in Psychology, Vol. 70. Amsterdam, New York, Oxford: North-Holland.

Feyereisen, P., & de Lannoy, J.-D. (1985). *Psychologie du geste.* Brussels and Liège: P. Mardaga.

Feyereisen, P., & Seron, X. (1982). Nonverbal communication and aphasia, a review: I. Comprehension. II. Expression. *Brain and Language, 16,* 191–212 & 213–236.

Feyereisen, P., Van de Wiele, M., & Dubois, F. (1988). The meaning of gestures: What can be understood without speech? *Cahiers de Psychologie Cognitive/European Bulletin of Cognitive Psychology, 8,* 3–25.

Field, T., Goldstein, S., Vega-Lahr, N., & Porter, K. (1986). Changes in imitative behavior during early infancy. *Infant Behavior and Development, 9,* 415–421.

Field, T., Vega-Lahr, N., Scafidi, F., & Goldstein, S. (1986). Effects of maternal unavailability on mother–infant interaction. *Infant Behavior and Development, 9,* 473–478.

Firth, R. (1970). Postures and gestures of respect. In J. Pouillon & P. Maranda (Eds.), *Echanges et communications: Mélanges offerts à C. Lévi-Strauss à l'occasion de son 60e anniversaire* (pp. 188–209). The Hague: Mouton. (Reprinted in T. Polhemus [Ed.], *Social aspects of the human body* [pp. 88–108]. Harmondsworth: Penguin, 1978)

Fisch, H. V., Frey, S., & Hirsbrunner, H. P. (1983). Analyzing nonverbal behavior in depression. *Journal of Abnormal Psychology, 92,* 307–318.

Fogel, A. (1981). The ontogeny of gestural communication: The first six months. In R. E. Stark (Ed.), *Language behavior in infancy and early childhood* (pp. 17–44). New York: Elsevier; Amsterdam: North-Holland.

Fogel, A. (1982). Early adult–infant interaction: Expectable sequences of behavior. *Journal of Pediatric Psychology, 7,* 1–22.

Fogel, A. (1985). Coordinative structures in the development of expressive behavior in early infancy. In G. Zivin (Ed.). *The development of expressive behavior: Biology–environment interactions* (pp. 249–267). New York: Academic Press.

Fogel, A. (1988). Cyclicity and stability in mother–infant face-to-face interaction: A comment on Cohn & Tronick (1988). *Developmental Psychology, 24,* 393–395.

Fogel, A., & Hannan, T. E. (1985). Manual actions of nine- to fifteen-week-old human infants during face-to-face interaction with their mothers. *Child Development, 56,* 1271–1279.

Fogel, A., & Thelen, E. (1987). Development of early expressive and communicative action: Reinterpreting the evidence from a dynamic systems perspective. *Developmental Psychology, 23,* 747–761.

Fogel, A., Toda, S., & Kawai, M. (1988). Mother–infant face-to-face interaction in Japan and the United States: A laboratory comparison using 3-month-old infants. *Developmental Psychology, 24,* 398–406.

Foldi, N. S., Cicone, M., & Gardner, H. (1983). Pragmatic aspects of communication in brain-damaged patients. In S. J. Segalowitz (Ed.), *Language functions and brain organization* (pp. 51–85). New York: Academic Press.

Fontaine, R. (1984a). Les imitations précoces: Problèmes méthodologiques et théoriques. *Cahiers de Psychologie Cognitive, 4,* 517–535.

Fontaine, R. (1984b). Imitative skills between birth and six months. *Infant Behavior and Development, 7,* 323–333.

Forsyth, G. A., Kushner, G. I., & Forsyth, P. D. (1981). Human facial expression judgment in a conversational context. *Journal of Nonverbal Behavior, 6,* 115–130.

Fossi, L., Faravelli, C., & Paoli, M. (1984). The ethological approach to the assessment of depressive disorders. *Journal of Nervous and Mental Disease, 172,* 332–341.

Frable, D. E. S. (1987). Sex-typed execution and perception of expressive movements. *Journal of Personality and Social Psychology, 53,* 391–396.

Freedle, R., & Lewis, M. (1977). Prelinguistic conversations. In M. Lewis & L. Rosenblum (Eds.), *Interaction, conversation, and the development of language* (pp. 157–185). New York: Wiley.

Freedman, N. (1977). Hands, words and mind: On the structuralization of body movement during discourse and the capacity for verbal representation. In N. Freedman & S. Grand (Eds.), *Communicative structures and psychic structures: A psychoanalytic interpretation of communication* (pp. 109–132). New York: Plenum.

Freedman, N., & Bucci, W. (1981). On kinetic filtering in associative monologue. *Semiotica, 34,* 225–249.

Freedman, N., O'Hanlon, J., Oltman, P., & Witkin, H. A. (1972). The imprint of psychological differentiation on kinetic behavior in varying communicative contexts. *Journal of Abnormal Psychology, 79,* 239–258.

Freedman, N., Van Meel, J. M., Barroso, F., & Bucci, W. (1986). On the development of communicative competence. *Semiotica, 62,* 77–105.

Freud, S. (1953). Fragment of an analysis of a case of hysteria. In J. Strachey (Ed. and Trans.), *The standard edition of the complete psychological works of Sigmund Freud* (Vol. 7, pp. 7–122). London: Hogarth Press. (Original work published 1905)

Frey, S., Hirsbrunner, H. P., Florin, A. M., Daw, W., & Crawford, R. (1983). A unified approach to the investigation of nonverbal and verbal behavior in communication research. In W. Doise & S. Moscovici (Eds.), *Current issues in European social psychology* (Vol. 1, pp. 143–199). Cambridge: Cambridge University Press.

Friedman, L. A. (1977). Formational properties of ASL. In L. A. Friedman (Ed.), *On the other hand: New perspectives on American Sign Language* (pp. 13–56). New York: Academic Press.

Friesen, W. V., Ekman, P., & Wallbott, H. (1979). Measuring hand movements. *Journal of Nonverbal Behavior, 4,* 97–112.

Fugita, S. S., Hogrebe, M. C., & Wexley, K. N. (1980). Perceptions of deception: Perceived expertise in detecting deception, successfulness of deception and nonverbal cues. *Personality and Social Psychology Bulletin, 6,* 637–643.

Furnham, A., Proctor, E., & Gunter, B. (1988). Memory for material presented in the media: The superiority of written communication. *Psychological Reports, 63,* 935–938.

Furnham, A., Trevethan, R., & Gaskell, G. (1981). The relative contribution of verbal, vocal and visual channels to person perception: Experiment and critique. *Semiotica, 37,* 39–57.

Fuson, K. C. (1988). *Children's counting and concepts of number.* New York: Springer.

Gainotti, G., & Lemmo, M. A. (1976). Comprehension of symbolic gestures in aphasia. *Brain and Language, 3,* 451–460.

Galifret-Granjon, N. J. (1974). Etude génétique des productions d'actes mimés sur ordre. *Psychiatrie de l'Enfant, 17,* 119–239.

Gallois, C., & Callan, V. J. (1986). Decoding emotional messages: Influence of ethnicity, sex, message type, and channel. *Journal of Personality and Social Psychology, 51,* 755–762.

Garcia, L. T., & Derfel, B. (1983). Perception of sexual experience: The impact of nonverbal behavior. *Sex Roles, 9,* 871–878.

Gardner, B. T., & Gardner, R. A. (1971). Two-way communication with an infant chimpanzee. In A. M. Schrier & F. Stollnitz (Eds.), *Behaviour of nonhuman primates* (Vol. 4, pp. 117–184). New York: Academic Press.

Gardner, B. T., & Gardner, R. A. (1980). Two comparative psychologists look at language acquisition. In K. E. Nelson (Ed.), *Children's language* (Vol. 2, pp. 331–369). New York: Gardner.

Garnica, O. K. (1978). Nonverbal concomitants of language input to children. In N. Waterson & C. Snow (Eds.), *The development of communication* (pp. 137–147). New York: Wiley.

Gatewood, J. B., & Rosenwein, R. (1981). Interactional synchrony: Genuine or spurious? A critique of recent research. *Journal of Nonverbal Behavior, 6,* 12–29.

Gifford, R., Ng, C. F., & Wilkinson, R. M. (1985). Nonverbal cues in the employment interview: Links between applicant qualities and interviewer judgments. *Journal of Applied Psychology, 70,* 729–736.

Gillespie, D. L., & Leffler, A. (1983). Theories of nonverbal behavior: A critical review of proxemics research. In R. Collins (Ed.), *Sociological theory, 1983* (pp. 120–154). San Francisco: Jossey Bass.

Ginsburg, G. P., & Kilbourne, B. K. (1988). Emergence of vocal alternation in mother–infant interchanges. *Journal of Child Language, 15,* 221–235.

Ginsburg, H. J., & Miller, S. M. (1981). Altruism in children: A naturalistic study of reciprocation and an examination of the relationship between social dominance and aid-giving behavior. *Ethology and Sociobiology, 2,* 75–83.

Ginsburg, H. J., Pollman, V. A., & Wanson, M. S. (1977). An ethological analysis of nonverbal inhibitors of aggressive behaviors in male elementary school children. *Developmental Psychology, 13,* 417–418.

Giovannini, D., & Ricci-Bitti, P. E. (1981). Culture and sex effect in recognizing emotion by facial and gestural cues. *Italian Journal of Psychology, 8,* 95–102.

Gitin, S. R. (1970). A dimensional analysis of manual expression. *Journal of Personality and Social Psychology, 15,* 271–277.

Givens, D. (1978). Greeting a stranger: Some commonly used nonverbal signals of aversiveness. *Semiotica, 22,* 351–367. (Reprinted in A. Kendon [Ed.], *Nonverbal communication, interaction, and gesture* [pp. 219–235]. The Hague: Mouton, 1981)

Glosser, G., & Wiener, M. (1990). Gestures and speech: Evidence from aphasia. In G. R. Hammond (Ed.), *The cerebral control of speech and limb movements* (pp. 257–277). Advances in Psychology, Vol. 70. Amsterdam, New York, Oxford: North-Holland.

Glosser, G., Wiener, M., & Kaplan, E. (1986). Communicative gestures in aphasia. *Brain and Language, 27,* 345–359.

Glosser, G., Wiener, M., & Kaplan, E. (1988). Variations in aphasic language behaviors. *Journal of Speech and Hearing Disorders, 53,* 115–124.

Goffman, E. (1959). *The presentation of self in everyday life.* Garden City, NY: Doubleday.

Goffman, E. (1971). *Relations in public.* New York: Basic Books.

Goldberg, S., & Rosenthal, R. (1986). Self-touching behavior in the job interview: Antecedents and consequences. *Journal of Nonverbal Behavior, 10,* 65–80.

Goldin-Meadow, S. (1979). Structure in a manual communication system developed without a conventional language model: Language without a helping hand. In H. Whitaker & H. A. Whitaker (Eds.), *Studies in neurolinguistics* (Vol. 4, pp. 125–209). New York: Academic Press.

Goldin-Meadow, S. (1982). The resilience of recursion: A study of a communication system developed without a conventional language model. In E. Wanner & L. R. Gleitman (Eds.), *Language acquisition: The state of the art* (pp. 51–77). Cambridge: Cambridge University Press.

Goldin-Meadow, S. (1985). Language development under atypical learning conditions: Replication and implications of a study of deaf children of hearing parents. In K. E. Nelson (Ed.), *Children's language* (Vol. 5, pp. 197–245). Hillsdale, NJ: Lawrence Erlbaum.

Goldin-Meadow, S., & Morford, M. (1985). Gesture in early child language: Studies of deaf and hearing children. *Merrill-Palmer Quarterly, 31,* 145–176.

Golinkoff, R. M. (1983). The preverbal negotiation of failed messages: Insights into the transition period. In R. M. Golinkoff (Ed.), *The transition from prelinguistic to linguistic communication* (pp. 57–78). Hillsdale, NJ: Lawrence Erlbaum.

Golinkoff, R. M. (1986). "I beg your pardon?": The preverbal negotiation of failed messages. *Journal of Child Language, 13,* 455–476.

Goodale, M. A. (1988). Hemispheric differences in motor control. *Behavioral Brain Research, 30,* 203–214.

Goodwin, C. (1981). *Conversational organization: Interaction between speakers and hearers.* New York: Academic Press.

Goodwin, M. H., & Goodwin, C. (1986). Gesture and coparticipation in the activity of searching a word. *Semiotica, 62,* 51–75.

Gopnik, A., & Meltzoff, A. N. (1986). Relations between semantic and cognitive development in the one-word stage: The specificity hypothesis. *Child Development, 57,* 1040–1053.

Gotlib, I. H. (1982). Self-reinforcement and depression in interpersonal interaction: The role of performance level. *Journal of Abnormal Psychology, 91,* 3–13.

Gottman, J. M., & Ringland, J. T. (1981). The analysis of dominance and bidirectionality in social development. *Child Development, 52,* 393–412.

Gould, S. J., & Lewontin, R. C. (1979). The spandrels of San Marco and the Panglossian paradigm: A critic of the adaptationist program. *Proceedings of the Royal Society of London, B205,* 581–595.

Gouzoules, S., Gouzoules, H., & Marler, P. (1984). Rhesus monkey (*Macaca mulatta*) screams: Representational signalling in the recruitment of agonistic aid. *Animal Behaviour, 32,* 182–193.

Graham, J. A., & Agryle, M. (1975). A cross-cultural study of the communication of extra-verbal meaning by gestures. *International Journal of Psychology, 10,* 57–67.

Graham, J. A., & Heywood, S. (1975). The effects of elimination of hand gestures and of verbal codability on speech performance. *European Journal of Social Psychology, 5,* 189–195.

Grammer, K., Schiefenhövel, W., Schleidt, M., Lorenz, B., & Eibl-Eibesfeldt, I. (1988). Patterns on the face: The eye brow flash in crosscultural comparison. *Ethology, 77,* 279–299.

Grand, S., Freedman, N., Steingart, I., & Buchwald, C. (1975). Communicative behavior in schizophrenia: The relation of adaptive styles to kinetic and linguistic aspects of interview behavior. *Journal of Nervous and Mental Disease, 161,* 293–306.

Grand, S., Marcos, L. R., Freedman, N., & Barroso, F. (1977). Relation of psycho-pathology and bilingualism to kinesic aspects of interview behavior in schizophrenia. *Journal of Abnormal Psychology, 86,* 492–500.

Grant, E. C. (1969). An ethological description of nonverbal behaviour during interviews. *British Journal of Medical Psychology, 41,* 177–184. (Reprinted in S. J. Hutt &. C. Hutt [Eds.], *Behaviour studies in psychiatry* [pp. 61–76]. Oxford: Pergamon, 1970)

Graves, R. (1983). Mouth asymmetry, dichotic ear advantage and tachistoscopic visual field advantage as measures of language lateralization. *Neuropsychologia, 21,* 641–649.

Graves, R., Goddglass, H., & Landis, T. (1982). Mouth asymmetry during spontaneous speech. *Neuropsychologia, 20,* 371–381.

Graves, R., Landis, T., & Simpson, C. (1985). On the interpretation of mouth asymmetry. *Neuropsychologia, 23,* 121–122.

Green, K. P. (1987). The perception of speaking rate using visual information from a talker's face. *Perception and Psychophysics, 42,* 587–593.

Green, R., Neuberg, D. S., & Finck, S. J. (1983). Sex-typed motor behaviors of "feminine" boys, conventionally masculine boys and conventionally feminine girls. *Sex Roles, 9,* 571–579.

Green, S., & Marler, P. (1979). The analysis of animal communication. In P. Marler & J. G. Vandenbergh (Eds.), *Handbook of behavioral neurobiology: Vol. 3. Social behavior and communication* (pp. 73–158). New York: Plenum.

Greenbaum, P. E., & Rosenfeld, H. M. (1980). Varieties of touching in greetings: Sequential structure and sex-related differences. *Journal of Nonverbal Behavior, 5,* 13–25.

Greenberg, M. T., & Marvin, R. S. (1982). Reactions of preschool children to an adult stranger: A behavioral system approach. *Child Development, 53,* 481–490.

Greene, R. L., & Crowder, R. G. (1984). Modality and suffix effects in the absence of auditory stimulation. *Journal of Verbal Learning and Verbal Behavior, 23,* 371–382.

Greenfield, P. M., & Smith, J. H. (1976). *The structure of communication in early language development.* New York: Academic Press.

Grosjean, F., & Gee, J. P. (1987). Prosodic structure and spoken word recognition. *Cognition, 25,* 135–155.

Grusec, J. E., & Abramovitch, R. (1982). Imitation of peers and adults in a natural setting: A functional analysis. *Child Development, 53,* 636–642.

Guillaume, P. (1926). *L'imitation chez l'enfant*. Paris: Alcan. (English trans.: *Imitation in children*. Chicago: University of Chicago Press, 1971)

Gunderson, V. M., & Lockard, J. S. (1980). Human postural signals as intention movements to depart: African data. *Animal Behaviour, 18,* 966–967.

Gutman, A. J., & Turnure, J. E. (1979). Mothers' production of hand gestures while communicating with their preschool children under various task conditions. *Developmental Psychology, 15,* 197–203.

Haaland, K. Y., Harrington, D. L., & Yeo, R. (1987). The effects of task complexity on motor performance in left and right CVA patients. *Neuropsychologia, 25,* 783–794.

Hadar, U. (1986). Forcefield analogy for communication involving movement of the head: An exercise in ecological semiotics. *Semiotica, 62,* 279–296.

Hadar, U. (1989). Two types of gesture and their role in speech production. *Journal of Language and Social Psychology, 8,* 221–228.

Hadar, U., Steiner, T. J., Grant, E. C., & Rose, F. C. (1983a). Head movement correlates of juncture and stress at sentence level. *Language and Speech, 26,* 117–129.

Hadar, U., Steiner, T. J., Grant, E. C., & Rose, F. C. (1983b). Kinematics of head movements accompanying speech during conversation. *Human Movement Science, 2,* 35–46.

Hadar, U. Steiner, T. J., Grant, E. C., & Rose, F. C. (1984). The timing of shifts of head postures during conversation. *Human Movement Science, 3,* 237–245.

Hadar, U., Steiner, T. J., & Rose, F. C. (1984). The relationship between head movements and speech dysfluencies. *Language and Speech, 27,* 333–342.

Hadar, U., Steiner, T. J., & Rose, F. C. (1985). Head movement during listening turns in conversation. *Journal of Nonverbal Behavior, 9,* 214–228.

Hager, J. C., & Van Gelder, R. S. (1985). Asymmetry of speech actions. *Neuropsychologia, 23,* 119–120.

Halberstadt, A. G., & Saitta, M. B. (1987). Gender, nonverbal behavior, and perceived dominance: A test of the theory. *Journal of Personality and Social Psychology, 53,* 257–272.

Hall, E. T. (1959). *The silent language*. New York: Doubleday.

Hall, J. A., Rosenthal, R., Archer, D., DiMatteo, M. R., & Rogers, P. L. (1978). Profile of nonverbal sensitivity. In P. McReynolds (Ed.), *Advances in psychological assessment* (Vol. 4, pp. 179–221). (Reprinted in S. Weitz [Ed.], *Nonverbal communication: Readings with commentary* [2nd ed., pp. 357–370]. New York: Oxford University Press, 1979)

Hall, P. M., & Hall, D. A. S. (1983). The handshake as interaction. *Semiotica, 45,* 249–264.

Halliday, M. A. K. (1973). *Explorations in the functions of language*. London: Arnold.

Halliday, M. A. K. (1975). *Learning how to mean: Explorations in the development of language*. London: Arnold.

Halliday, S., & Leslie, J. C. (1986). A longitudinal semi-cross-sectional study of the development of mother–child interaction. *British Journal of Developmental Psychology, 4,* 211–222.

Hampson, E., & Kimura, D. (1984). Hand movement asymmetries during verbal and nonverbal tasks. *Canadian Journal of Psychology, 38,* 102–125.

Hannan, T. E. (1982). Young infants' hand and finger expressions: An analysis of category reliability. In T. Field & A. Fogel (Eds.), *Emotion and early interaction* (pp. 253–265). Hillsdale, NJ: Lawrence Erlbaum.

Hannan, T. E. (1987). A cross-sequential assessment of the occurrences of pointing in 3- to 12-month-old human infants. *Infant Behavior and Development, 10,* 11–22.

Hannan, T. E., & Fogel, A. (1987). A case-study assessment of "pointing" during the first three months of life. *Perceptual and Motor Skills, 65,* 187–194.

Harding, C. G. (1982). Development of the intention to communicate. *Human Development, 25,* 140–151.

Harper, R. G., Wiens, A. N., & Matarazzo, J. D. (1978). *Nonverbal communication: The state of the art.* New York: Wiley.

Harrigan, J. A. (1985). Listener's body movements and speaking turns. *Communication Research, 12,* 233–250.

Harrigan, J. A., Kues, J. R., Steffen, J. J., & Rosenthal, R. (1987). Self touching and impressions of others. *Personality and Social Psychology Bulletin, 13,* 497–512.

Harrigan, J. A., Kues, J. R., & Weber, J. G. (1986). Impressions of hand movements: Self-touching and gestures. *Perceptual and Motor Skills, 63,* 503–516.

Harrigan, J. A., Oxman, T. E., & Rosenthal, R. (1985). Rapport expressed through nonverbal behavior. *Journal of Nonverbal Behaviour, 9,* 95–110.

Harrigan, J. A., & Steffen, J. J. (1983). Gaze as turn-exchange signal in group conversation. *British Journal of Social Psychology, 22,* 67–68.

Harris, L. J. (1989). Hand preference in gestures and signs in the deaf and hearing: Some notes on early evidence and theory. *Brain and Cognition, 10,* 189–219.

Harris, M., Jones, D., & Grant, J. (1983). The nonverbal context of mothers' speech to infants. *First Language, 4,* 21–30.

Harris, M., Jones, D., Brooks, S., & Grant, J. (1986). Relations between the nonverbal context of maternal speech and rate of language development. *British Journal of Developmental Psychology, 4,* 261–268.

Harris, M. J., & Rosenthal, R. (1985). Mediation of interpersonal expectancy effects: 31 meta-analyses. *Psychological Bulletin, 97,* 363–386.

Hatta, T., & Dimond, S. J. (1984). Differences in face touching by Japanese and British people. *Neuropsychologia, 22,* 531–534.

Hausfater, G., & Takacs, D. (1987). Structure and function of hindquarter presentations in yellow baboons (*Papio cynocephalus*). *Ethology, 74,* 297–319.

Hayes, L. A., & Watson, J. S. (1981). Neonatal imitation: Fact or artifact? *Developmental Psychology, 17,* 655–660.

Healey, J. M., Liederman, J., & Geschwind, N. (1986). Handedness is not a unidimensional trait. *Cortex, 22,* 33–53.

Heath, C. C. (1982). The display of recipiency: An instance of a sequential relationship in speech and body movement. *Semiotica, 42,* 147–167.

Heath, C. (1984). Participation in the medical consultation: The co-ordination of verbal and non-verbal behaviour between the doctor and the patient. *Sociology of Health and Illness, 6,* 311–338.

Heath, C. (1985). The consultation's end: The coordination of speech and body movement. *International Journal of the Sociology of Language, 51,* 27–42.

Hécaen, H. (1978). Les apraxies idéomotrices: Essai de dissociation. In H. Hécaen & M. Jeannerod (Eds.), *Du contrôle moteur à l'organisation du geste* (pp. 343–358). Paris: Masson.

Hedge, B. J., Everitt, B. S., & Frith C. D. (1978). The role of gaze in dialogue. *Acta Psychologica, 42,* 453–475.

Heilman, K. M., Rothi, L., & Kertesz, A. (1983). Localization of apraxia-producing lesions. In A. Kertesz (Ed.), *Localization in neuropsychology* (pp. 371–392). New York: Academic Press.

Heilman, K. M., Rothi, L., & Valenstein, E. (1982). Two forms of indeomotor apraxia. *Neurology, 32,* 342–346.

Heimann, M., Nelson, K. E., & Schaller, J. (1989). Neonatal imitation of tongue protrusion and mouth opening: Methodological aspects and evidence of early individual differences. *Scandinavian Journal of Psychology, 30,* 90–101.

Hellige, J. B. (1983). Hemisphere × task interaction and the study of laterality. In J. B. Hellige (Ed.), *Cerebral hemisphere asymmetry: Method, theory, and application* (pp. 411–443). New York: Praeger.

Herder, J. G. (1772). *Abhandlung über den Ursprung der Sprache.* Berlin: Voss.

Herrmann, M., Reichle, T., Lucius-Hoene, G., Wallesch, C. W., & Johannsen-Horbach, H. (1988). Nonverbal communication as a compensatory strategy for severely nonfluent aphasics? A quantitative approach. *Brain and Language, 33,* 41–54.

Hertz, R. (1909). La prééminence de la main droite, étude sur la polarité religieuse. *Revue Philosophique, 68,* 553–580. (English trans. in R. Needham [Ed.], *Essays on dual symbolic classification.* Chicago: University of Chicago Press, 1973)

Heslin, R., & Alper, T. (1983). Touch: A bonding gesture. In J. M. Wiemann & R. P. Harrison (Eds.), *Nonverbal interaction* (pp. 47–75). London: Sage.

Heslin, R., & Boss, D. (1980). Nonverbal intimacy in airport arrival and departure. *Personality and Social Psychology Bulletin, 6,* 248–252.

Heslin, R., & Patterson, M. L. (1982). *Nonverbal behavior and social psychology.* New York: Plenum Press.

Hewes, G. W. (1957). The anthropology of posture. *Scientific American, 196*(2), 122–132.

Hewes, G. W. (1973). Primate communication and the gestural origin of language. *Current Anthropology, 14,* 5–24.

Hewes, G. W. (1976). The current status of the gestural theory of language origin. *Annals of the New York Academy of Sciences, 280,* 482–504.

Hinde, R. A. (1970). *Animal behaviour: A synthesis of ethology and comparative psychology* (2nd ed.). New York: McGraw Hill.

Hinde, R. A. (1976). Interactions, relationships and social structure. *Man* (N.S.), *11,* 1–17.

Hinde, R. A. (1983). Ethology and child development. In M. M. Haith & J. J. Campos (Eds.), *Handbook of child psychology: Vol. 2. Infancy and developmental psychobiology* (pp. 27–93). New York: Wiley.

Hinde, R. A. (1985). Expression and negotiation. In G. Zivin (Ed.), *The development of expressive behavior: Biology–environment interactions* (pp. 103–116). New York: Academic Press.

Hinde, R. A., & Herrmann, J. (1977). Frequencies, durations, derived measures and their correlations in studying dyadic and triadic relationships. In H. R. Schaffer (Ed.), *Studies in mother–infant interaction* (pp. 19–46). New York: Academic Press.

Hiscock, M. (1986). Lateral eye movements and dual-task performance. In H. J. Hannay (Ed.), *Experimental techniques in human neuropsychology* (pp. 264–308). New York: Oxford University Press.

Hiscock, M., & Bergstrom, K. J. (1981). Ocular motility as an indicator of verbal and visuospatial processing. *Memory and Cognition, 9,* 332–338.

Hobbs, J. R., & Evans, D. A. (1980). Conversation as planned behavior. *Cognitive Science, 4,* 349–377.

Hockett, C. F., & Altmann, S. A. (1968). A note on design features. In T. A. Sebeok (Ed.), *Animal communication* (pp. 61–72). Bloomington: Indiana University Press.

Hocking, J. E., & Leathers, D. G. (1980). Nonverbal indicators of deception: A new theoretical perspective. *Communication Monographs, 47,* 119–131.

Hoff-Ginsberg, E., & Shatz, M. (1982). Linguistic input and the child's acquisition of language. *Psychological Bulletin, 92,* 3–26.

Hold, B. (1977). Rank and behaviour: An ethological study of preschool children. *Homo, 28,* 158–188.

Hoots, M. A., McAndrew, F. T., & François, G. R. (1989). Decoding of gestures by kindergarten, first-, and third-grade children. *Journal of Genetic Psychology, 150,* 117–118.

Houston, A. I. (1982). Transitions and time sharing. *Animal Behaviour, 30,* 615–625.

Hulme, C., Monk, A., & Ives, S. (1987). Some experimental studies of multisensory teaching: The effects of manual tracing on children's paired associate learning. *British Journal of Developmental Psychology, 5,* 299–307.

Hutt, C., & Hutt, S. J. (1965). Effects of environmental complexity on stereotyped behaviour in children. *Animal Behaviour, 13,* 1–4.

Hutt, C., & Hutt, S. J. (1968). Stereotypies and their relation to arousal: A study of autistic children. *Human Development, 11,* 277–286. (Reprinted in S. J. Hutt & C. Hutt [Eds.], *Behaviour studies in psychiatry* [pp. 175–204]. Oxford: Pergamon, 1970)

Ingram, D. (1975). Motor asymmetries in young children. *Neuropsychologia, 13,* 95–102.

Inhelder, B., Lézine, I., Sinclair, H., & Stambak, M. (1972). Les débuts de la fonction symbolique. *Archives de Psychologie, 41,* 187–243.

Jackson, J. P. (1974). The relationship between the development of gestural imagery and the development of graphic imagery. *Child Development, 45,* 432–438.

Jacobson, S. W. (1979). Matching behavior in the young infant. *Child Development, 50,* 425–430.

Jaffe, J., & Feldstein, S. (1970). *Rhythm of dialogues.* New York: Academic Press.

Jaffe, J., Stern, D. N., & Peery, J. C. (1973). "Conversational" coupling of gaze behavior in prelinguistic human development. *Journal of Psycholinguistic Research, 2,* 321–329.

Jakobson, R. (1972). Motor signs for "yes" and "no." *Language in Society, 1,* 91–96.

Jancovic, M. A., Devoe, S., & Wiener, M. (1975). Age-related changes in hand and arm movements as non-verbal communication: Some conceptualizations and an empirical exploration. *Child Development, 46,* 922–928.

Janssen, P., & Kraaimaat, F. (1980). Disfluency and anxiety in stuttering and non-stuttering adolescents. *Behavioural Analysis and Modification, 4,* 116–126.

Jason, G. W. (1983). Hemispheric asymmetries in motor function: I. Left-hemisphere specialization for memory but not performance. II. Ordering does not contribute to left-hemisphere specialization. *Neuropsychologia, 21,* 35–45 & 47–58.

Jason, G. W. (1985). Gesture fluency after focal cortical lesions. *Neuropsychologia, 23,* 463–481.

Jeannerod, M. (1984). The timing of natural prehension movement. *Journal of Motor Behavior, 16,* 235–254.

Jeannerod, M. (1988). *The neural and behavioural organization of goal-directed movements.* Oxford: Clarendon Press.

Jodelet, D. (1984). The representation of the body and its transformations. In R. M. Farr & S. Moscovici (Eds.), *Social representations* (pp. 211–238). Cambridge: Cambridge University Press.

Johnson, H. G., Ekman, P., & Friesen, W. V. (1975). Communicative body movements: American emblems. *Semiotica, 15,* 335–353. (Reedition in A. Kendon [Ed.], *Nonverbal communication, interaction, and gesture* [pp. 401–419]. The Hague: Mouton, 1981)

Johnston, T. D. (1988). Developmental explanation and the ontogeny of bird song: Nature/nurture redux. *Behavioral and Brain Sciences, 11,* 617–663.

Jones, I.H., & Pansa, M. (1979). Some nonverbal aspects of depression and schizophrenia occurring during the interview. *Journal of Nervous and Mental Disease, 167,* 402–409.

Jones, M. R. (1943). Studies in nervous movements: 1. The effect of arithmetic on the frequencies and patterning of movements. 2. The effects of inhibition of micturition on the frequency and patterning of movement. *Journal of General Psychology, 29,* 47–62 & 303–312.

Jones, N., Kearins, J., & Watson, J. (1987). The human tongue show and observers' willingness to interact: Replication and extensions. *Psychological Reports, 60,* 759–764.

Jormakka, L. (1976). The behaviour of children during a first encounter. *Scandinavian Journal of Psychology, 17,* 15–22.

Jurich, A. P., & Jurich, J. A. (1974). Correlations among nonverbal expressions of anxiety. *Psychological Reports, 34,* 199–204.

Kaitz, M., Meschulach-Sarfaty, O., Auerbach, J., & Eidelman, A. (1988). A reexamination of newborns' ability to imitate facial expressions. *Developmental Psychology, 24,* 3–7.

Kaye, K. (1977). Toward the origin of dialogue. In H. R. Schaffer (Ed.), *Studies in mother–infant interaction* (pp. 89–117). New York: Academic Press.

Kaye, K., & Fogel, A. (1980). The temporal structure of face-to-face communication between mothers and infants. *Developmental Psychology, 18,* 454–464.

Keating, C. F. (1985). Human dominance signals: The primate in us. In S. L. Ellyson & J. F. Dovidio (Eds.), *Power, dominance, and nonverbal behavior* (pp. 89–108). New York: Springer.

Keele, W. (1981). Behavioral analysis of movement. In V. B. Brooks (Ed.), *Handbook of physiology: Section 1. The nervous system: Vol. 2. Motor control* (pp. 1391–1414). Bethesda, MD: American Physiological Society.

Kehrer, H. E., & Tente, D. (1969). Observations on displacement activities in children. *Journal of Child Psychology and Psychiatry, 10,* 259–268.

Keller, H., & Schölmerich, A. (1987). Infant vocalizations and parental reactions during the first 4 months of life. *Developmental Psychology, 23,* 62–67.

Keller, H., Schölmerich, A., & Eibl-Eibesfeldt, I. (1988). Communication patterns in adult–infant interactions in Western and non Western cultures. *Journal of Cross-cultural Psychology, 19,* 427–445.

Kelso, J. A. S., Tuller, B., & Harris, K. S. (1983). A "dynamic pattern" perspective on the control and coordination of movement. In P. F. MacNeilage (Ed.), *The production of speech* (pp. 137–173). New York: Springer.

Kemp, N. J., & Rutter, D. R. (1982). Cuelessness and the content and style of conversation. *British Journal of Social Psychology, 21,* 43–49.

Kemp, N. J., & Rutter, D. R. (1986). Social interaction of blind people: An experimental analysis. *Human Relations, 39,* 195–210.

Kemp, N. J., Rutter, D. R., Dewey, M. E., Harding, A. G., & Stephenson, G. M. (1984). Visual communication and impression formation. *British Journal of Social Psychology, 23,* 133–145.

Kempler, D. (1988). Lexical and pantomime abilities in Alzheimer's disease. *Aphasiology, 2,* 147–159.

Kendon, A. (1967). Some functions of gaze direction in social interaction. *Acta Psychologica, 26,* 22–63.

Kendon, A. (1970). Movement coordination in social interaction: Some examples described. *Acta Psychologica, 32,* 100–125.

Kendon, A. (1972a). Review of "Kinesics and context." *American Journal of Psychology, 85,* 447–455.

Kendon, A. (1972b). Some relationships between body motion and speech: An analysis of an example. In A.W. Siegman & B. Hope (Eds.), *Studies in dyadic communication* (pp. 177–210). New York: Pergamon.

Kendon, A. (1973). The role of visible behaviour in the organization of social interaction. In M. von Cranach & I. Vine (Eds.), *Social communication and movement* (pp. 29–74). New York: Academic Press.

Kendon, A. (1975a). Gesticulation, speech and the gesture theory of language origins. *Sign Language Studies, 9,* 349–373. (Reprinted in M. R. Key [Ed.], *The relationship of verbal and nonverbal communication* [pp. 207–227]. Paris & The Hague: Mouton, 1980)

Kendon, A. (1975b). Some functions of the face in a kissing round. *Semiotica, 15,* 299–334. (Reprinted in A. Kendon [Ed.], *Nonverbal communication, interaction, and gesture* [pp. 321–356]. The Hague: Mouton, 1981)

Kendon, A. (1980). A description of a deaf-mute sign language from the Enga Province of Papua Guinea with some comparative discussion. Part I: The formational properties of Enga signs. *Semiotica, 31,* 1–34.

Kendon, A. (1981). Current issues in the study of "nonverbal communication." In A. Kendon (Ed.), *Nonverbal communication, interaction, and gesture* (pp. 1–53). The Hague: Mouton.

Kendon, A. (1982a). The organization of behavior in face-to-face interaction: Observations on the development of a methodology. In K. R. Scherer & P. Ekman (Eds.), *Handbook of methods in nonverbal behavior research* (pp. 440–505). Cambridge: Cambridge University Press.

Kendon, A. (1982b). The study of gesture: Some observations on its history. *Semiotic Inquiry, 2,* 45–62.

Kendon, A. (1983). Gesture and speech: How they interact. In J. M. Wiemann & R. P. Harrison (Eds.), *Nonverbal interaction* (pp. 13–45) (Sage Annual Reviews of Communication Research, Vol. 11). London: Sage.

Kendon, A. (1985). Some uses of gestures. In D. Tannen & M. Saville-Troike (Eds.), *Perspectives on silence* (pp. 215–233). Norwood, NJ: Ablex.

Kendon, A. (1986). Some reasons for studying gesture. *Semiotica, 62,* 3–28.

Kendon, A., & Ferber, A. (1973). A description of some human greetings. In R. P. Michael & J. H. Crook (Eds.), *Comparative ecology and behaviour of primates* (pp. 591–688). New York: Academic Press.

Kenner, A. N. (1984). The effect of task differences, attention, and personality on the frequency of body-focused hand movements. *Journal of Nonverbal Behavior, 8,* 159–171.

Kenner, A. N. (1989). Personality and body-focused hand movements. *Perceptual and Motor Skills, 68,* 907–913.

Kenny, D. A., & Malloy, T. E. (1988). Partner effects in social interaction. *Journal of Nonverbal Behavior, 12,* 34–57.

Kimura, D. (1973). Manual activity during speaking. I. Right-handers. II. Left-handers. *Neuropsychologia, 11,* 45–50 & 51–55.

Kimura, D. (1976). The neural basis of language qua gesture. In H. Whitaker & H. A. Whitaker (Eds.), *Studies in neurolinguistics* (Vol. 2, pp. 145–156). New York: Academic Press.

Kimura, D. (1982). Left-hemisphere control of oral and brachial movements and their relation to communication. *Philosophical Transactions of the Royal Society of London, B298,* 135–149.

Kimura, D. (1988). Review of "What the hands reveal about the brain" by Howard Poizner, Edward S. Klima and Ursulla Bellugi. *Language and Speech, 31,* 375–378.

Kimura, D., & Humphrys, C. A. (1981). A comparision of left- and right-arm movements during speaking. *Neuropsychologia, 19,* 807–812.

Kinsbourne, M. (1986). Brain organization underlying orientation and gestures: Normal and pathological cases. In J. L. Nespoulous, P. Perron, & A. R. Lecours (Eds.), *The biological foundations of gestures: Motor and semiotic aspects* (pp. 65–76). Hillsdale, NJ: Lawrence Erlbaum.

Kinsbourne, M., & Hiscock, M. (1983). Asymmetries of dual-task performances. In J. B. Hellige (Ed.), *Cerebral hemisphere asymmetry: Method, theory, and application* (pp. 255–334). New York: Praeger.

Kirch, M. S. (1987). *Deutsche Gebärdensprache.* Hamburg: Buske.

Kirk, L., & Burton, M. (1976). Physical versus semantic classification of nonverbal forms: A cross-cultural experiment. *Semiotica, 17,* 315–337. (Reprinted in A. Kendon [Ed.], *Nonverbal communication, interaction, and gesture* [pp. 459–481]. The Hague: Mouton, 1981)

Klatzky, R. L., McCloskey, B. P., Doherty, S., Pellegrino, J., & Smith, T. (1987). Knowledge about hand shaping and knowledge about objects. *Journal of Motor Behavior, 19,* 187–213.

Klatzky, R. L., Pellegrino, J. W., McCloskey, B. P., & Doherty, S. (1989). Can you squeeze a tomato? The role of motor representations in semantic sensibility judgments. *Journal of Memory and Language, 28,* 56–77.

Klein, Z. (1984). Sitting postures in male and female. *Semiotica, 48,* 119–131.

Kleinke, C. L. (1986). Gaze and eye-contact: A research review. *Psychological Bulletin, 100,* 78–100.

Klima, E. S., & Bellugi, U. (1979). *The signs of language.* Cambridge: Harvard University Press.

Knapp, M. L., Hart, R. P., Friedrich, G. W., & Shulman, G. M. (1973). The rhetoric of good-bye: Verbal and nonverbal correlates of human leave-taking. *Speech Monographs, 40,* 182–198.

Knowlson, J. R. (1965). The idea of gesture as a universal language in the XVIIth and XVIIIth centuries. *Journal of the History of Ideas, 26,* 495–508.

Koepke, J. E., Hamm, M., Legerstee, M., & Russell, M. (1983). Neonatal imitation: Two failures to replicate. *Infant Behavior and Development, 6,* 97–102.

Kraaimaat, F., & Janssen, P. (1985). Are the accessory facial movements of the stutterer learned behaviours? *Perceptual and Motor Skills, 60,* 11–17.

Krauss, R. M. (1981). Impression formation, impression management, and nonverbal behavior. In E. T. Higgins, C. P. Herman, & M. P. Zanna (Eds.), *Social cognition: The Ontario symposium* (Vol. 1, pp. 323–341). Hillsdale, NJ: Lawrence Erlbaum.

Krauss, R. M., Apple, W., Morency, N., Wenzel, C., & Winton, W. (1981). Verbal, vocal and visible factors in judgments of another's affect. *Journal of Personality and Social Psychology, 40,* 312–320.

Krauss, R. M., Garlock, C. M., Bricker, P. D., & McMahon, L. E. (1977). The role of audible and visible back channel responses in interpersonal communication. *Journal of Personality and Social Psychology, 35,* 523–529.

Kraut, R. (1980). Humans as lie detectors: Some second thoughts. *Journal of Communication, 30*(4), 209–216.

Kraut, R. E., & Poe, D. (1980). Behavioral roots of person perception: The deception judgments of customs inspectors and laymen. *Journal of Personality and Social Psychology, 39,* 784–798.

Kristeva, J. (1968). Le geste, pratique ou communication? *Langages, 10,* 48–64.

(English trans. in T. Polhemus [Ed.], *Social aspects of the human body* [pp. 264–284]. Harmondsworth: Penguin, 1978)

Krout, M. H. (1935a). Autistic gestures: An experimental study in symbolic movements. *Psychological Monographs, 46*, 1–126.

Krout, M. H. (1935b). The social and psychological significance of gestures. *Journal of Genetic Psychology, 47*, 385–411.

Kudoh, T., & Matsumoto, D. (1985). Cross-cultural examination of the semantic dimensions of body postures. *Journal of Personality and Social Psychology, 48*, 1440–1446.

Kumin, L., & Lazar, M. (1974). Gestural communication in pre-school children. *Perceptual and Motor Skills, 38*, 708–710.

Kupfer, D. J., Maser, J. D., Blehar, M. C., & Miller, R. (1987). Behavioral assessment in depression. In J. D. Maser, (Ed.), *Depression and expressive behavior* (pp. 1–15). Hillsdale, NJ: Lawrence Erlbaum.

LaFrance, M. (1979). Nonverbal synchrony and rapport: Analysis by the cross-lag panel technique. *Social Psychology Quarterly, 42*, 66–70.

LaFrance, M. (1985). Postural mirroring and intergroup relations. *Personality and Social Psychology Bulletin, 11*, 207–217.

LaFrance, M., & Ickes, W. (1981). Posture mirroring and interactional involvement: Sex and sex typing differences. *Journal of Nonverbal Behavior, 5*, 139–154.

LaFrance, M., & Mayo, C. (1976). Racial differences in gaze behavior during conversations: Two systematic observational studies. *Journal of Personality and Social Psychology, 33*, 547–552.

LaFrance, M., & Mayo, C. (1978). Cultural aspects of nonverbal communication. *International Journal of Intercultural Relations, 2*, 71–89.

LaFreniere, P., & Charlesworth, W. R. (1983). Dominance, attention and affiliation in a preschool group: A nine-month longitudinal study. *Ethology and Sociobiology, 4*, 55–67.

Lavergne, J., & Kimura, D. (1987). Hand movement asymmetry during speech: No effect of speaking topic. *Neuropsychologia, 25*, 689–693.

Lecompte, W. A. (1981). The ecology of anxiety: Situational stress and role of self-stimulation in Turkey. *Journal of Personality and Social Psychology, 40*, 712–721.

Leffler, A., Gillespie, D. L., & Conaty, J. C. (1982). The effects of status differentiation on nonverbal behavior. *Social Psychology Quarterly, 45*, 153–161.

Legerstee, M., Corter, C., & Kienapple, K. (1990). Hand, arm, and facial actions of young infants to a social and nonsocial stimulus. *Child Development, 61*, 774–784.

Lehmkuhl, G., Poeck, K., & Willmes, K. (1983). Ideomotor apraxia and aphasia: An examination of types and manifestations of apraxic symptoms. *Neuropsychologia, 21*, 199–212.

LeMay, A., David, R., & Thomas, A. P. (1988). The use of spontaneous gesture by aphasic patients. *Aphasiology, 2*, 137–145.

Lempers, J. D. (1979). Young children's production and comprehension of nonverbal deictic behaviors. *Journal of Genetic Psychology, 135*, 93–102.

Lempers, J. D., Flavell, E. R., & Flavell, J. H. (1977). The development in very young children of knowledge concerning visual perception. *Genetic Psychology Monographs, 95*, 3–53.

Lempert, H., & Kinsbourne, M. (1985). Possible origin of speech in selective orienting. *Psychological Bulletin, 97*, 62–73.

Lenneberg, E. H. (1967). *Biological foundations of language.* New York: Wiley.

Leroi-Gourhan, A. (1964). *Le geste et la parole: Vol. 1. Technique et langage.* Paris: Albin Michel.

Lesko, W. A., & Schneider, F. W. (1978). Effects of speaking order and speaker gaze level on interpersonal gaze in a tryad. *Journal of Social Psychology, 104,* 185–195.

Leung, E. H. L., & Rheingold, H. L. (1981). Development of pointing as a social gesture. *Developmental Psychology, 17,* 215–220.

Levelt, W. J. M., Richardson, G., & La Heij, W. (1985). Pointing and voicing in deictic expressions. *Journal of Memory and Language, 24,* 133–164.

Levinson, S. C. (1983). *Pragmatics.* Cambridge: Cambridge University Press.

Lewis, M., Stanger, C., & Sullivan, M. W. (1989). Deception in 3-year-olds. *Developmental Psychology, 25,* 439–443.

Lewis, M., & Sullivan, M. W. (1985). Imitation in the first six months of life. *Merrill-Palmer Quarterly, 31,* 315–333.

Lickiss, K. P., & Wellens, A. R. (1978). Effects of visual accessibility and hand restraint on fluency of gesticulation and effectiveness of message. *Perceptual and Motor Skills, 46,* 925–926.

Lieberman, P. (1984). *The biology and evolution of language.* Cambridge: Harvard University Press.

Lieberman, P. (1985). On the evolution of human syntactic ability: Its preadaptive bases. Motor control and speech. *Journal of Human Evolution, 14,* 657–668.

Littlepage, G. E., & Pineault, M. A. (1979). Detection of deceptive factual statements from the body and the face. *Personality and Social Psychology Bulletin, 5,* 325–328.

Lock, A. (1980). *The guided reinvention of language.* New York: Academic Press.

Lock, A., Young, A., Service, V., & Chandler, P. (1990). Some observations on the origins of the pointing gesture. In V. Volterra & C. J. Erting (Eds.), *From gesture to language in hearing and deaf children* (pp. 42–55). Berlin: Springer.

Lockard, J. S., & Adams, R. M. (1980). Courtship behaviors in public: Different age/sex roles. *Ethology and Sociobiology, 1,* 245–253.

Lockard, J. S., Allen, D. J., Schiele, B. J., & Wilmer, M. J. (1978). Human postural signals: Stance, weight-shifts and social distance as intention movements to depart. *Animal Behaviour, 26,* 219–224.

Lorenz, K. (1950). Part and parcel in animal and human societies. (English trans. in K. Lorenz, *Studies in animal and human behaviour, Vol. 2* [pp. 115–195]. London: Methuen, 1973)

Losey, G. S. (1978). Information theory and communication. In P. W. Colgan (Ed.), *Quantitative ethology* (pp. 43–98). New York: Wiley.

Loveland, K. A., & Landry, S. H. (1986). Joint attention and language in autism and developmental language delay. *Journal of Autism and Developmental Disorders, 16,* 335–349.

Lumsden, C. J., & Wilson, E. O. (1982). Précis of *Genes, mind, and culture. Behavioral and Brain Sciences, 5,* 1–38.

MacDonald, J., & McGurk, H. (1978). Visual influences on speech perception processes. *Perception and Psychophysics, 24,* 253–257.

Machida, S. (1986). Teacher accuracy in decoding nonverbal indicants of comprehension and noncomprehension in Anglo- and Mexican-American children. *Journal of Educational Psycholollgy, 78,* 454–464.

Macnamara, J. (1977). From sign to language. In J. Macnamara (Ed.), *Language learning and thought* (pp. 11–35). New York: Academic Press.

MacNeilage, P. F., Studdert-Kennedy, M. G., & Lindblom, B. (1984). Functional precursors to language and its lateralization. *American Journal of Physiology, R15,* 912–914.

MacNeilage, P. F., Studdert-Kennedy, M. G., & Lindblom, B. (1987). Primate handedness reconsidered. *Behavioral and Brain Sciences, 10,* 247–303.

Mahl, G. F. (1967). Some clinical observations on nonverbal behavior in interviews. *Journal of Nervous and Mental Disease, 144,* 482–505.

Major, B., Schmidlin, A. M., & Williams, L. (1990). Gender patterns in social touch: The impact of setting and age. *Journal of Personality and Social Psychology, 58,* 634–643.

Mandel, M. (1977). Iconic devices in ASL. In L. A. Friedman (Ed.), *On the other hand: New perspectives on American Sign Language* (pp. 57–107). New York: Academic Press.

Manstead, A. S. R., Wagner, H. I., & MacDonald, C. J. (1984). Face, body, and speech as channels of communication in the detection of deception. *Basic and Applied Social Psychology, 5,* 317–332.

Manstead, A. S. R., Wagner, H. I., & MacDonald, C. J. (1986). Deceptive and nondeceptive communication: Sending experience, modality, and individual abilities. *Journal of Nonverbal Behavior, 10,* 147–167.

Marcon, R. A. (1986). Variation in children's nonverbal communication as a function of listener and second-language development. *Journal of Genetic Psychology, 146,* 459–468.

Marcos, L. R. (1979a). Hand movements and non-dominant fluency in bilinguals. *Perceptual and Motor Skills, 48,* 207–214.

Marcos, L. R. (1979b). Nonverbal behavior and thought processing. *Archives of General Psychiatry, 36,* 940–943.

Marler, P. (1976). Social organization, communication and graded signals: The chimpanzee and the gorilla. In P. P. G. Bateson & R. A. Hinde (Eds.), *Growing points in ethology* (pp. 239–279). Cambridge; Cambridge University Press.

Marler, P. (1984). Animal communication: Affect or cognition? In K. R. Scherer & P. Ekman (Eds.), *Approaches to emotion* (pp. 345–368). Hillsdale, NJ: Lawrence Erlbaum.

Marler, P., & Peters, S. (1980). Birdsong and speech: Evidence for special processing. In P. Eimas & J. Miller (Eds.), *Perspectives on the study of speech* (pp. 75–112). Hillsdale, NJ: Lawrence Erlbaum.

Marslen-Wilson, W., Levy, E., & Tyler, L. K. (1982). Producing interpretable discourse: The establishment and maintenance of reference. In R. J. Jarvella & W. Klein (Eds.), *Speech, place and action* (pp. 339–378). New York: Wiley.

Martinsen, H., & Smith, L. (1989). Studies of vocalization and gesture in the transition to speech. In S. von Tetzchner, L. S. Siegel, & L. Smith (Eds.), *The social and cognitive aspects of normal and atypical language development* (pp. 95–112). New York: Springer.

Massaro, D. W. (1987). Speech perception by ear and eye. In B. Dodd & R. Campbell (Eds.), *Hearing by eye: The psychology of lipreading* (pp. 53–83). Hove, England: Lawrence Erlbaum.

Massaro, D. W. (1989). Multiple book review of *Speech perception by ear and eye: A paradigm for psychological inquiry. Behavioral and Brain Sciences, 12,* 741–794.

Masur, E.F. (1982). Mother's responses to infant's object-related gestures: Influence on lexical development. *Journal of Child Language, 9,* 23–30.

Masur, E. F. (1983). Gestural development, dual-directional signaling, and the transition to words. *Journal of Psycholinguistic Research, 12,* 93–109.

Masur, E. F. (1987). Imitative interchanges in a social context: Mother–infant matching behavior at the beginning of the second year. *Merrill-Palmer Quarterly, 33,* 453–473.

Masur, E. F., & Ritz, E. G. (1984). Patterns of gestural, vocal, and verbal imitation performance in infancy. *Merrill-Palmer Quarterly, 30,* 369–392.

Mathon, C. (1969). Pour une sémiologie du geste en Afrique occidentale. *Semiotica, 3*, 245–255.

Matsumoto, D., & Kudoh, T. (1987). Cultural similarities and differences in the semantic dimensions of body postures. *Journal of Nonverbal Behavior, 11*, 166–179.

Maurus, M., & Pruscha, H. (1973). Classification of social signals in squirrel monkeys by means of cluster analysis. *Behaviour, 47*, 106–128.

Mauss, M. (1935). Les techniques du corps. *Journal de Psychologie Normale et Pathologique, 32*, 271–293. (English trans. in *Economy and Society, 2*, 70–88 [1973])

Maxwell, G. M., Cook, M. W., & Burr, R. (1985). The encoding and decoding of liking from behavioral cues in both auditory and visual channels. *Journal of Nonverbal Behavior, 9*, 239–263.

Mayer, N. K., & Tronick, E. Z. (1985). Mother's turn-giving signals and infant turn-taking in mother–infant interaction. In T. M. Field & N. A. Fox (Eds.), *Social perception in infants* (pp. 199–216). Norwood, NJ: Ablex.

Maynard, S. K. (1987). Interactional functions of a nonverbal sign: Head movement in Japanese dyadic casual conversation. *Journal of Pragmatics, 11*, 589–606.

Mayo, C., & LaFrance, M. (1978). On the acquisition of nonverbal communication: A review. *Merrill-Palmer Quarterly, 24*, 213–228.

McArthur, L. Z., & Baron, R. M. (1983). Toward an ecological theory of social perception. *Psychological Review, 90*, 215–238.

McCleery, R. H. (1983). Interactions between activities. In T. R. Haliday & P. J. B. Slater (Eds.), *Animal behaviour* (Vol. 1, pp. 134–167). Oxford: Blackwell.

McClenney, L., & Neiss, R. (1989). Posthypnotic suggestion: A method for the study of nonverbal communication. *Journal of Nonverbal Behavior, 13*, 37–45.

McCloskey, M., & Caramazza, A. (1988). Theory and methodology in cognitive neuropsychology: A response to our critics. *Cognitive Neuropsychology, 5*, 583–623.

McCune-Nicolich, L. (1981). Toward symbolic functioning: Structure of early pretend games and potential parallels with language. *Child Development, 52*, 785–797.

McDowall, J. J. (1978a). Accuracy of boundary detection by observers of filmed movements. *Perceptual and Motor Skills, 47*, 1091–1100.

McDowall, J. J. (1978b). Interactional synchrony: A reappraisal. *Journal of Personality and Social Psychology, 36*, 963–975.

McDowall, J. J. (1978c). Microanalysis of filmed movement: The reliability of boundary detection by observers. *Environmental Psychology and Nonverbal Behavior, 3*, 77–88.

McFarland, D. J. (1971). *Feedback mechanisms in animal behaviour.* New York: Academic Press.

McFarland, D. J. (1974). Time sharing as a behavioral phenomenon. *Advances in the Study of Behaviour, 5*, 201–225.

McFarland, D. J. (1983). Behavioural transitions: A reply to Roper. Time sharing: a reply to Houston. *Animal Behaviour, 31*, 305–308.

McFarland, D. J., & Houston, A. (1981). *Quantitative ethology: The state space approach.* London: Pitman.

McGinley, H., Blau, G. L., & Takai, M. (1984). Attraction effects of smiling and body position: A cultural comparison. *Perceptual and Motor Skills, 58*, 915–922.

McGinley, H., McGinley, P., & Nicholas, K. (1978). Smiling, body position and interpersonal attraction. *Bulletin of the Psychonomic Society, 12*, 21–24.

McGinley, H., Nicholas, K., & McGinley, P. (1978). Effects of body position and attitude similarity on interpersonal attraction and opinion change. *Psychological Reports, 42*, 127–138.

McGrew, W. C. (1972). *An ethological study of children's behaviour.* New York: Academic Press.

McGrew, W. C., & Tutin, C. E. G. (1978). Evidence for a social custom in wild chimpanzees? *Man* (N.S.), *13*, 234–251.

McKenzie, B., & Over, R. (1983). Young infants fail to imitate facial and manual gestures. *Infant Behavior and Development, 6*, 85–95.

McLeod, P. L., & Rosenthal, R. (1983). Micromomentary movement and the decoding of face and body cues. *Journal of Nonverbal Behavior, 8*, 83–90.

McNeill, D. (1975). Semiotic extension. In L. E. Solso (Ed.), *Information processing and cognition: The Loyola symposium* (pp. 351–380). Hillsdale, NJ: Lawrence Erlbaum.

McNeill, D. (1979). *The conceptual basis of language.* Hillsdale, NJ: Lawrence Erlbaum.

McNeill, D. (1985). So you think gestures are nonverbal? *Psychological Review, 92*, 350–371.

McNeill, D. (1986). Iconic gestures of children and adults. *Semiotica, 62*, 107–128.

McNeill, D. (1987a). *Psycholinguistics: A new approach.* New York: Harper & Row.

McNeill, D. (1987b). So you do think gestures are nonverbal! Reply to Feyereisen (1987). *Psychological Review, 94*, 499–504.

McNeill, D. (1989). A straight path – to where? Reply to Butterworth and Hadar. *Psychological Review, 96*, 175–179.

McNeill, D., & Levy, E. (1982). Conceptual representations in language activity and gesture. In J. Jarvella & W. Klein (Eds.), *Speech, place, and action* (pp. 271–295). New York: Wiley.

McNeill, D., Levy, E. T., & Pedelty, L. L. (1990). Speech and gesture. In G. R. Hammond (Ed.), *The cerebral control of speech and limb movements* (pp. 203–256). Advances in Psychology, Vol. 70. Amsterdam, New York, Oxford: North-Holland.

Mehrabian, A. (1972). *Nonverbal communication.* Chicago: Aldine; New York: Atherton.

Mehrabian, A., & Friedman, S. L. (1986). An analysis of fidgeting and associated individual differences. *Journal of Personality, 54*, 406–429.

Meier, R. P., & Newport, E. L. (1990). Out of the hands of babes: On a possible sign advantage in language acquisition. *Language, 16*, 1–23.

Meltzoff, A. N. (1988). Imitation, objects, tools, and the rudiments of language in human ontogeny. *Human Evolution, 3*, 45–64.

Meltzoff, A. N., & Moore, M. K. (1983). The origins of imitation in infancy: Paradigm, phenomena and theories. In L. Lipsitt (Ed.), *Advances in infancy research* (Vol. 2, pp. 265–301). Norwood, NJ: Ablex.

Meltzoff, A. N., & Moore. M. K. (1989). Imitation in newborn infants: Exploring the range of gestures imitated and the underlying mechanism. *Developmental Psychology, 25*, 954–962.

Messer, D. J. (1978). The integration of mothers' referential speech with joint play. *Child Development, 49*, 781–787.

Messer, D. J. (1981). Non-linguistic information which could assist the young child's interpretation of adult speech. In W. P. Robinson (Ed.), *Communication in development* (pp. 39–62). New York: Academic Press.

Messer, D. J. (1983). The redundancy between adult speech and nonverbal behavior: A contribution to acquisition? In R. M. Golinkoff (Ed.), *The transition from prelinguistic to linguistic communication* (pp. 147–165). Hillsdale, NJ: Lawrence Erlbaum.

Messer, D. J., & Vietze, P. M. (1984). Timing and transitions in mother–infant gaze. *Infant Behavior and Development, 7,* 169–181.

Messer, D. J., & Vietze, P. M. (1988). Does mutual influence occur during mother–infant social gaze? *Infant Behavior and Development, 11,* 97–110.

Meyerson, I. (1986). Etude du mouvement et du geste chez l'homme. *Journal de Psychologie Normale et Pathologique, 81,* 103–129.

Michael, G., & Willis, F. N. (1968). The development of gestures as a function of social class, education and sex. *Psychological Record, 18,* 515–519.

Miller, L., & Bart, W. M. (1986). Patterns of nonverbal behavior among adolescents responding to a formal reasoning task. *Journal of Psychology, 120,* 51–57.

Miller, L. C., Lechner, R. E., & Rugs, D. (1985). Development of conversational responsiveness: Preschoolers' use of responsive listener cues and relevant comments. *Developmental Psychology, 21,* 473–480.

Montagner, H., Henry, J. C., Lombardot, M., Restoin, A., Bolzoni, D., Durand, M., Humbert, Y., & Moyse, A. (1978). Behavioural profiles and corticosteroid excretion rhythms in young children. Part 1: nonverbal communication and setting up of behavioural profiles in children from 1 to 6 years. In V. Reynolds & N. G. Blurton-Jones (Eds.), *Human behaviour and adaptation* (pp. 207–228). London: Taylor & Francis.

Montepare, J. M., Goldstein, S. B., & Clausen, A. (1987). The identification of emotion from gait information. *Journal of Nonverbal Behavior, 11,* 33–42.

Montepare, J. M., & Zebrowitz-McArthur, M. (1988). Impressions of people created by age-related qualities of their gaits. *Journal of Personality and Social Psychology, 55,* 547–556.

Moore, M. M. (1985). Nonverbal courtship patterns in women: Context and consequences. *Ethology and Sociobiology, 6,* 237–247.

Moore, M. M., & Butler, D. L. (1989). Predictive aspects of nonverbal courtship behavior in women. *Semiotica, 76,* 205–215.

Morais, J. (1982). The two sides of cognition. In J. Mehler, M. Garrett, & E. Walkes (Eds.), *Perspectives in mental representations* (pp. 277–309). Hillsdale, NJ: Lawrence Erlbaum.

Morgan, B. J. T., Simpson, M. J. A., Hanby, J. P., & Hall-Craggs, J. (1976). Visualizing interaction and sequential data in animal behaviour: Theory and application of cluster-analysis methods. *Behaviour, 56,* 1–43.

Morgan, M. J., & McManus, I. C. (1988). The relationship between brainedness and handedness. In F. C. Rose, R. Whurr, & M. A. Wyke (Eds.), *Aphasia* (pp. 85–130). London: Whurr.

Morris, D., Collett, P., Marsch, P., & O'Shaughnessy, M. (1979). *Gestures, their origins and distribution.* London: J. Cape.

Morsbach, H. (1973). Aspects of nonverbal communication in Japan. *Journal of Nervous and Mental Disease, 157,* 262–277.

Mundy, P., Sigman, M., Kasari, C., & Yirmiya, N. (1988). Nonverbal communication skills in Down syndrome children. *Child Development, 59,* 235–249.

Mundy, R., Sigman, M., Ungerer, J., & Sherman, T. (1986). Defining the social deficits of autism: The contribution of nonverbal communication measures. *Journal of Child Psychology and Psychiatry, 27,* 657–669.

Mundy, P., Sigman, M., Ungerer, J., & Sherman, T. (1987). Nonverbal communication and play correlates of language development in autistic children. *Journal of Autism and Developmental Disorders, 17,* 349–364.

Murphy, C. M. (1978). Pointing in a context of a shared activity. *Child Development, 49,* 371–380.

Murphy, C. M., & Messer, D. J. (1977). Mothers, infants and pointing: A study of a gesture. In H. R. Schaffer (Ed.), *Studies in mother–infant interaction* (pp. 325–354). New York: Academic Press.

Murray, L., & Trevarthen, C. (1986). The infant's role in mother–infant communication. *Journal of Child Language, 13,* 15–29.

Natale, M., & Bolan, R. (1980). The effect of Velten's mood induction procedure for depression on hand movement and head-down posture. *Motivation and Emotion, 4,* 323–333.

Nelson, K. (1987). What's in a name? Reply to Seidenberg & Petitto. *Journal of Experimental Psychology: General, 116,* 293–296.

Nelson, K. (1988). Chimp communication without conditioning. *Behavioral and Brain Sciences, 11,* 461–462.

Nespoulous, J. L. (1979). Geste et discours: Étude du comportement gestuel spontané d'un aphasique en situation de dialogue. *Etudes de Linguistique Appliquée, 2,* 100–121.

Ninio, A., & Bruner, J. S. (1978). The achievement and antecedents of labelling. *Journal of Child Language, 5,* 1–15.

Nishida, T. (1980). The leaf-clipping display: A newly discovered expressive gesture in wild chimpanzees. *Journal of Human Evolution, 9,* 117–128.

Noirot, E. (1983). Réflexions sur les stratégies de recherche dans le domaine du développement humain précoce. *Enfance, 1*(2), 169–195.

Noirot, E. (1989). Communication par mouvements de tête: Conséquences et signification. *Archives de Psychologie, 57,* 215–252.

Noller, P. (1985). Video primacy – A further look. *Journal of Nonverbal Behavior, 9,* 28–47.

O'Connor, B. P., & Gifford, R. (1988). A test among models of nonverbal immediacy reactions: Arousal labeling, discrepancy-arousal, and social cognition. *Journal of Nonverbal Behavior, 12,* 6–33.

O'Leary, M. J., & Gallois, C. (1985). The last ten turns: Behavior and sequencing in friend's and stranger's conversational endings. *Journal of Nonverbal Behavior, 9,* 8–27.

Olswang, L. B., & Carpenter, R. L. (1982). The ontogenesis of agent. I. Cognitive notion. II. Linguistic expression. *Journal of Speech and Hearing Research, 25,* 297–306 & 306–314.

Oster, H., Daily, L., & Goldenthal, P. (1989). Processing facial affect. In A. W. Young & H. D. Ellis (Eds.), *Handbook of research on face processing* (pp. 107–161). Amsterdam: North-Holland.

O'Sullivan, M., Ekman, P., Friesen, W., & Scherer, K. (1985). Why you say it and how you say it: The contribution of speech content and voice quality to judgment of others. *Journal of Personality and Social Psychology, 48,* 54–62.

Overton, W. F., & Jackson, J. P. (1973). The representation of imagined objects in action sequences: A developmental study. *Child Development, 44,* 309–314.

Packer, M. J. (1983). Communication in early infancy: Three common assumptions examined and found inadequate. *Human Development, 26,* 233–248.

Page, J. L. (1985). Relative translucency of ASL signs representing three semantic classes. *Journal of Speech and Hearing Disorders, 50,* 241–247.

Parker, S. T. (1985). A social-technological model for the evolution of language. *Current Anthropology, 26,* 617–639.

Patterson, C. J., Cosgrove, J. M., & O'Brien, R. G. (1980). Nonverbal indicants of comprehension and noncomprehension in children. *Developmental Psychology, 16,* 38–48.

Patterson, F. G. (1978). The gestures of a gorilla: Language acquisition in another pongid. *Brain and Language, 5,* 72–97.

Patterson, F. G., Tanner, J., & Mayer, N. (1988). Pragmatic analysis of gorilla utterances: Early communicative development in gorilla Koko. *Journal of Pragmatics, 12,* 35–54.

Patterson, M. L. (1982). A sequential functional model of nonverbal exchange. *Psychological Review, 89,* 231–249.

Patterson, M. L. (1983). *Nonverbal behavior: A functional perspective.* New York: Springer.

Pawlby, S. J. (1977). Imitative interaction. In M. R. Schaffer (Ed.), *Studies in mother–infant interaction* (pp. 203–224). New York: Academic Press.

Pea, R. D. (1980). The development of negation in early child language. In D. R. Olson (Ed.), *The social foundations of language and thought* (pp. 156–186). New York: Norton.

Pearl, M. C., & Schulman, S. R. (1983). Techniques for the analysis of social structures in animal societies. *Advances in the Study of Behavior, 13,* 107–146.

Pechman, T., & Deutsch, W. (1982). The development of verbal and nonverbal devices for reference. *Journal of Experimental Child Psychology, 34,* 330–341.

Peery, J. C. (1980). Neonate–adult head movement: No and yes revisited. *Developmental Psychology 16,* 245–250.

Peirce, C. S. (1974). Elements of logic. In C. Hartshorne & P. Weiss (Eds.), *Collected papers of Charles Sanders Peirce* (Vols. 1 & 2). Cambridge: Belknap Press of the Harvard University Press. (Originally published 1932)

Perkins, R. E. (1986). The checklist of sex role motor behavior applied to a European population in a natural setting. *Behavioral Assessment, 8,* 285–300.

Perrett, D. I., Harries, M. H., Bevan, R., Thomas, S., Benson, P. J., Mistlin, A. J., Chitty, A. J., Hietanen, J. K., & Ortega, J. E. (1989). Frameworks of analysis for the neural representation of animate objects and actions. *Journal of Experimental Biology, 146,* 87–113.

Petersen, M. R. (1982). The perception of species-specific vocalizations by primates: A conceptual framework. In C. T. Snowdon, C. H. Brown, & M. R. Petersen (Eds.), *Primate communication* (pp. 171–211). Cambridge: Cambridge University Press.

Peterson, L. N., & Kirshner, H. S. (1981). Gestural impairment and gestural ability in aphasia: A review. *Brain and Language, 14,* 333–348.

Petitto, L. (1987). On the autonomy of language and gesture: Evidence from the acquisition of personal pronouns in American Sign Language. *Cognition, 27,* 1–52.

Petitto, L. (1988). "Language" in the prelinguistic child. In F. Kessel (Ed.), *The development of language and language researchers: Essays in honor of Roger Brown* (pp. 187–221). Hillsdale, NJ: Lawrence Erlbaum.

Petty, R. E., & Cacioppo, J. T. (1983). The role of bodily response in attitude measurement and change. In J. T. Cacioppo & R. E. Petty (Eds.), *Social psychophysiology, a source book* (pp. 51–101). New York: Guilford.

Petty, R. E., Wells, G. L., Heesacker, M., Brock, T. C., & Cacioppo, J. T. (1983). The effect of recipient posture on persuasion: A cognitive response analysis. *Personality and Social Psychology Bulletin, 9,* 209–222.

Piaget, J. (1951). *Play, dreams, and imitation in childhood.* New York: Norton. (Original work published 1946)

Piaget, J. (1952). *The origins of intelligence in children* (Margaret Cook, Trans.). New York: International Universities Press. (Original work published 1936)

Piaget, J. (1954). *The child's construction of reality.* New York: Basic Books. (Original work published 1937)

Plooij, F. X. (1978). Some basic traits of language in wild chimpanzees? In

A. Lock (Ed.), *Action, gesture and symbol: The emergence of language* (pp. 111–131). New York: Academic Press.

Plooij, F. X. (1979). How wild chimpanzee babies trigger the onset of mother–infant play and what the mother makes of it. In M. Bullowa (Ed.), *Before speech: The beginning of interpersonal communication* (pp. 223–243). Cambridge: Cambridge University Press.

Plume, K. H., Zelhart, P. F., & Markley, R. P. (1985). Nonverbal communication between motor vehicle drivers: Waves in Kansas. *Psychological Record, 35,* 315–321.

Poizner, H., & Battison, R. (1980). Cerebral asymmetry for sign language: Clinical and experimental evidence. In H. Lane & F. Grosjean (Eds.), *Recent perspectives on American Sign Language* (pp. 79–101). Hillsdale, NJ: Lawrence Erlbaum.

Poizner, H., Klima, E. S., & Bellugi, U. (1987). *What the hands reveal about the brain.* Cambridge: MIT Press.

Poling, T. H. (1978). Sex differences, dominance and physical attractiveness in the use of nonverbal emblems. *Psychological Reports, 43,* 1087–1092.

Polsky, R. H., & McGuire, M. T. (1979). An ethological analysis of manic-depressive disorders. *Journal of Nervous and Mental Disease, 167,* 56–65.

Posner, M. I., Nissen, M. J., & Klein, R. M. (1976). Visual dominance: An information processing account of its origins and significance. *Psychological Review, 83,* 157–171.

Premack, D. (1985). "Gavagai!" or the future history of the animal language controversy. *Cognition, 19,* 207–296.

Premack, D., & Woodruff, G. (1978). Does the chimpanzee have a theory of mind? *Behavioral and Brain Sciences, 1,* 515–526.

Prutting, C. A., & Kirchner, D. M. (1987). A clinical appraisal of the pragmatic aspects of language. *Journal of Speech and Hearing Disorders, 52,* 105–119.

Quinn, J. G., & Ralston, G. E. (1986). Movement and attention in visual working memory. *Quarterly Journal of Experimental Psychology, 38A,* 689–703.

Radeau, M., & Bertelson, P. (1987). Auditory-visual interaction and the timing of inputs: Thomas (1941) revisited. *Psychological Research, 49,* 17–22.

Ragsdale, J. D., & Silvia, C. F. (1982). Distribution of kinesic hesitation phenomena in spontaneous speech. *Language and Speech, 25,* 185–190.

Rapcsak, S. Z., Croswell, S. C., & Rubens, A.B. (1989). Apraxia in Alzheimer's disease. *Neurology, 39,* 664–669.

Ratner, N., & Bruner, J. S. (1978). Games, social exchanges and the acquisition of language. *Journal of Child Language, 5,* 391–401.

Read, B., & Cherry, L. (1978). Preschool children's production of directive forms. *Discourse Processes, 1,* 233–245.

Reeder, G. D., & Fulks, J. L. (1980). When actions speak louder than words: Implications schemata and the attribution of ability. *Journal of Experimental Social Psychology, 16,* 33–46.

Reisberg, D., McLean, J., & Goldfield, A. (1987). Easy to hear but hard to understand: A lipreading advantage with intact auditory stimuli. In B. Dodd & R. Campbell (Eds.), *Hearing by eye: The psychology of lipreading* (pp. 97–113). Hove, England: Lawrence Erlbaum.

Reithinger, N. (1987). Generating referring expressions and pointing gestures. In G. Kempen (Ed.), *Natural language generation: New results in artificial intelligence, psychology and linguistics* (pp. 71–81). Dordrecht: M. Nijhoff.

Rekers, G. A., Sanders, J. A., & Strauss, C. C. (1981). Developmental differentiation of adolescent body gestures. *Journal of Genetic Psychology, 138,* 123–131.

Ricci-Bitti, P. E. (1976). Communication by gesture in South and North Italians. *Italian Journal of Psychology, 3,* 117–125.

Ricci-Bitti, P. E., Argyle, M., & Giovannini, D. (1979). Emotional arousal and gestures. *Italian Journal of Psychology, 6*, 59–67.

Richer, J. (1976). The social avoidance behaviour of autistic children. *Animal Behaviour, 24*, 898–906.

Riddoch, M. J., & Humphreys, G. W. (1987). Visual object processing in optic aphasia: A case of semantic access agnosia. *Cognitive Neuropsychology, 4*, 131–185.

Riggio, R. E., & Friedman, H. S. (1986). Impression formation: The role of expressive behavior. *Journal of Personality and Social Psychology, 50*, 421–427.

Riggio, R. E., Friedman, H. S., & DiMatteo, M. R. (1981). Nonverbal greetings: Effects of the situation and personality. *Personality and Social Psychology Bulletin, 7*, 682–689.

Riggio, R. E., Tucker, J., & Widaman, K. F. (1987). Verbal and nonverbal cues as mediators of deception ability. *Journal of Nonverbal Behavior, 11*, 126–145.

Rimé, B. (1982). The elimination of visible behaviour from social interactions: Effects on verbal, nonverbal and interpersonal variables. *European Journal of Social Psychology, 12*, 113–129.

Rimé, B. (1983). Nonverbal communication or nonverbal behavior? Towards a cognitive–motor theory of nonverbal behavior. In W. Doise & S. Moscovici (Eds.), *Current issues in European social psychology* (Vol. 1, pp. 85–135). Cambridge: Cambridge University Press.

Rimé, B., Bouvy, H., Leborgne, B., & Rouillon, F. (1978). Psychopathy and nonverbal behavior in interpersonal situations. *Journal of Abnormal Psychology, 87*, 636–647.

Rimé, B., & Gaussin, J. (1982). Sensibilité des comportements non verbaux aux variations de la densité de communication. *L'Année Psychologique, 82*, 173–187.

Rimé, B., & Schiaratura, L. (1991). Gesture and speech. In R. Feldman & B. Rimé (Eds.), *Fundamentals of nonverbal behavior* (pp. 239–281). New York: Cambridge University Press.

Rimé,. B., Schiaratura, L., Hupet, M., & Ghysselinckx, A. (1984). Effects of relative immobilization on the speaker's nonverbal behavior and on the dialogue imagery level. *Motivation and Emotion, 8*, 311–325.

Riseborough, M. G. (1981). Physiographic gestures as decoding facilitators: Three experiments exploring a neglected facet of communication. *Journal of Nonverbal Behavior, 5*, 172–183.

Riseborough, M. G. (1982). Meaning in movement: An investigation into the interrelationship of physiographic gestures and speech in seven-year-olds. *British Journal of Psychology, 73*, 497–503.

Riskind, J. H. (1984). They stoop to conquer: Guiding and self-regulatory functions of physical posture after success and failure. *Journal of Personality and Social Psychology, 47*, 479–493.

Riskind, J. H., & Gotay, C. C. (1982). Physical posture: Could it have regulatory or feedback effects on motivation and emotion? *Motivation and Emotion, 6*, 273–298.

Ristau, C. A., & Robbins, D. (1982). Language in the great apes: A critical review. *Advances in the Study of Behavior, 12*, 141–255.

Rocissano, L., & Yatchmink, Y. (1984). Joint attention in mother–toddler interaction: A study of individual variation. *Merrill-Palmer Quarterly, 30*, 11–31.

Rodger, R. S., & Rosenbrugh, D. (1979). Computing a grammar for sequences of behavioural acts. *Animal Behaviour, 27*, 737–749.

Rodgon, M. M., & Kurdek, L. A. (1977). Vocal and gestural imitation in 8-, 14- and 20-month-old children. *Journal of Genetic Psychology, 131*, 115–123.

Rögels, P. L. J. M., Roelen, E., & Van Meel, J. M. (1990). The function of self-touching, posture shift, and motor discharge in children from 3 to 6 years of age. *Perceptual and Motor Skills, 70,* 1169–1178.

Rogers, W. T. (1978). The contribution of kinesic illustrators toward the comprehension of verbal behavior within utterances. *Human Communication Research, 5,* 54–62.

Rogers, W. T. (1979). The relevance of body motion cues to both functional and dysfunctional communicative behavior. *Journal of Communication Disorders, 12,* 273–282.

Röhrich, L. (1960). Gebärdensprache und Sprachgebärde. In W. D. Hand & G. O. Arlt (Eds.), *Humaniora, essays in literature, folklore, bibliography, honoring H. Taylor* (pp. 121–149). Locust Valley, NY: J. J. Augustin.

Roper, R., & Hinde, R. A. (1978). Social behavior in a play group: Consistency and complexity. *Child Development, 49,* 570–579.

Roper, T. J. (1980). "Induced" behaviour as evidence of nonspecific motivational effects. In F. M. Toates & T. R. Halliday (Eds.), *Analysis of motivational processes* (pp. 221–242). New York: Academic Press.

Roper, T. J. (1984). Response of thirsty rats to absence of water: Frustration, desinhibition or compensation? *Animal Behaviour, 32,* 1225–1235.

Rosenfeld, H. M. (1966a). Approval seeking and approval inducing functions of verbal and nonverbal response in dyads. *Journal of Personality and Social Psychology, 4,* 597–605.

Rosenfeld, H. M. (1966b). Instrumental affiliative functions of facial and gestural expression. *Journal of Personality and Social Psychology, 4,* 65–72.

Rosenfeld, H. M. (1967). Nonverbal reciprocation of approval: An experimental analysis. *Journal of Experimental Social Psychology, 3,* 102–111.

Rosenfeld, H. M. (1978). Conversational control functions of nonverbal behavior. In A. W. Siegman & S. Feldstein (Eds.), *Nonverbal behavior and communication* (pp. 291–328). Hillsdale, NJ: Lawrence Erlbaum.

Rosenfeld, H. M. (1982). Measurement of body motion and orientation. In K. R. Scherer & P. Ekman (Eds.), *Handbook of methods in nonverbal behavior research* (pp. 199–286). Cambridge: Cambridge University Press.

Rosenfeld, H. M., & Hancks, M. (1980). The nonverbal context of verbal listener responses. In M. R. Key (Ed.), *The relationship of verbal and nonverbal communication* (pp. 193–206). The Hague: Mouton.

Rosenfeld, H. M., Shea, M., & Greenbaum, P. (1979). Facial emblems of "right" and "wrong": Topographical analysis and derivation of a recognition test. *Semiotica, 26,* 15–33. (Reprinted in A. Kendon [Ed.], *Nonverbal communication, interaction, and gesture* [pp. 483–501]. The Hague: Mouton, 1981)

Rosenthal, R. (1982). Conducting judgment studies. In K. R. Scherer & P. Ekman (Eds.), *Handbook of methods in nonverbal behavior research* (pp. 287–361). Cambridge: Cambridge University Press.

Rosenthal, R., & DePaulo, B. M. (1979). Sex differences in eavesdropping of nonverbal cues. *Journal of Personality and Social Psychology, 37,* 273–295.

Rothi, L. J. G., & Heilman, K. M. (1984). Acquisition and retention of gestures by apraxic patients. *Brain and Cognition, 3,* 426–437.

Rothi, L. J. G., Heilman, K. M., & Watson, R. T. (1985). Pantomime comprehension and ideomotor apraxia. *Journal of Neurology, Neurosurgery, and Psychiatry, 48,* 207–210.

Rothi, L. J. G., Mack, L., & Heilman, K. M. (1986). Pantomime agnosia. *Journal of Neurology, Neurosurgery, and Psychiatry, 49,* 451–454.

Rowell, T. E., & Olson, D. K. (1983). Alternative mechanisms of social organization in monkeys. *Behaviour, 86,* 31–54.

Roy, E. A. (1982). Action and performance. In A. W. Ellis (Ed.), *Normality and pathology in cognitive functions* (pp. 295–298). London: Academic Press.

Ruggieri, V., Celli, C., & Crescenzi, A. (1982). Self-contact and gesturing in different stimulus situations: Relationships with cerebral dominance. *Perceptual and Motor Skills, 54,* 1003–1010.

Rutter, D. R. (1977). Visual interaction and speech patterning in remitted and acute schizophrenic patients. *British Journal of Social and Clinical Psychology, 16,* 357–361.

Rutter, D. R. (1984). *Looking and seeing: The role of visual communication in social interaction.* New York: Wiley.

Rutter, D. R. (1987). *Communicating by telephone.* Oxford: Pergamon.

Rutter, D. R., & Durkin, K. (1987). Turn-taking in mother–infant interaction: An examination of vocalization and gaze. *Developmental Psychology, 23,* 54–61.

Rutter, D. R., & O'Brien, P. (1980). Social interaction in withdrawn and aggressive maladjusted girls: A study of gaze. *Journal of Child Psychology and Psychiatry, 21,* 59–66.

Rutter, D. R., & Stephenson, G. M. (1977). The role of visual communication in synchronizing conversation. *European Journal of Social Psychology, 7,* 29–37.

Rutter, D. R., Stephenson, G. M., & Dewey, M. E. (1981). Visual communication and the content and style of conversation. *British Journal of Social and Clinical Psychology, 20,* 41–52.

Sackett, G. P. (1987). Analysis of sequential social interaction data: Some issues, recent developments, and a causal inference model. In J. D. Osofsky (Ed.), *Handbook of infant development* (2nd ed., pp. 855–878). New York: Wiley.

Sackin, S., & Thelen, E. (1984). An ethological study of peaceful associative outcomes to conflict in preschool children. *Child Development, 55,* 1098–1102.

Sacks, H., Schegloff, E. A., & Jefferson, G. A. (1974). A simplest systematics for the organization of turn-taking for conversation. *Language, 50,* 696–735.

Sade, D. S. (1972). Sociometrics of *Macaca mulatta:* I. Linkages and cliques in grooming matrices. *Folia Primatologica, 18,* 196–223.

Safadi, M., & Valentine, C. A. (1990). Contrastive analyses of American and Arab nonverbal and paralinguistic communication. *Semiotica, 82,* 269–292.

Sainsbury, P., & Wood, E. (1977). Measuring gesture: Its cultural and clinical correlates. *Psychological Medicine, 7,* 63–72.

Saitz, R., & Cervenka, E. (1973). *Handbook of gestures: Colombia and the United States* (2nd ed.). The Hague: Mouton.

Salmaso, D., & Longoni, A. M. (1985). Problems in the assessment of hand preference. *Cortex, 21,* 533–549.

Salz, E., & Dixon, D. (1982). Let's pretend: The role of motoric imagery in memory for sentences and words. *Journal of Experimental Child Psychology, 34,* 77–92.

Sanders. R. J. (1985). Teaching apes to ape language: Explaining the imitative and nonimitative signing of a chimpanzee (*Pan troglodytes*). *Journal of Comparative Psychology, 99,* 197–210.

Sapir, E. (1949). The unconscious patterning of behavior in society. In D. G. Mandelbaum (Ed.), *Selected writings of Edward Sapir in language, culture, and personality.* Berkeley and Los Angeles: University of California Press. (Originally published 1927)

Savage-Rumbaugh, S. (1987). Communication, symbolic communication, and language. *Journal of Experimental Psychology: General, 116,* 288–292.

Savage-Rumbaugh, S., McDonald, K., Sevcik, R. A., Hopkins, W. D., & Rubert, E. (1986). Spontaneous symbol acquisition and communicative use by pigmy chimpanzees (*Pan paniscus*). *Journal of Experimental Psychology: General, 115,* 211–235.

Savage-Rumbaugh, E. S., Pate, J. L., Lawson, J., Smith, S. T., & Rosenbaum, S. (1983). Can a chimpanzee make a statement? *Journal of Experimental Psychology: General, 112,* 457–492.

Savage-Rumbaugh, E. S., Wilkerson, B. J., & Bakeman, R. (1977). Spontaneous gestural communication among conspecifics in the pigmy chimpanzee (*Pan paniscus*). In G. H. Bourne (Ed.), *Progress in ape research* (pp. 97–116). New York: Academic Press.

Savin-Williams, R. C., Small, S. A., & Zeldin, R. S. (1981). Dominance and altruism among adolescent males: A comparison of ethological and psychological methods. *Ethology and Sociobiology, 2,* 167–176.

Saxe, G. B., & Kaplan, R. (1981). Gesture in early counting: A developmental analysis. *Perceptual and Motor Skills, 53,* 851–854.

Scaife, M., & Bruner, J. S. (1975). The capacity for joint visual attention in the infant. *Nature, 253,* 265–266.

Schaffer, H. R., & Crook, C. K. (1980). Child compliance and maternal control techniques. *Developmental Psychology, 16,* 54–61.

Schaffer, H. R., Hepburn, A., & Collis, G. M. (1983). Verbal and nonverbal aspects of mothers' directives. *Journal of Child Language, 10,* 337–355.

Scheflen, A. E. (1964). The significance of posture in communication systems. *Psychiatry, 27,* 316–331.

Scheflen, A. E. (1965). Quasi-courtship behavior in psychotherapy. *Psychiatry, 28,* 245–257.

Scheflen, A. E. (1968). Human communication: Behavioral programs and their integration in interaction. *Behavioral Science, 13,* 44–55.

Scheflen, A. E., & Scheflen, A. (1972). *Body language and social order: Communication as behavioral control.* Englewood Cliffs, NJ: Prentice-Hall.

Schegloff, E. A. (1984). On some gestures' relation to talk. In J. H. Atkinson & J. Heritage (Eds.), *Structures of social action: Studies in conversation analysis* (pp. 266–296). Cambridge: Cambridge University Press.

Scherer, K. R. (1979). Nonlinguistic vocal indicators of emotion and psychopathology. In C. E. Izard (Ed.), *Emotion in personality and psychopathology* (pp. 495–529). New York: Plenum.

Scherer, K. R. (1984). The nonverbal.dimension: A fad, a field, or a behavioral modality? In H. Tajfel (Ed.), *The social dimension: European developments in social psychology* (Vol. 1, pp. 160–183). Cambridge: Cambridge University Press.

Scherer, K. R. (1985). Vocal affect signalling: A comparative approach. *Advances in the study of behavior, 15,* 189–244.

Scherer, K. R. (1986). Vocal affect expression: A review and a model for future research. *Psychological Bulletin, 99,* 143–165.

Scherer, K. R., Scherer, U., Hall, J. A., & Rosenthal, R. (1977). Differential attribution of personality based on multichannel presentation of verbal and nonverbal cues. *Psychological Research, 39,* 221–247.

Scherer, K. R., & Wallbott, H. G. (1985). Analysis of nonverbal behavior. In T. A. Van Dijk (Ed.), *Handbook of discourse analysis* (Vol. 2, pp. 199–230). New York: Academic Press.

Schiffrin, D. (1974). Handwork as ceremony: The case of the handshake. *Semiotica, 12,* 189–202. (Reprinted in A. Kendon [Ed.], *Nonverbal communication, interaction, and gesture* [pp. 237–250]. The Hague: Mouton, 1981)

Schmidt, R. A. (1988). *Motor control and learning: A behavioral emphasis* (2nd ed.) Champaign, IL.: Human Kinetics Publishers.

Schmidt, R. A., Gielen, S. C. A. M., & Van den Heuvel, P. J. M. (1984). The locus of intersensory facilitation in reaction time. *Acta Psychologica, 57*, 145–164.

Schmitt, J. C. (1990). *La raison des gestes dans l'Occident médiéval.* Paris: Gallimard.

Schnur, E., & Shatz, M. (1984). The role of maternal gesturing in conversations with one-year-olds. *Journal of Child Language, 11*, 29–41.

Schwartz, B., Tesser, A., & Powell, E. (1982). Dominance cues in nonverbal behavior. *Social Psychology Quarterly, 45*, 114–120.

Schwartz, L. M., Foa, U. G., & Foa, E. B. (1983). Multichannel nonverbal communication: Evidence for combinatory rules. *Journal of Personality and Social Psychology, 45*, 274–281.

Scott, P. A., & Charteris, J. (1986). Gesture identification: Southern African ratings compared with European responses. *International Journal of Psychology, 21*, 753–768.

Sebeok, T. A. (1972). *Perspectives in zoosemiotics.* The Hague: Mouton.

Seidenberg, M. S., & Petitto, L. A. (1979). Signing behavior in apes: A critical review. *Cognition, 7*, 177–215.

Seidenberg, M. S., & Petitto, L. A. (1987). Communication, symbolic communication and language: Comment on Savage-Rumbaugh et al. (1986). *Journal of Experimental Psychology: General, 116*, 279–296.

Seiss, R. (1965). Beobachtungen zur Frage der Uebersprungbewegungen in menschlichen Verhalten. *Psychologische Beiträge, 8*, 3–97.

Sergent, J. (1983). The role of the input in visual hemispheric asymmetries. *Psychological Bulletin, 93*, 481–514.

Seyfarth, R. M., Cheney, D. L., & Marler, P. (1980). Vervet monkeys' alarm calls: Semantic communication in a free ranging primate. *Animal Behaviour, 28*, 1070–1094.

Shallice, T. (1988a). *From neuropsychology to mental structure.* Cambridge: Cambridge University Press.

Shallice, T. (1988b). Specialisation within the semantic system. *Cognitive Neuropsychology, 5*, 133–142.

Shatz, M. (1982). On mechanisms of language acquisition: Can features of the communicative environment account for development? In E. Wanner & L. R. Gleitman (Eds.), *Language acquisition: The state of the art* (pp. 102–127). Cambridge: Cambridge University Press.

Shatz, M. (1983). Contributions of mother and mind to the development of communicative competence: A status report. In M. Perlmutter (Ed.), *Minnesota symposium on child psychology* (Vol. 17, pp. 33–59). Hillsdale, NJ: Lawrence Erlbaum.

Shatz, M. (1987). Bootstrapping operations in child language. In K. E. Nelson & A. Van Kleck (Eds.), *Children's language* (Vol. 6, pp. 1–22). Hillsdale, NJ: Lawrence Erlbaum.

Sherzer, J. (1973). Verbal and nonverbal deixis: The pointed lip gesture among the San Blas Cuna. *Language in Society, 2*, 117–131.

Shore, C., O'Connell, B., & Bates, E. (1984). First sentences in language and symbolic play. *Developmental Psychology, 20*, 872–880.

Short, J., Williams, E., & Christie, B. (1976). *The social psychology of telecommunications.* New York: Wiley.

Shrout, P. E., & Fiske, D. W. (1981). Nonverbal behaviors and social evaluation. *Journal of Personality, 49*, 115–128.

Shutter, R. (1979). A study of nonverbal communication among Jews and Protestants. *Journal of Social Psychology, 109*, 31–41.

Siegman, A. W., & Reynolds, M. A. (1983a). Effects of mutual invisibility and topical intimacy on verbal fluency in dyadic communication. *Journal of Psycholinguistic Research, 12,* 443–455.

Siegman, A. W., & Reynolds, M. A. (1983b). Speaking without seeing, or the effect of interviewer absence on interviewee disclosure time. *Journal of Psycholinguistic Research, 12,* 595–602.

Sigelman, C. K., Adams, R. A., Meeks, S. R., & Purcell, M. A. (1986). Children's nonverbal responses to a physically disabled person. *Journal of Nonverbal Behavior, 10,* 173–186.

Sigman, M., Mundy, P., Sherman, T., & Ungerer, J. (1986). Social interactions of autistic, mentally retarded, and normal children and their caregivers. *Journal of Child Psychology and Psychiatry, 27,* 647–656.

Ska, B., & Nespoulous, J. L. (1987). Pantomimes and aging. *Journal of Clinical and Experimental Neuropsychology, 9,* 754–766.

Slater, P. J. B. (1978). Data collection. In P. W. Colgan (Ed.), *Quantitative ethology* (pp. 7–24). New York: Wiley.

Slater, P. J. B. (1983). The study of communication. In T. R. Halliday & P. J. B. Slater, *Animal behaviour: Vol. 2. Communication* (pp. 9–42). Oxford: Blackwell.

Sluckin, A. M., & Smith, P. K. (1977). Two approaches to the concept of dominance in preschool children. *Child Development, 48,* 917–923.

Smith, A., McFarland, D. H., & Weber, C. M. (1986). Interactions between speech and finger movements: An exploration of the dynamic pattern perspective. *Journal of Speech and Hearing Research, 29,* 471–480.

Smith, L. (1987a). Nonverbal competency in aphasic stroke patients' conversation. *Aphasiology, 1,* 127–139.

Smith, L. (1987b). Fluency and severity of aphasia and nonverbal competency. *Aphasiology, 1,* 291–295.

Smith, P. K. (1973). Temporal clusters and individual differences in the behaviour of preschool children. In R. P. Michael & J. H. Crook (Eds.), *Comparative ecology and behaviour of primates* (pp. 751–798). New York: Academic Press.

Smith, P. K., & Connolly, K. J. (1980). *The ecology of preschool behaviour.* Cambridge: Cambridge University Press.

Smith, W. J. (1977). *The behavior of communicating: An ethological approach.* Cambridge: Harvard University Press.

Smith, W. J., Chase, J., & Lieblich, A. K. (1974). Tongue showing: A facial display of humans and other primates species. *Semiotica, 11,* 201–246. (Reprinted in A. Kendon [Ed.], *Nonverbal communication, interaction, and gesture* [pp. 503–548]. The Hague: Mouton, 1981)

Smyth, M. M., Pearson, N. A., & Pendleton, L. R. (1988). Movement and working memory: Patterns and positions in space. *Quarterly Journal of Experimental Psychology, 40A,* 497–514.

Smyth, M. M., & Pendleton, L. R. (1989). Working memory for movements. *Quarterly Journal of Experimental Psychology, 41A,* 235–250.

Smyth, M. M., & Pendleton, L. R. (1990). Space and movement in working memory. *Quarterly Journal of Experimental Psychology, 42A,* 291–304.

Sogon, S., & Masutani, M. (1989). Identification of emotion from body movements: A cross-cultural study of Americans and Japanese. *Psychological Reports, 65,* 35–46.

Sousa-Poza, J. F., & Rohrberg, R. (1977). Body movement in relation to type of information (person- and nonperson-oriented) and cognitive style (field dependence). *Human Communication Research, 4,* 19–29.

Sousa-Poza, J. F., Rohrberg, R., & Mercure, A. (1979). Effects of type of information (abstract–concrete) and field dependence on asymmetry of hand movements during speech. *Perceptual and Motor Skills, 48,* 1323–1330.

Sparhawk, C. M. (1978). Contrastive–identificational features of Persian gestures. *Semiotica, 24,* 49–86. (Reprinted in A. Kendon [Ed.], *Nonverbal communication, interaction, and gesture* [pp. 421–458]. The Hague: Mouton, 1981)

Stebbins, G. L., & Ayala, F. J. (1981). Is a new evolutionary synthesis necessary? *Science, 213,* 967–971.

Steele, J. (1989). Hominid evolution and primate social cognition. *Journal of Human Evolution, 18,* 421–432.

Steenhuis, R. E., & Bryden, M. P. (1989). Different dimensions of hand preference that relate to skilled and unskilled activities. *Cortex, 25,* 289–304.

Steingart, I., Grand, S., Margolis, R., Freedman, N., & Buchwald, C. (1976). A study of the representation of anxiety in chronic schizophrenia. *Journal of Abnormal Psychology, 85,* 535–542.

Steklis, H. D. (1985). Primate communication, comparative neurology, and the origin of language re-examined. *Journal of Human Evolution, 14,* 157–163.

Stern, D. N. (1974). The goal and structure of mother–infant play. *Journal of American Child Psychiatry, 13,* 402–421.

Stern, D. N., Bender, E. P. (1974). An ethological study of children approaching a strange adult: Sex differences. In R. C. Friedman, R. M. Richard, & R. D. Vande Wiele (Eds.), *Sex differences in behavior* (pp. 233–254). New York: Wiley.

Stern, D. N., Hofer, L., Haft, W., & Dore, J. (1985). Affect attunement: The sharing of feeling states between mother and infant by means of intermodal fluency. In T. M. Field & N. A. Fox (Eds.), *Social perception in infants* (pp. 249–268). Norwood, NJ: Ablex.

Stern, D. N., Jaffe, J., Beebe B., & Bennett, S. L. (1975). Vocalizing in unison and in alternation: Two modes of communication within the mother–infant dyad. *Annals of the New York Academy of Sciences, 263,* 89–100.

Sternberg, R. J., & Smith, C. (1985). Social intelligence and decoding skills in nonverbal communication. *Social Cognition, 3,* 168–192.

Stevenson, M. B., Roach, M. A., VerHoeve, J. N., & Leavitt, L. A. (1990). Rhythms in the dialogue of infant feeding: Preterm and term infants. *Infant Behavior and Development, 13,* 51–70.

Stier, D. S., & Hall, J. A. (1984). Gender differences in touch: An empirical and theoretical review. *Journal of Personality and Social Psychology, 47,* 440–459.

Stiff, J. B., Miller, G. R., Sleight, C., Mongeau, P., Garlick, R., & Rogan, R. (1989). Explanations for visual cue primacy in judgments of honesty and deceit. *Journal of Personality and Social Psychology, 56,* 555–564.

Stine, E. A. L., Wingfield, A., & Myers, S. D. (1990). Age differences in processing information from television news: The effects of bisensory augmentation. *Journal of Gerontology: Psychological Sciences, 45,* P1–P8.

Stokoe, W. C. (1980). Sign language structure. *Annual Review of Anthropology, 9,* 365–390.

Storrs, D., & Kleinke, C. L. (1990). Evaluation of high and equal status male and female touchers. *Journal of Nonverbal Behavior, 14,* 87–95.

Strayer, F. F. (1980). Current problems in the study of human dominance. In D. R. Omark, F. F. Strayer, & D. G. Freedman (Eds.), *Dominance relations: An ethological view of human conflict and social interaction* (pp. 443–452). New York: Garland.

Strayer, F. F., & Strayer, J. (1976). An ethological analysis of social agonism and dominance relations among preschool children. *Child Development, 47,* 980–989.

Suarez, S. D., & Gallup, G. G. (1986). Face touching in primates: A closer look. *Neuropsychologia, 24,* 597–600.

Summerfield, A. B., & Lake, J. A. (1977). Nonverbal and verbal behaviours associated with parting. *British Journal of Psychology, 68*, 133–136.

Summerfield, Q. (1987). Some preliminaries to a comprehensive account of audio-visual speech perception. In B. Dodd & R. Campbell (Eds.), *Hearing by eye: The psychology of lipreading* (pp. 3–51). Hove, England: Lawrence Erlbaum.

Sutton, D., Trachy, R. E., & Lindeman, R. C. (1981). Vocal and nonvocal discriminative performances in monkeys. *Brain and Language, 14*, 93–105.

Symons, D. K., & Moran, G. (1987). The behavioral dynamics of mutual responsiveness in early face-to-face mother–infant interactions. *Child Development, 58*, 1488–1495.

Tartter, V. C. (1983). The effects of symmetric and asymmetric dyadic visual access on attribution during communication. *Language and Communication, 3*, 1–10.

Taylor, S. E., & Thompson, S. C. (1982). Stalking the elusive "vividness effect." *Psychological Review, 89*, 155–181.

Taylor, T. J., & Cameron, D. (1987). *Analysing conversation: Rules and units in the structure of talk*. Oxford: Pergamon.

Tepper, D. T., & Haase, R. F. (1978). Verbal and nonverbal communication of facilitative conditions. *Journal of Counseling Psychology, 25*, 35–44.

Terrace, H. S., Petitto, L. A., Sanders, R. J., & Bever, T. G. (1979). Can an ape create a sentence? *Science, 206*, 891–902.

Terrace, H. S., Petitto, L. A., Sanders, R. J., & Bever, T. G. (1980). On the grammatical capacity of apes. In K. E. Nelson (Ed.), *Children's language* (Vol. 2, pp. 371–495). New York: Gardner.

Tfouni, L. V., & Klatzky, R. L. (1983). A discourse analysis of deixis: Pragmatic, cognitive and semantic factors in the comprehension of "this," "that," "here" and "there." *Journal of Child Language, 10*, 123–133.

Thal, D., & Bates, E. (1988). Language and gesture in late talkers. *Journal of Speech and Hearing Research, 31*, 115–123.

Thayer, S. (1986). History and strategy of research on social touch. *Journal of Nonverbal Behavior, 10*, 12–28.

Thelen, E. (1979). Rhythmical stereotypies in norman human infants. *Animal Behaviour, 27*, 699–715.

Thelen, E. (1980). Determinants of amounts of stereotyped behavior in normal human infants. *Ethology and Sociobiology, 1*, 141–150.

Thelen, E. (1981a). Kicking, rocking and waving: Contextual analysis of rhythmical stereotypies in normal human infants. *Animal Behaviour, 29*, 3–11.

Thelen, E. (1981b). Rhythmic behavior in infancy: An ethological perspective. *Developmental Psychology, 17*, 237–257.

Thomas, A. P., & Bull, P. (1981). The role of pre-speech posture change in dyadic interaction. *British Journal of Social Psychology, 20*, 105–111.

Thomas, E. A. C., & Martin, J. A. (1976). Analyses of parent–infant interaction. *Psychological Review, 83*, 141–156.

Thompson, L. A., & Massaro, D. W. (1986). Evaluation and integration of speech and pointing gestures during referential understanding. *Journal of Experimental Child Psychology, 42*, 144–168.

Thompson, T. L. (1982). Gaze toward and avoidance of the handicapped: A field experiment: *Journal of Nonverbal Behavior, 6*, 188–196.

Tinbergen, N. (1951). *The study of instinct*. Oxford: Oxford University Press.

Toates, F. M., & Archer, J. (1978). A comparative review of motivational systems using classical control theory. *Animal Behaviour, 26*, 368–380.

Todor, J. I., & Smiley, A. L. (1985). Performance differences between the hands: Implications for studying disruption to limb praxis. In E. A. Roy (Ed.),

Neuropsychological studies of apraxia and related disorders (pp. 309–344). Amsterdam: North-Holland.

Tomasello, M., George, B. L., Kruger, A. C., Jeffrey, M., & Evans, F. A. (1985). The development of gestural communication in young chimpanzees. *Journal of Human Evolution, 14,* 175–186.

Tomasello, M., Gust, D., & Frost, G. T. (1989). A longitudinal investigation of gestural communication in young chimpanzees. *Primates, 30,* 35–50.

Trevarthen, C. (1977). Descriptive analyses of infant communicative behaviour. In H. R. Schaffer (Ed.), *Studies in mother–infant interaction* (pp. 227–270). New York: Academic Press.

Trevarthen, C. (1979). Communication and cooperation in early infancy: A description of primary intersubjectivity. In M. Bullowa (Ed.), *Before speech: The beginning of interpersonal communication* (pp. 321–347). Cambridge: Cambridge: University Press.

Trevarthen, C. (1980). The foundations of intersubjectivity: Development of interpersonal and cooperative understanding in infants. In D. R. Olson (Ed.), *The social foundations of language and thought: Essays in honor of J. S. Bruner* (pp. 316–342). New York: W. W. Norton.

Trevarthen, C. (1986). Form, significance and psychological potential of hand gestures in infants. In J. L. Nespoulous, P. Perron, & A. R. Lecours (Eds.), *The biological foundation of gesture: Motor and semiotic aspects* (pp. 149–202). Hillsdale, NJ: Lawrence Erlbaum.

Trevarthen, C., & Hubley, P. (1978). Secondary intersubjectivity: Confidence, confiding and acts of meaning in the first year. In A. Lock (Ed.), *Action, gesture and symbol: The emergence of language* (pp. 183–229). New York: Academic Press.

Trimboli, A., & Walker, M. B. (1987). Nonverbal dominance in the communication of affect: A myth? *Journal of Nonverbal Behavior, 11,* 180–190.

Tronick, E., Als, H., & Adamson, L. (1979). The communicative structure of face-to-face interaction. In M. Bullowa (Ed.), *Before speech: The beginning of interpersonal communication* (pp. 349–372). Cambridge: Cambridge University Press.

Tronick, E., Als, H., & Brazelton, T. B. (1980). Monadic phases: A structural descriptive analysis of infant–mother face-to-face interaction. *Merrill-Palmer Quarterly, 26,* 3–24.

Tronick, E. Z., & Cohn, J. F. (1989). Infant–mother face-to-face interaction: Age and gender differences in coordination and the occurrence of miscoordination. *Child Development, 60,* 85–92.

Trout, D. L., & Rosenfeld, H. M. (1980). The effect of postural lean and body congruence on the judgment of psychotherapeutic rapport. *Journal of Nonverbal Behavior, 4,* 176–190.

Turner, M. L., LaPointe, L. B., Cantor, J., Reeves, C. H., Griffeth, R. H., & Engle, R. W. (1987). Recency and suffix effects found with auditory presentation and with mouthed visual presentation: They are not the same thing. *Journal of Memory and Language, 26,* 138–164.

Ulrich, G., & Harms, K. (1979). Videoanalytic study of manual kinesics and its lateralization in the course of treatment of depressive syndromes. *Acta Psychiatrica Scandinavica, 59,* 481–492.

Vaid, J., Bellugi, U., & Poizner, H. (1989). Hand dominance for signing: Clues to brain lateralization of language. *Neuropsychologia, 27,* 949–960.

Van Engeland, H., Bodnar, F. A., & Bolhuis, G. (1985). Some qualitative aspects of the social behaviour of autistic children: An ethological approach. *Journal of Child Psychology and Psychiatry, 26,* 879–893.

Van Hoof, J. A. R. A. M. (1982). Categories and sequences of behavior: Methods for description and analysis. In K. R. Scherer & P. Ekman (Eds.), *Handbook of methods in nonverbal behavior research* (pp. 362–439). Cambridge: Cambridge University Press.

Van Meel, J. M. (1982). The nature and development of the kinesic representational system. In B. de Gelder (Ed.), *Knowledge and representation* (pp. 210–216). London: Routledge & Kegan Paul.

Varney, N. R. (1978). Linguistic correlates of pantomime recognition in aphasic patients. *Journal of Neurology, Neurosurgery, and Psychiatry, 41*, 564–568.

Varney, N. R. (1982). Pantomime recognition defect in aphasia: Implications for the concept of asymbolia. *Brain and Language, 15*, 32–39.

Varney, N. R., & Benton, A. L. (1982). Qualitative aspects of pantomime recognition defect in aphasia. *Brain and Cognition, 1*, 132–139.

Varney, N. R., & Damasio, H. (1987). Locus of lesion in impaired pantomime recognition. *Cortex, 23*, 699–703.

Varney, N. R., Damasio, H., & Adler, S. (1989). The role of individual difference in determining the nature of comprehension defects in aphasia. *Cortex, 25*, 47–55.

Vauclair, J. (1990). Primate cognition: From representation to language. In S. T. Parker & K. R. Gibson (Eds.), *"Language" and intelligence in monkeys and apes* (pp. 312–329). Cambridge: Cambridge University Press.

Vaughn, B. E., & Waters, E. (1981). Attention structure, sociometric status and dominance: Interrelation, behavioral correlates and relationships to social competence. *Developmental Psychology, 17*, 275–288.

Venus, C. A., & Canter, G. J. (1987). The effect of redundant cues on comprehension of spoken messages by aphasic adults. *Journal of Communication Disorders, 20*, 477–491.

Vinter, A. (1985a). La capacité d'imitation à la naissance: Elle existe, mais que signifie-t-elle? *Canadian Journal of Psychology, 39*, 16–33.

Vinter, A. (1985b). *L'imitation chez le nouveau-né.* Neuchâtel: Delachaux et Niestlé.

Vinter, A. (1986). The role of movement in eliciting early imitation. *Child Development, 57*, 66–71.

Vogelaar, L. M. E., & Silverman, M. S. (1984). Nonverbal communication in crosscultural counseling: A literature review. *International Journal for the Advancement of Counseling, 7*, 41–57.

Volkmar, F. R., Hoder, E. L., & Cohen, D. J. (1985). Compliance, "negativism," and the effects of treatment structure in autism: A naturalistic, behavioral study. *Journal of Child Psychology and Psychiatry, 26*, 865–877.

Volkmar, F. R., Hoder, E. L., & Siegel, A.E. (1980). Discrepant social communication. *Developmental Psychology, 16*, 495–505.

Volkmar, F. R., & Siegel, A. E. (1979). Young children's responses to discrepant social communication. *Journal of Child Psychology and Psychiatry, 20*, 139–149.

Volterra, V., & Caselli, M. C. (1986). First stage of language acquisition through two modalities in deaf and hearing children. *Italian Journal of Neurological Science, Suppl. 5*, 109–115.

Vrugt, A., & Kerkstra, A. (1984). Sex differences in nonverbal communication. *Semiotica, 50*, 1–41.

Vygotsky, L. S. (1962). *Thought and language.* New York: Wiley. (Second Russian edition published 1956)

Waldron, J. (1975). Judgments of like–dislike from facial expression and body posture. *Perceptual and Motor Skills, 41*, 799–804.

Walker, M. B., & Nazmi, M. K. (1979). Communicating shapes by words and gestures. *Australian Journal of Psychology, 31*, 137–143.

Walker, M. B., & Trimboli, C. (1983). The expressive function of the eye flash. *Journal of Nonverbal Behavior, 8,* 3–13.

Wallbott, H. G. (1982). Contributions of the German "Expression Psychology" to nonverbal communication research: Part III. Gait, gestures, and body movement. *Journal of Nonverbal Behavior, 7,* 20–32.

Wallbott, H. G. (1985). Hand movement quality: A neglected aspect of nonverbal behavior in clinical judgment and person perception. *Journal of Clinical Psychology, 41,* 345–359.

Wallbott, H. G., & Scherer, K. R. (1986). Cues and channels in emotion recognition. *Journal of Personality and Social Psychology, 51,* 690–699.

Walsh, D. G., & Hewitt, J. (1985). Giving men the come-on: Effect of eye contact and smiling in a bar environment. *Perceptual and Motor Skills, 61,* 873–874.

Walters, K. L., & Walk, R. D. (1988). Perception of emotion from moving body cues in photographs. *Bulletin of the Psychonomic Society, 26,* 112–114.

Wampold, B. E. (1984). Tests of dominance in sequential categorical data. *Psychological Bulletin, 96,* 424–429.

Watson, O. M. (1970). *Proxemic behavior: A cross-cultural study.* The Hague: Mouton.

Waxer, P. H. (1977). Nonverbal cues for anxiety: An examination of emotional leakage. *Journal of Abnormal Psychology, 86,* 306–314.

Waxer, P. H. (1981). Channel contribution in anxiety displays. *Journal of Research in Personality, 15,* 44–56.

Waxer, P. H. (1983). Emotional deceit: False words versus false actions. *Motivation and Emotion, 7,* 365–376.

Weiner, S. L., & Ehrlichman, H. (1976). Ocular motility and cognitive processes. *Cognition, 4,* 31–43.

Weisfeld, G. E., & Beresford, J. M. (1982). Erectness of posture as an indicator of dominance or success in humans. *Motivation and Emotion, 6,* 113–131.

Werner, H., & Kaplan, B. (1963). *Symbol formation: An organismic-developmental approach to language and the expression of thought.* New York: J. Wiley.

Westman, R. S. (1977). Environmental languages and the functional bases of animal behavior. In B. A. Hazlett (Ed.), *Quantitative methods in the study of animal behavior* (pp. 145–201). New York: Academic Press.

Wetherby, A. M. (1986). Ontogeny of communicative functions in autism. *Journal of Autism and Developmental Disorders, 16,* 295–316.

Whiten, A., & Byrne, R. W. (1988). Tactical deception in primates. *Behavioral and Brain Sciences, 11,* 233–273.

Wickler, W. (1967). Socio-sexual signals and their intraspecific imitation among primates. In D. Morris (Ed.), *Primate ethology* (pp. 69–147). London: Weidenfeld & Nicolson.

Wickler, W. (1976). The ethological analysis of attachment: Sociometric, motivational and sociophysiological aspects. *Zeitschrift für Tierpsychologie, 42,* 12–28.

Wickler, W. (1986). *Dialekte im Tierreich.* Münster: Aschendorff.

Wiener, M., Devoe, S., Rubinow, S., & Geller, J. (1972). Nonverbal behavior and nonverbal communication. *Psychological Review, 79,* 185–214.

Wiens, A. N., Harper, R. G., & Matarazzo, J. D. (1980). Personality correlates of nonverbal interview behavior. *Journal of Clinical Psychology, 36,* 205–215.

Wilcox, M. J., & Howse, P. (1982). Children's use of gestural and verbal behavior in communicative misunderstandings. *Applied Psycholinguistics, 3,* 15–27.

Wild, H., Johnson, W. R., & McBrayer, D. J. (1983). Gestural behavior as a response to external stimuli. *Perceptual and Motor Skills, 56,* 547–550.

Wiley, R. H. (1983). The evolution of communication: Information and manipulation. In T. R. Halliday & P. J. B. Slater, *Animal behaviour: Vol. 2. Communication* (pp. 156–189). Oxford: Blackwell.

Wilkinson, L. C., Rembold, K. L. (1981). The form and function of children's gestures accompanying verbal directives. In P. Dale & D. Ingram (Eds.), *Child language: An international perspective* (pp. 175–186). Baltimore: University Park Press.

Williams, D. G. (1973). So-called nervous habits. *Journal of Psychology, 83,* 103–109.

Williams, E. (1977). Experimental comparisons of face-to-face and mediated communication: A review. *Psychological Bulletin, 84,* 963–976.

Willis, F. N., & Reeves, D. L. (1976). Touch interaction in junior high school students in relation to sex and race. *Developmental Psychology, 12,* 91–92.

Wilson, C., & Williams, E. (1977). Watergate words: A naturalistic study of media and communication. *Communication Research, 4,* 169–178.

Wilson, E. O. (1975). *Sociobiology: The new synthesis.* Cambridge: Belknap Press of Harvard University Press.

Wolf, M. E., & Goodale, M. A. (1987). Oral asymmetries during verbal and nonverbal movements of the mouth. *Neuropsychologia, 25,* 375–396.

Wolfgang, A., & Bhardwaj, A. (1984). 100 years of nonverbal study. In A. Wolfgang (ed.), *Nonverbal behavior: Perspectives, applications, intercultural insights* (pp. 461–469). New York: Lewinston.

Woodall, W. G., & Burgoon, J. K. (1981). The effects of nonverbal synchrony on message comprehension and persuasiveness. *Journal of Nonverbal Behavior, 5,* 207–223.

Woodall, W. G., & Folger, J. P. (1981). Encoding specificity and nonverbal cue context: An expansion of episodic memory research. *Communication Monographs, 48,* 39–53.

Woodall, W. G., & Folger, J. P. (1985). Nonverbal cue context and episodic memory: On the availability and endurance of nonverbal behaviors as retrieval cues. *Communication Monographs, 52,* 319–333.

Wundt, W. (1973). *The language of gestures.* The Hague: Mouton. (Originally published 1900)

Wyler, F., Graves, R., & Landis, T. (1987). Cognitive task influence on relative hemispheric motor control: Mouth asymmetry and lateral eye movements. *Journal of Clinical and Experimental Neuropsychology, 9,* 105–116.

Young, A. W., Lock, A. J., & Service, V. (1985). Infant's hand preferences for actions and gestures. *Developmental Neuropsychology, 1,* 17–27.

Young, D. W. (1980). Meanings of counselor nonverbal gestures: Fixed or interpretative? *Journal of Counseling Psychology, 27,* 447–452.

Young, G., Segalowitz, S. J., Corter, C. M., & Trehub, S. E. (1983). Overview. In G. Young, S. J. Segalowitz, C. M. Corter, & S. E. Trehub (Eds.), *Manual specialization and the developing brain* (pp. 3–12). New York: Academic Press.

Zimmer, H. D., & Engelkamp, J. (1985). Modality-specific representation systems and inference: Task-dependent activation processes in the motor memory. In G. Rickheit & H. Stohner (Eds.), *Inferences in text processing* (pp. 137–157). Amsterdam: Elsevier.

Zinober, B., & Martlew, M. (1985). Developmental changes in four types of gesture in relation to acts and vocalizations from 10 to 21 months. *British Journal of Developmental Psychology, 3,* 293–306.

Zivin, G. (1977). On becoming subtle: Age and social rank changes in the use of a facial gesture. *Child Development, 48,* 1314–1321.

Zuckerman, M., Blanck, P. D., DePaulo, B. M., & Rosenthal, R. (1980). Developmental changes in decoding discrepant and nondiscrepant nonverbal cues. *Developmental Psychology, 16,* 220–228.

Zuckerman, M., DePaulo, B. M., & Rosenthal, R. (1981). Verbal and nonverbal communication of deception. In L. Berkowitz (Ed.), *Advances in experimental social psychology* (Vol. 14, pp. 1–59). New York: Academic Press.

Zuckerman, M., & Driver, R. E. (1985). Telling lies: Verbal and nonverbal correlates of deception. In A. W. Siegman & S. Feldstein (Eds.), *Nonverbal communication: An integrated perspective* (pp. 129–147). Hillsdale, NJ: Lawrence Erlbaum.

Zuckerman, M., Miserandino M., & Bernieri, F. (1983). Civil inattention exists – in elevators. *Personality and Social Psychology Bulletin, 9*, 578–586.

Subject index

D